Signs of Agni Yoga

FIERY WORLD

III

FIERY WORLD

III

1935

Agni Yoga Society
319 West 107th Street
New York NY 10025
www.agniyoga.org

Reprinted 2017. Updated August 2021.
Translated from Russian by the Agni Yoga Society.

Now we may begin the approach to the Fiery World, affirming the supermundane signs. We have repeatedly pointed out the urgency of the development of necessary earthly qualities. The Teaching always proceeds along two currents which, when they meet, form the complete line of attainment. While many earthly qualities are not easy to attain, the super-earthly conditions may appear to be abstract; but they are an existing reality. He who is accustomed to think on a planetary scale knows how real is the life in the World of Fire, in the World of Radiance, in the World of Attainment.

Thus, let us begin the third part of *Fiery World*.

FIERY WORLD

Part III

1. One should not only reconcile the Fiery World with Infinity, but also hold firmly to the concept of the Hierarchy. The Beauty of the Fiery World is crowned by the steps of Hierarchy, which ascends into the Infinite Light.

One should not feel grieved if only a few consciously ascend the steps of Light. These giants are surrounded by such magnets that they attract others who are carried along involuntarily, unaware of the difficult path.

2. You yourselves gather strength ascending the new step. Only very few can travel the path of Light, rejoicing as each aspiration is directed to the Lords. One may grow true wings of the spirit when the entrusted treasure is realized.

3. Much of that which is sacred and great will not necessarily appear so outwardly. The dimensions assume true magnitude in the inner consciousness. One may foresee various conditions, but one cannot foreknow how or when the Messenger will come. People by their own conventional measures impede the transcendental manifestations. Think not that this word is antiquated, for indeed now more than ever is the radiation of spirit being denied. But without a sun neither the Macrocosm nor the microcosm can exist. You know that the movements of the Luminaries could not possibly be more propitious. One may wait for centuries for such conjunctions, and just now not centuries but a mere few years are enough to determine the new boundary lines for humanity. Not many perceive these Cosmic structures; so much the more must the few fully comprehend the striking events indicated by the Luminaries. One must fully realize the greatness of the hour; and for this solemnity is ordained. If you sense it—good for you!

4. It is correct to think that between the earthly plane and the Fiery World there is coordination; but the causes of all developments are invisible. Thus one may look upon temporary anguish on the earthly plane as a threshold to great joy. One may send quietly a fiery wave into the earthly domain, but thunder is heard on the far-off worlds. Therefore all dimensions are reached by varying potentialities of the waves. Verily, all creative energies are active both on the earthly plane and in the Fiery World. The conducting current is one, but people cannot always understand the extending significance of an action.

5. Unknown are the causes of actions on the earthly plane. Only to the consciousness of an Adept is the understanding of the essential nature of all occurrences accessible. Thus, humanity can absorb only a minute grain of Truth. Therefore let us speak about the Fiery Law with deep reverence.

6. In the actions of the hostile ones there can be observed an expenditure of superfluous energies. Perplexed, these people can only look upon the facts as if reflected in a distorting mirror. Thus, motivated by an evil will, they employ an improper focus of vision. Only the followers of the Hierarchy of Good can harness all energies into a channel of good. Indeed, only the fiery consciousness can take in the horizon of the World; therefore the events which are sweeping away the old accumulations elude the enemy. The manifestation of foresight really can be applied only through the focus of vision of the builders. Thus, the Fiery World has been predestined by the Bearers of Light.

7. I give this farewell bidding to the disciple: "Let thy prayer be—'Thee, O Lord, I shall serve in everything, always and everywhere. Let my path be marked by the attainment of selflessness.'" When the disciple realizes in his heart the joy of the path, a path which knows no friction because all is transformed in the joy of Service, then it is possible to open before him the Great Gates. Amidst higher concepts the disciple must remember in his heart the records of Light. Amidst the frightening manifestations the disciple must remember about the records of darkness. There is inscribed upon the Shield of Light—"Lord, I come alone, I come in a manifested achievement, I shall reach the goal, I shall reach it!" And there is inscribed upon the Shield of Light honesty, devotion and self-abnegation. But fearful are the records of darkness. Let the hand of the disciple refrain from inscribing upon these permanent scrolls lie, hypocrisy, betrayal, selfhood.

8. Among the manifestations which are particularly harmful for ascent may be noted half-way service. It is impossible to advance without casting away this terrible half-wayness. It must be remembered that, having once chosen the Teacher, the disciple must always act with an understanding of all the harmful effects of half-wayness. Not only is an obvious betrayal (against which one can openly fight with a sword) dangerous, but these pernicious burrowings of half-wayness are so harmful. One must direct the consciousness of people along the path of honesty. People must understand that the most important thing is the honesty of Service. How can one affirm the growth of the spirit, how can one prove devotion to Hierarchy, how can one purify the consciousness? By observing this one law—

honesty of Service. Thus let us always keep in mind the harm of half-wayness. The records of darkness contain all half-way decisions and actions; therefore, on the fiery path one should remember the consequences of half-wayness. If it were possible to make manifest all the records of the Subtle World, humanity would be terrified at the gray shadows around destruction, half-wayness, betrayal, incitement to strife, blasphemy, intolerance and selfhood. Thus, on the fiery path let us remember about the danger of half-wayness and its undermining effect.

9. Sources which are responsive to subtle energies are very sensitive. Hence that quality which reveals itself mostly in pure currents is so very important. Likewise, as the results of chemical experiments vary with the use of different vessels, substances and combinations, the manifestations of subtle receptivity are also quite diverse. An organism filled with imperil will admit only a small particle of the sending. An organism which is saturated with selfhood will impart a dreadful coloration which distorts the sending. An organism imbued with malevolence will carry the distorted sending to a neighbor. Thus the distortion in the reception of a sending results from certain qualities in the receiver. You were justified in asking why do We not put a stop to such distortions. It is because there are records of writings by human hands so monstrous as to represent the Mahatmas of the East as issuing condemnation upon retiring for the night. So think those who seek the condemnation of a neighbor. Indeed, people attribute to the Mahatmas even slander. People ascribe to Us all their earthly qualities.

10. Let us continue about sendings and receivings. The ability is given to a fiery spirit to receive subtle energies. Only the fiery consciousness is able to conduct a current of subtle energies. Therefore the records must be scrutinized with a great deal of discrimination. It is because humanity has become accustomed to visualizing the Highest on a low plane, that the Images of the Lords have acquired such distorted forms. Indeed, people have become used to the thought that the Higher should serve the lower, but they do not realize that only the understanding of Service gives one the right to a manifested link of the Chain. Thus it is the distorted understanding of Sendings that produces the results which litter the space. We know of cases wherein the Higher Ones called a disciple "Mahatma" but some recipients of the gray variety perverted this great sending to the point of ugliness. Therefore We shall give a fair warning against all distortion and false records. When We call a disciple "Mahatma" We affirm a great potentiality. But what does a medium or a recipient poisoned with imperil reveal? Thus, it is necessary to purify the profane human actions and to destroy these records in the future. In the Fiery World only the fiery consciousness can be a true recipient of Our Sendings.

11. History makes note of all pseudo-prophets and imposters. But all spiritual imposters and false sources have not been sufficiently pointed out. If into the basis of the State could be put the spiritual principle, it would be possible to follow all the pernicious effects of false sources. One may understand the records of darkness to include all the false sources and the evil intentions of the imposters. With justice it has been asked, "Why disparage the Higher Teaching?" There is only one answer—the imposters live in Maya. And in order to secure a grain for the Common Weal, a manifestation of tolerance is needed. With sorrow do We issue forgiveness to these imposters, for they live in

Maya and they will depart into Maya. This is also true with regard to the distortion of Sendings.

12. Among the traducers of the Teaching one should notice a particular kind of people who assign for themselves the obligation of standing in custody of the Truth. But it is the prerogative of the fiery consciousness to manifest Truth. The self-appointed guardians of the Truth are at great pains to take for the Truth only that which is agreeable to them. Hence, there are so many vilifiers of the Teaching and of all enlightened beginnings. It is correct to point out the anathema and maledictions which are proclaimed by such guardians of Truth. How much of the Beautiful has been destroyed by these dark efforts! Why is it that these forces of darkness cannot stand Our Indications? Because Our Teaching is all-embracing, all-pervading, and of primal origin. Darkness contends especially with the Source which is close to the Hierarchy of Light. If We will trace all the false sources one will become convinced to what extent they are supported by human consciousness. The sowers of doubts and distortions continually voice interdiction of Truth and all Light. But the Fiery World also has its Fiery Guardians. Woe to the pseudo-guardians and woe to those who litter the space with pseudo-teachings. Woe to those who in an unworthy manner have given and are giving to the World a conception of Hierarchy which belittles the Luminous Images. Thus let us combat the distortions.

13. Great is the creativeness of the purification of consciousness. Everywhere are such accumulations! Without the purification of consciousness humanity cannot advance. And We can save only when the consciousness has been purified. Therefore We intensify so greatly all Our energies.

14. It is asked why We do not put a stop to the false sources. Why do We not expose those who distort the Sendings? If one were to stop by force the current in whose wake humanity is proceeding, fanaticism would turn into brutality. Thus, the evil free will flows like lava, engulfing also those who rise against the Good, as history reveals. Surely, violent manifestations of force cannot carve a righteous path for humanity. Hence, all the subtle energies can be accepted only by a fiery consciousness. Thus, tolerance is truly the lot of the fiery consciousness. Of course, one should purify wherever there are accumulations of filth, and the lot of the fiery consciousness is to purify the records of space. Among the accumulated pages of human writings there will have to be noted those pernicious records which have clouded the brains of even well-meaning people. Thus on the path to the Fiery World one should understand the great significance of receptivity of higher energies and of subtle sendings.

15. Among the receivers of the Teaching there are many channels; each channel has its own special characteristic and designation. But the ocean of thought of the Teaching can be given only through the source nearest of all to it. There are many branches and means for the communication, and special qualities of the channels indicate the limitations of the receivers. Those fiery receivers who can contain the ocean of thought of the Teaching function as the chief unifiers between the Higher Forces and the World. It is not difficult to investigate how these Hiero-Inspirations have proceeded, nor is it difficult to trace how the Bearers of the Fiery Consciousness have proceeded. Therefore one should observe, and place an achievement of light over and above the manifestations of limitation. In this achievement the fiery understanding of humanity can truly be affirmed.

16. In the days of Armageddon all energies are extraordinarily tense. The attraction of all possibilities for the actions of Good requires great intensification. Verily, all Cosmic forces are in action, creating all necessary conditions. How can the consciousness become awakened without an impetus, without striving for a change from the present mode of life? Of course the builders are carrying the entire burden of what takes place, and it is essential to realize that the battle of Armageddon is great and that all constructive manifestations for the great Plan are likewise great. Therefore let us bless all those who create obstacles, because Our energies are thereby developed and joined to the constructiveness of Light. It may be asked, "Is it impossible to do without cataclysms? Is it impossible to be without terrors and calamities? Is it impossible to be without miseries?" We must then remind about the spatial accumulations, and human engenderings which must be expiated. Thus, the Forces of Light are solicitous about the great fiery transmutation. Thus, on the way to the Fiery World one should bear in mind that in the time of Armageddon a purification of space takes place.

17. The affirmation of the vital power of the Teaching is especially important in this epoch in which there appears a dividing line between creators and true seekers on the one hand, and the deniers of Truth on the other. Someone acknowledges the present, the past and the future; someone sees everything in the refraction of Maya; someone wishes to attain a higher manifestation through the denial of Hierarchy; someone regards himself as a traveller without a Guide—thus multi-colored are the grimaces of the spirit. Therefore one should constantly reiterate about the creative origins, and transform the human consciousness through the vital power of the Teaching. We direct all Our efforts toward the regeneration of the spirit. This fiery transmutation holds the key to Our labor. During the epoch of fiery regeneration one should reveal the vital power of the Teaching; because the denial of the laws obscures one's thinking and allows dissolution to creep in. Thus, humanity must realize the courage of absorbing the transmutation of the Fiery World in all reality.

18. Humanity does not ponder over the degeneration of many nations. There are evil-minded nations which are obviously corrupt and decaying, before the very eyes of the World! One may even trace upon the physical structure of its individuals a nation's degeneration: jaws, cheekbones, arms, legs, ears as well as other symptoms reflect the process. An evil-minded nation also becomes a nursery of diseases of the spirit and body. But during the fiery creativeness and transmutation of the spirit the potentiality of progress and development of a nation will be disclosed to men. He who will not accept the Fiery Baptism, who will not follow the Origin of Light, will depart into the chaos of dissolution. One may observe the moral sinking and affirm that only the Fiery World offers the needed purification.

19. As there is not enough room for all on a summit, whoever ascends it will likewise discover that the ascent cannot take place with a heavy load. Furthermore, there is no place on the peak for anything superfluous. The ascending spirit must constantly bear in mind the necessity to break away from the attachments to everyday life. The slopes are steep, and one should remember also that only the foot of the Mountain is broad. At the base there is room for worldly

things, but the Summit is sharp-pointed and too small for all human possessions. Mundane occurrences are best seen from the Summit; hence, everyone should remember about the Summit, but should also not forget about the steep slopes. During the ascent, in courage, firmness and creativeness, one should remember that the Summit itself is small but the horizon vast. The higher one ascends the broader and more powerful is the vision; and the more powerful the vision the stronger the fusion into oneness. Thus let us remember the farewell bidding given for the ascent.

20. Verily, the higher the more effectual the coalescence into oneness. Likewise, as a man travelling on his way to a mountain top breaks away from attractions of the world below, so is the traveller in the manifested Fiery Right liberated from all burdensome memories which life had imposed.

21. The Teaching is given in endless succession, for the purpose of affirmation of fiery revelations and the carrying out of highest laws, and, following the same principle as that governing magnetic poles, can be given only to a fiery spirit that has been aligned with Hierarchy for thousands of years. The intensified fiery action extends for thousands of years. The fusion of consciousness is forged over a span of thousands of years. The united path is carved and paved in thousands of years. Hearts are merged in one Great Service in thousands of years. Immutable is the Cosmic Law, and it should be understood that the succession of the Teaching is affirmed through millenniums. There are many who attempt to infringe upon this great right, but a Cosmic Right is given to a creator in the Fiery World. Therefore humanity must purify consciousness for the understanding of the great Right of succession.

22. Verily one should accept the symbol of the

Summit as the goal in the ascent of the spirit. Each disciple should remember that avoiding of the Summit leads the traveller away from the path. Each excessive burden will hinder the traveller. The Summit is sharp-pointed, and each needless attachment to the earthly world brings the traveller to a halt. It is difficult to halt on the slope, so let us remember about the Summit when beginning the ascent. It is difficult to reach the Summit if the spirit does not grasp the fundamentals of Hierarchy. Thus, on the Fiery Path there is no lone-liness nor emptiness; only a breaking away from the earthly world and an irresistible attraction toward the Fiery World.

23. The World is striving for the crowning perfection. Manifold are the paths of the search. The closest to perfection will be the path of Beauty. Religion has given a striving for Nirvana, but it is distorted by misleading concepts. Many quests were deflected by the misunderstanding of the concepts of Karma and Reincarnation. He who sought perfection could have found through Beauty the powerful laws of Being. Yet if one should take all distorted manifestations of life and line them up with Beauty one would find the law of perfection. If we take the unbalanced conditions of all principles introduced into life and line them up with Beauty, we shall arrive at the law of Being. When we observe the life of the planet with all its prejudices, we see that we must inevitably arrive at the victorious crowning through Beauty. One should become accustomed to the realization of the victorious crowning. Such thinking will bring one to the Fiery World.

24. One of the great concepts, often incorrectly interpreted, is precisely the great concept of humility. It has been interpreted as non-resistance to evil; it has been interpreted as good-heartedness, as compassion, but very few accepted it as self-denial. For only self-denial and self-sacrifice can give understanding of humility. Truly, We see the giants of spirit and the heroes who devote themselves fully to the humble tasks for the good of humanity. We know of great experiments being humbly carried out in the earthly laboratories for the benefit of humanity. We know the great fiery experiments of those who dedicate their lives wholly and humbly to the benefit of mankind. We know manifestations on the path to the Fiery World which inspire all surroundings. Truly manifold is humility manifested through self-sacrifice and self-renunciation. Heroism is a manifestation of various aspects of humility. Thus the records of space are filled with great deeds of humility. Invaluable are these fiery flights of the spirit. Thus, verily, the heroes of humility drain the cup of poison for the good of mankind.

25. As the highest humility and the highest self-renunciation, should one accept the Image of Those bearing the full Chalice of self-sacrifice. They carry a heavy burden in the heart. They bear the brunt of the tension manifested by humanity. They carry the burden of the entire discrepancy. Such humility is redemption. Who will give himself wholly to the achievement of drinking the cup of poison? Who will take upon himself the Fiery Shield for the good of humanity? Who will resolve to accept the fiery energies? Who will manifest the understanding of the entire Cosmic tension? Verily, he who is in consonance with the Higher Forces. Mankind is accustomed to demand Good, but very rarely does man think of giving. Hence the humility of a saint who carries a fiery chalice is regarded as the highest humility. The fiery chalice holds the essence of the saving of the spirit of mankind and the atonement. Thus, let us remember and manifest understanding.

26. For such fiery humility the spirit must be tempered through thousands of years and must live in constant achievement. Thus takes place the final bid for the planet, and in this great Battle We manifest Our Might. Therefore Our humility is so fiery. It is not easy for a fiery spirit to manifest humility. The fiery spirit is like a furnace, like a flaming torch, and self-denial and self-sacrifice are its lot upon the last step. Therefore the last sojourn on Earth is so hard. Each threshold means a painful step. Thus do We forge the great future.

27. The dominance of the spirit and the dominance of the heart are understood so little that it is necessary to broaden these concepts for the advancement of humanity. Often lack of understanding of these great principles creates a disturbance of the earthly equilibrium. The best example is the gap between East and West. Thus, in the East one does not understand that the domination of spirit does not mean inaction and that domination of the heart is not lack of will. And the West has destroyed both these concepts and affirmed the domination of matter as the basis of life. One cannot advance without the dominance of spirit and of heart. One should accept into daily usage the formula of inspired matter. Then spirit, heart and matter will enter life. The Fiery World affirms domination of spirit in its entire Cosmic span. If the scientists would but understand the great significance of the domination of the spirit, how many useful investigations could be given to humanity! But the "bookmen" do not acknowledge the most powerful force, namely, the domination of spirit. Therefore each subtle approach to science, to art, must be evaluated as true fiery thinking. Let us remember about the dominance of spirit on the path to the Fiery World.

28. Man himself affirms that power which governs his being. This power will consist of the principal qualities of the spirit. People live under the dominion of various potentials. One may distinguish the manifestations of construction and destruction. Those who live under the power of Beauty are attracted toward constructiveness. They create by their potentiality the mastery of spirit. They regenerate life through Beauty. But how terrible is the life of those who live by the power of destruction! Of course, speaking of the power of destruction, one should have in mind the power of selfhood, which is opposed to the power of Beauty. Thus one should understand clearly that a man either casts himself into an abyss or is uplifted into Infinity. The domination of spirit and heart is a great cosmic law. Therefore the Fiery World creates through the power of spirit.

29. Today, on Our Day, I shall tell how the power of Beauty summons into the World of Fiery Completion. Creativeness through the power of Cosmic Love is infinite. The space resounds with the affirmation of the law of Cosmic Love. The rays are intertwined in powerful unity. Only by united Rays was it possible to arrest the many earthquakes which We have stopped. Thus for the World the experiment of Agni Yoga is being affirmed as a fiery transmutation. But for the Higher World there exists the knowledge of the cosmic law which manifests the experiment of Agni Yoga as a preparation for the acceptance of the Ray of the great Cosmic Right. Thus, the Fiery World makes manifest the essential nature of the Cosmic Right.

30. Only a broadened consciousness can understand the power of creativeness of the invisible Cosmic Ray. The power of this Ray is the law of the Fiery World. The vibrations of rays have been shown. Thus, for instance, the tension of will, striving of spirit, joy and all other manifestations of spirit and heart send forth their own rays. In this one should remember that the substance of radiations does not replace the Cosmic Ray, for in this Ray is contained the entire potentiality of actions. Rays consciously directed represent cosmic power. How many great structures could have been affirmed by a lofty tension of spirit and purity of heart! How powerful then would have been the unified rays! But if the spirit be not directed toward the grandeur of the Cosmic Origins, it cannot receive the power of the Cosmic Ray. A great future can be realized only through reception of the Cosmic Ray.

31. I shall speak about the great Cosmic Ray in connection with the manifestation of unity. On the last earthly step, before the victorious crowning, a conformity of the fierily transmuted centers with the Cosmic Ray is established. Each visible tension has its corresponding cosmic designation. Thus the centers are saturated with fire for admittance of the great Cosmic Ray, which adapts all the bodies for the final rending from Earth. The subtle, the physical and the astral bodies thus take on one and the same image of Beauty. This is the greatest action of the Cosmic Ray, and the Fiery Right attracts this mysterious Cosmic Ray. In this lies the supreme cosmic Mystery and the greatest manifestation of Cosmos!

32. The struggle of the spirit is a step toward recovery. During stagnation of the spirit and the persistence of conceit and self-justification, the spirit cannot advance. Therefore the fiery baptism presupposes the struggle of the spirit. Naturally, intensified questing leads toward the struggle of the spirit. One may observe how people rise and sink in spirit. One may observe how a spirit which possesses a full synthesis becomes engrossed in its searching and does not man-

ifest the quality of completeness. One may also perceive in a specialist a person who finds in his labors self-sufficiency and a feeling of crowned completeness. This is likewise true of the so-called "business ability" in contrast to a free swing of thought and creativeness. Hence, it is so important to discern in people their potentialities, because the manifestation of a genius is not always visible to those who are limited by self-sufficiency. Therefore it is also necessary to develop respect for the labor and the research of those who possess a synthesis. On the path to the Fiery World synthesis and the manifestation of the struggle of the spirit are needed.

33. Amidst the wrestlings of the spirit there should be especially noted the feeling of dissatisfaction. The spirit which possesses a synthesis can, of course, affirm its strength. But precisely these fiery receivers do not know the feeling of satisfaction. Thus, one may often observe in life that conventionality precludes acceptance of the Bearers of Synthesis. The multitude always evaluates evidence alone. One may only regret that people so limit themselves by creating such narrow boundaries. One may pity those who are unwilling to understand the creativeness of thought. You spoke correctly about thought and straight-knowledge. The thought reigns above all Samadhi. The higher, the more powerful. The more flaming the thought the more useful the manifestation. Truly, thought is all-powerful and limitless.

34. Amidst fiery struggles the spirit manifests anguish. Especially on the final step does the spirit know these struggles. Anguish is a manifestation of the Subtle World, and absence of self-satisfaction is knowledge of the future. During the division of the spirit this feeling is particularly strong.

35. So much is said about co-operation, but so little is comprehended! This is one of the most misconstrued concepts, because in a human community the idea of united labor is so distorted. Life in the community of co-workers has in view no forcing of feelings, of obligations, of constraints, but an affirmation of united work in the name of manifested Good. If the human community would accept the law of united labor as the law of life, to what an extent human consciousness could become purified! For the rhythm of a common task can unite various specialists and individuals who differ in their qualities. The law is simple, but how many distortions surround it! The manifestation of the human nearness of the spirit is conditioned by many causes, spiritual as well as karmic, but under the ray of labor a community may be organized with the aid of the law of co-operation. Therefore it is necessary to educate the co-workers through labor and by the affirmation that each co-worker is a part of the whole. However, one should exclude incorrect thinking about the personal. Such interpretation can help a community to become affirmed as a single channel. So many sad happenings can be avoided through the expansion of consciousness and by the subtle understanding that it is inadmissible to encroach upon the heart of another being. Thus, on the path to the Fiery World the co-workers should understand that one may advance only through the law of Common Labor—there is no other measure! The subtle is attained only by the subtle; and the subtle threads of the heart resound only in a tension of many thousands of years. Therefore, let the co-workers especially realize this single path. Precisely, the law of united labor permits no infringement upon the heart of another.

36. In the community one should remember

about the sacredness of feelings. One should especially remember that it is inadmissible to evoke forcibly the subtle feeling in a fellow worker. One should not develop subtle vibrations in the heart by outside demands. Only an inner, merited action gives birth to a conformable vibration. Rarely is this life of spirit found amidst choking earthly vibrations. Yet this manifestation—when spirit resounds in harmony with spirit—is so beautiful! First of all, in the development of the consciousness of the community one should affirm the understanding of co-operation. In this understanding the community can become strengthened, and the worm of self-pity will vanish. Thus do We administer advice to the disciples, affirming the joy of labor without encroachment upon the heart of another. Long since was it said: "One cannot be dear by force!" This is also a cosmic formula. But one can greatly purify the path of concerted labor. Thus let the disciples remember the manifestation of co-operation as an important step in the daily life of the community.

37. The achievement of the spirit consists in that amidst earthly difficulties and struggles the spirit develops the higher striving. The spirit cannot become affirmed amidst conditions of well-being or abundance. Therefore the co-workers can prove the strength of their spirit and striving amidst daily labors and difficulties. How could one attain the highest state, attain refinement of consciousness, without spiritual labor? So many blessed cares are on the path of purification of consciousness! Each action which rends the spirit from earthly desires is a higher affirmation. The path to the Fiery World leads through the labors of spirit, through earthly privations; and highest achievements come through departure from earthly manifestations in quest of the higher ones. Thus, when it is

said, "the achievement of spirit will be with those who have known the struggle and search for knowledge," it means this will be a fiery attainment. Thus let us remember upon the path to the Fiery World.

38. The most powerful path of manifested reciprocity is the one of the spirit manifesting a subtle flow of energy. The most subtle reciprocity is through spirit-understanding. The force of the reciprocity of spirit-understanding is incomparable to anything. Of course, in spiritual construction one must make use of many channels, but one should distinguish between the channels which are governed by the will from without and from within. The great Source of spirit-understanding is the most subtle and the most high affirmation. The outside source is simply a channel through which one may send—even paralyzing the will. But there is so much inaccurate information, because one may not too often paralyze the will. Besides, these channels are very unilateral, whereas in the cosmic structure they are like a single retort. Hence, it is so important to cognize the power of spirit-understanding. Mediums, and other sources as well, receive only partial sendings which crowd the space. The solicitude of Hierarchy is expressed in sendings to the workers, but if they do not transmit that which is sent to the community the channel is impure. Would Hierarchy send visions for one worker alone? Again, the channel is impure. Therefore it is so difficult to broaden the consciousness.

39. The essence of fiery advancement comes from various affirmations of spirit. The chief factor will be the development of self-activity. In self-activity will be contained love for Hierarchy; in it will be contained a feeling of responsibility and a true understanding of Service. Thus when We speak of self-activity, one should understand that it includes all qualities of higher affirmation. When a co-worker takes upon himself the development of self-activity, his field of action becomes unlimited. Hierarchy becomes the fiery impetus of all his actions. No attacks, near or far, are frightening to the co-worker, because he knows fiery service. Therefore it is so important to purify one's consciousness from selfhood. But the co-worker must be prepared to accept all difficulties, knowing that Service to Hierarchy is the highest attainment.

40. Only after a long search do we find that which belongs to the spirit and the heart. Only lengthy quests lead to crowning.

41. Kingliness of spirit is contained in fiery consciousness, precisely as discipline of the spirit, as an affirmed synthesis, and as a manifestation of broad understanding. Thus, only slaves in spirit are afraid of everything which is fiery, because each manifestation of Fire scorches them. One may trace how regally the revealed co-worker proceeds, illumined by the Fire of consciousness. One should note not only the achievements of apparent heroism, but also the great path of kingliness of the spirit amidst daily life. It is impossible to err in the potentiality of the regal Bearer of Fire. We know these great heroes who saturate the space and all surroundings with their fire and inspire others to achievement. Thus, it is necessary in life to watch the subtle actions of the kingly spirit. One should subtly discern heroism, because we do not always see the fiery heroism of the spirit; and the basis of heroism is not always revealed to the eye of the ordinary man. How beautiful is the path of a kingly spirit!

42. How differently is the manifestation of heroism commonly understood. One should remember that a hero is not always proclaimed by a trumpet blast. Not in universal glamour does a hero of the spirit proceed, but in true draining of the chalice of poison. To those who demand more, more is often given, to meet their requirement, but earthly gifts are no affirmation of higher gifts. Verily a hero of the spirit proceeds by another path. His burden will be the Burden of the World. And how wonderful is the countenance of the hero of the spirit, proceeding impetuously onward in silence and in solitude! The fiery creativeness of the hero of the spirit is comparable only to the Fire of the highest tension, because the higher flame is invisible. The space intensifies greatly the rays of the creators of the spirit. Is not the image of the Giving One an image of the miracle-working Heart? Thus let us remember on the path to the Fiery World.

43. The heart of a hero knows self-sacrifice in the name of Common Good. It knows self-renunciation and Great Service. The path of the hero is not always strewn with wreaths of human gratitude. The path of the hero proceeds by thorny ways. Therefore, one should always revere the path of self-renunciation, because each advancement upon the face of the Earth which affirms heroism of the spirit guarantees a new beginning. How many heroes of the spirit could have been seen upon mankind's path as torch-bearers! But these fires of the spirit are unnoticeable to the eye of ignorance. Thus, on the path to the Fiery World one should revere the heroes of everyday life who saturate life with an achievement in each hour. The community of labor should cultivate these heroes, because the pillars of a nation stand erect only on the qualities of heroism of the spirit and the heart. He who knows the heroism of self-renunciation will not be a chance hero of an hour—the records of space will mark forever the labors of the hero of the spirit.

44. If people would ponder deeply about the steps of evolution, they would come to the conclusion that the laws are infinitely multiform. It is so simple, it would seem, to investigate the process of all growths and refinements, but humanity notices only that which can be traced within a frame of everyday understanding.

Can people then grasp the magnitude of laws which balance the entire Cosmos? Earthly measure is not applicable to the grandeur of Cosmos; and the lack of success of all the investigations can be attributed to this lack of understanding. It is impossible to limit the Unlimited! Thinking can penetrate the depth of Cosmos when the spirit is imbued with the understanding of the essential nature of Fire, its infinite power and unlimited properties. If humanity could grasp the essentiality and magnitude of fiery constructiveness, then all the steps of evolution would lead to the affirmation of great laws. Everything movable travels a spiral path toward great refinement. Therefore on the path to the Fiery World one should know about the infinitude of the laws.

45. If humanity would understand evolution, then indeed it would arrive at the comprehension of the Fiery Right. Only the Fiery Right can create cosmically. Thus can be accomplished the steps of a mighty evolution. The entire equilibrium of Cosmos is maintained upon the fiery unification of the First Causes.

46. Though the good effects of good intentions, of good thoughts and actions are elusive, still, according to the law of causality, everything produces an effect. This law is immutable and sublime. The affirmation of causality in each action gives a broadening of consciousness; for not fear, but discernment, of actions gives the proper direction. How beautiful is the law which gives life to every good and to each creative beginning! Indeed, the structure of the Cosmos is aggrandized by all the origins of each hour. Verily, the heroes of the spirit know how their striving of each day links them with the construction of life. Thus the law of causality can direct the thinking towards an understanding of the infinitude of the Fiery World; when the spirit senses that it is a link in a Cosmic Chain, as the effect of a cause and the cause of a new effect. Man will be able to realize a great deal through this simple understanding of the law of cause and effect. On the path to the Fiery World let us remember about the eternal motion of our actions.

47. How sublime is the law of Causality! In it is contained the answer to every question. The human mind is confused by the problem of misfortunes, but the law of Causality brings one to the law of Karma. Man is exasperated at calamities, but the law of Causality points out to him the sources of same. Man is bewildered by strange disturbances of equilibrium, but the Cosmic law invokes Higher Justice. He who is aligned with the law of Causality in his spirit, is already allied with Truth. If schools and churches would proclaim the law of Causality, the consciousness would be then on a higher level, as that which is separated from the foundations of Existence, cannot advance. It is right to affirm that a primary cause cannot exist without the one Fire of Being; and Cosmic Construction proceeds in like manner, uniting those things which by right belong together. Thus, everything is unified in the Cosmos. The law of Causality must be accepted in all its might.

48. How man does limit the Fiery Right! He does not even understand that he is going against the very affirmation of Existence. How many wondrous manifested laws are concealed from man! Thus each sacred principle must be guarded. Close by is the revelation, yet it is difficult to broaden the consciousness. Thus the sacred is cognized by that spirit which is close to the Fiery Law. Unification is affirmation of the Cosmic law of Causality. A fiery vortex generates a powerful spatial tension; therefore all human calculations are unreliable. Indeed, to humanity it has been given according to its consciousness; that is the reason Truth is concealed, but the affirmation of Fiery Right rules in space. Thus We, the Arhats, sacredly guard in the heart the law of Cosmic Right. Cosmic structure is impossible without fiery fusion—upon this we shall end.

49. Since times immemorial the Chalice has been a symbol of Service. The gifts of Higher Forces are gathered in the Chalice and given from the Chalice. The symbol of the Chalice has always stood for self-sacrifice. Whoever bears the Chalice bears Achievement. Each lofty deed can be marked by the symbol of the Chalice. Everything most lofty, everything for the good of humanity, should bear this symbol. The Chalice of the Grail, and the Chalice of the Heart which has dedicated itself to the Great Service, is a most Cosmic Magnet. The Heart of the Cosmos is reflected in this great symbol. All images of Heroes of the Spirit may be represented as bearing the Chalice. The whole universe is reflected in the Chalice of the fiery spirit. The Chalice contains the accumulations of centuries which are gathered around the seed of the spirit. It is necessary to accept the affirmation of the Chalice as a great symbol in everyday life. Small children, and all youth, should be taught to think about the Chalice. One should understand the entire diversity of forms of the great symbol, the Chalice.

50. In life, which is unified by the law of Cosmic

Right, it is possible to trace how the cup of poison is drained in attaining the great Cosmic Right. The spirit bears all the affirmed chalices through self-sacrifice. The great chalice of Beauty is revealed as a crowning to the spirit through the Fiery Right. Verily, great is the time, because final energies are being intensified on a final step. Rightly has it been said—"The heart will not long endure if the attraction is often repeated." The heart of the Arhat drains the Chalice of abnegation on the final step. Our life Chalice is filled and reveals the path to Our Cosmic Existence.

51. What has been spoken about the masses and about their lack of understanding of statesmanship was correct. One must add to this the fact of the absence of national leaders. It is necessary to develop in the nation a sense of responsibility, in order that the voice of the people be truly the voice of a community. The development of the sense of leadership has degenerated! The soul of a nation is hidden, and he who represents the state must possess the whole synthesis of the nation. It will be impossible to admit in the future such manifestations as the appearance of those arbitrary leaders who have overrun the planet. The right of leadership belongs to a spirit linked with the Forces of Light. Therefore, according to the Higher Law, there can be no accidental leaders. When the consciousness has become expanded, then will become possible the affirmation of the great law of Leadership. In each field there should be applied a subtle understanding of the law of Leadership. Thus, statesmanship must be manifest in the entire structure of life. The act of violation of the national feeling by the pronouncements of the leader results in grave consequences. Hence, it is fitting to honor the great Leadership which is bestowed by the special right of the state spirit of the nation. On the path to the Fiery World let us honor the Leader.

52. Least of all do people understand success. Usually, when the success of a task commissioned by the Hierarchy, and imbued with the help of the Hierarchy, is attributed by the spirit steeped in selfhood to its own merit, the success turns into a heartache of the spirit. When a co-worker requires adoration of himself for fulfillment of the task given him, he closes by this very act the records of the space. The records of life passing on in all earthly glory reveal so many beggars in spirit! A co-worker who presents to the community the idea that the Hierarchy will act in accordance with the affirmation of the successful co-worker introduces truly a belittlement of the Hierarch. How difficult it is to introduce among the co-workers the true concept of success! Indeed, only humility of the spirit and the feeling of gratitude are appropriate. Who gave all possibilities? Who has given the direction? Who has manifested all good? Only the Hierarch, only the Leader, only the Forces of Light. Successful co-worker, examine thy armor; on each link is inscribed—Hierarchy. Not I myself, nor mine, but Thine, O Lord!

Hence, on the path to the Fiery World one should remember that humility is the companion of success. Co-worker, pretend not to luck, for fiery energies are subtle, and crude egotism does not contain the fires. Thus, let us remember about humility when we wish to be truly successful.

53. You spoke rightly about coarseness, and how powerless are the subtle energies against coarseness. No structure can stand upon pillars of coarseness. Therefore each manifestation saturated with coarseness will not be durable, retrogression is inevitable. Complete disintegration will follow where the worm of coarseness eats away the foundation. Every human action is subject to this same danger. A coarse action may be covered with a thousand lusts, and is not to be concealed from the records of space. Every government should be concerned with the elimination of this horror. Every community must contend with this plague. No closely knit community can show evidence of coarseness in its midst. The nation brought up on coarseness must undergo a fiery transmutation; and he who has permitted such disintegration will be karmically responsible. Likewise the co-workers who dwell in coarseness will have to pass through a special purification. Actually, coarseness is a frightful infection, which develops decomposition in the surroundings. Hence, no government can be successful if it is a nursery of microbes of coarseness. Likewise, a co-worker will not be truly successful if coarseness grips his spirit. Thus, let us remember in the construction upon the path to the Fiery World.

54. Let Us explain how to understand tolerance. When We speak about a higher tolerance, We mean that Hierarchy can show leniency because the heart of the Hierarch is all-containing; it feels everything and knows all impulses and intentions, and weighs all the good and the bad. In His leniency the Higher Spirit descends into the sphere of the consciousness of the disciple, and by His indulgence and tolerance uplifts the disciple. But not thus must the co-worker accept the indications about tolerance. For the disciple who is intolerant toward his surroundings, the needed quality cannot be called leniency. When the development of this wonderful quality, tolerance, is indicated to him, it means that first of all he must exclude censure. The indication about tolerance does not mean to have always command over one's fellow-worker; it does

not mean that the spirit is on such a level that it can condemn those who surround him. The indication about tolerance first of all must awaken in the disciple the understanding of the fact that the spirit must be freed from egoism, because selfhood carries the most frightful monstrosities. Hence, only the spirit of a disciple freed from selfhood can manifest leniency. On the path to the Fiery World one should understand the true significance of tolerance.

55. Daring of the spirit is the beginning of ascent. The manifestation of true daring indicates to the spirit how to affirm the measuring scale of all actions, as well as the direction, because daring admits no faint-heartedness. Daring eradicates all tendency toward betrayal. Whoever has realized in spirit true daring knows the beauty of Service. The daring one knows the path of attainment and fears nothing. His life is filled with devotion to Hierarchy. Each co-worker can reflect upon the beauty of fiery daring, for it frees the spirit from all worldly chains. The daring one is not afraid of solitude, for in spirit he feels a bond with the Hierarchy of Light. The daring one knows that the joy of the spirit is contained only in achievement. The daring one is in need of no human recognition, for his achievement is a crown self-woven by labor and striving. Only the heroes of spirit know true attainment. Thus, the daring one will be freed from selfhood. He knows true Service for the good of mankind. On the path to the Fiery World let us remember daring.

56. No advancement is possible, no construction is possible, without the strongest expenditures of energies on the part of Hierarchy, when the co-workers are clouded with personal feelings. The co-workers must remember the first law, which affirms the first step— the expulsion of feelings of personal vengeance, for the

feeling of revenge is a powerful manifestation of the unscrupulousness of selfhood. For the sake of personal vengeance the co-worker may give up that of greatest value. When a co-worker forgets, due to selfhood, the affirmation which he must forge in his spirit in order not to forget Service, the harm may become indelible. Primitive man lived and believed in vengeance, but the consciousness has broadened and man can no longer dwell with such black concepts. He who knows the meaning of Karma can understand that a man takes revenge only on himself. A co-worker will not become affirmed through selfhood and infringement upon the heart of his fellow-man. And a successful co-worker must not impose respect, but must merit it. A king of the spirit must first of all reveal himself in a small circle of life. The growth of dimensions proceeds from within, and the spirit may bedeck itself with all the crowns of human glory and still remain a beggar. Thus let it be remembered by those who are diseased with selfhood and self-conceit. On the path to the Fiery World these chains are not fitting.

57. If humanity would regard everything positive with the same attention as everything negative, then much more could be manifest in cosmic construction. For instance, mania, obsession and evil use of hypnotism have entered into the consciousness; even though only partially understood, nevertheless they have become implanted. But positive manifestations are little realized. It is customary to accept the fact that people acting under the influence of mania or obsession have acquired quite a force, which is demonstrated by the action. Why, then, is it not possible to direct the consciousness to the all-powerful influence of the spirit! It is necessary to bring into daily life the understanding of the magnetism of the spirit. All the nega-

tive forces put together are not to be compared with the power of the magnet of the spirit. On the path to the Fiery World one must learn to evaluate the magnet of the spirit.

58. A man can easily regain a right level of consciousness if the spirit is imbued with great reverence for the Invisible World. All denials arise out of destructive thoughts about the Invisible. If people would accustom themselves to thinking about the Subtle World and the great magnet of the spirit, then each spirit would understand how important it is to practice prophylaxis of the aura. When it is customary to consider all manifestations of the magnet of the spirit as suggestion, then indeed the most powerful actions of man are lost.

Indeed, the leaders of the spirit do not practice suggestion nor hypnotism, and great faith in Hierarchy is not illusion but the life of the Subtle World. The manifestation of followers and pupils is a consequence of the magnet of the spirit of the Hierarch. Thus let us remind all faint-hearted and obsessed ones, who are not averse to employ blasphemy and betrayal. Nothing is worse than lack of understanding of the Hierarchic Principles of Existence. Let us manifest understanding for the magnet of the spirit on the path to the Fiery World.

59. The most widespread cult is the cult of self-service. The champions of this cult always have stopped at nothing, and the aspects of their attempts are as varied as they are numerous. In the crooked mirrors of these champions of evil one can observe how monstrously distorted are good beginnings. Truly these followers of self-service stop at nothing, beginning with the smallest actions which gratify selfhood and ending with the plundering of the Highest gifts. Self-service can reveal itself in a most unexpected display; for instance, a pseudo heir imposes a veto on a spatial decision. It is impossible to enumerate all the distortions resulting from self-service. Who will take upon himself the sacrificial labor? He who represents the Heavenly Forces on Earth; He who knows the fiery Cult of Renunciation; He who knows Cosmic Service. Co-workers, manifest understanding of the harm of self-service. Thus let the successful co-worker remember on the path to the Fiery World. Sacrificial labor is the crown of the spirit.

60. Religion and science must not be considered separate in their essential nature. Subtle study of matter and the atom leads to the conclusion that vital energy is not electricity but Fire. Thus science and religion merge upon a single principle. Matter is affirmed as a fiery substance, and no thoughtful spirit will deny that the higher force is Fire. Science cannot destroy the concept of the divinity of Fire, nor can religion impose an interdiction on the subtle analyses made by science. In this way, then, the understanding and the harmony of the concepts of religion and science are affirmed. A subtle parallel can be drawn between science and religion, which will reveal all the higher stages. Therefore, it is so important that scholars should be in possession of subtle occult receptivity. But only a refined organism can possess this divine perception which is not developed from without but from within. Therefore, all the great discoveries for the good of humanity will not emanate from enormous laboratories, but will be discovered by the spirit of scholars who are in possession of the synthesis. We, the Brothers of Humanity, see the results which direct all quests along the right channel. Of course, the gift of the synthesis is not always bestowed, but those selfless zealots who do possess the synthesis are in no need of specialization. We see and foretell great results from the synthesis of spirit of the zealots. On the path to the Fiery World one must revere the Bearers of Synthesis.

61. Many channels feed into the mouth of a river.

The river receives waters from the mountains and carries them through many channels to eventually swell the sea. Often the mouth of the river is hidden and unnoticeable; often it is inconspicuous and narrow; often it is underground; yet whatever kind of mouth the river may have, it feeds the currents of the sea. In its role in life, the heart may be closely compared to the river's mouth, although its synthesizing function is not always apparent. Though the synthesis may seem unmanifested, still it is impossibleto arrest the force of the estuary's current; likewise it is impossible to arrest the creativeness of the synthesis of the heart, for the elements of this synthesis are fed into it through the paths of subtle energies; and the outflow of the subtle energies resulting from the synthesis also is a most subtle process. The divisibility of the spirit best demonstrates this fine process. The divisibility of the spirit is linked with divisibility of energies, and, if manifested on a high level, may involve the divisibility of centers. One group of centers acts upon the earthly plane, the other returns a subtle fluid to the Fiery World. In the transmutation of the centers it is always necessary to have in mind this powerful divisibility of the spirit.

Great is the labor of the subtle energies of the centers, and it can never stop. One may only replace one process by another. When the high Agni Yogi devotes his energies to the task of great cosmic construction, in this giving is contained a great fiery transmutation. In such instances manifestations on a physical plane cannot be clearly expressed, and the high Agni Yogi can listen to his own thoughts because his consciousness will carry impressions of the Subtle World and his work in it. These thoughts are, as it were, remembrances of the creative work of the centers and of the spirit. It is said, "a thought suddenly flashed"—but We say, "the spirit has recalled." Thus one may affirm the work of a high Agni Yogi. On the path to the Fiery World it must be remembered that synthesis is like a river's mouth and each specialization is like one channel.

62. How can the imagination be properly defined? Usually people take the imagination to be their own invention of forms, but the imagination itself has its roots and distinctions. One may find the core of the imagination in the "chalice," as the precipitation of many lives. However, the imagination is nourished not only by the remembrances of past lives, but also by the action of the present. When the spirit participates in the life of the far-off Worlds, or in the Subtle World, or in the Astral World, then frequently the memories of these experiences are reflected as imagination. Often scholars obtain formulas, or direction, precisely through a communion with the Subtle World. Thought and striving are also kindled by the Subtle Spheres. But a spirit possessing the synthesis not only takes from the treasury of the "chalice," but also is a true co-worker of Cosmic Forces. How many inexplicable causes of unquenchable imagination there are, and how many unexplainable manifestations of heart anguish! Usually, when strength is being spent for a structure, and the divisibility of the spirit is active, heart anguish is inevitable. Furthermore, the heart is a most powerful reservoir for assisting others. There are strong examples of great saints who nourished the far

and near with a wealth of currents. The Agni Yogi is such a nutritive agent. On the path to the Fiery World let us sensitively and cautiously refer to the heart which knows fiery anguish.

63. Verily, Divine Force descends upon the Earth at large and is divinely directed upward in the individual human spirit. This Divine Communion is a manifestation of the union of Worlds, union of Spirit, union of Karma. Many communions can be discerned on the earthly plane. Many Divine Sparks have been scattered, but a Divine Communion is eternal. The source of Eternal Communion is spirit and actions, bound by the powerfully manifest Cosmic Law.

64. When the Divine unites the spheres, all energies manifest a maximum tension. All great events can take place only during great tension. Likewise, all cosmic transmutations—physical, spiritual and planetary—can be affirmed only when all fiery energies are received. It can be traced scientifically how all events are transpiring under high tension, how light and shadow are accentuated. If humanity does not evince enough penetration to perceive the path of Good, it is possible even through the manifested workings of evil to indicate great battles and achievement. Verily, it is possible to trace the path of Good by the actions of darkness! The realization of equilibrium alone must direct humanity to the understanding of the great Cosmic Law. Only the union of Great Higher Forces can produce equilibrium. For we know how the attraction of the Luminaries acts: their energies are reciprocally compressed. The World is one; Macrocosm and microcosm are one. And the manifested spirit intensifies its forces for destruction and for construction in equal measure. Not less powerfully can the spirit act as a creator; and creative forces are intensified by the forces of the Higher Worlds. Thus united are Macrocosm and microcosm.

65. All statecraft and social order can be affirmed upon cosmic law. Science gives all the directions, and only sensitivity of application is needed to reveal the many aspects which are for construction. If instead of so-called innovations and new statutes humanity would turn its attention to the cosmic laws, it would be possible to establish equilibrium, which now is being violated more and more, beginning with the law of conception and extending up to cosmic consummation. The affirmed laws are one. Upon all planes it is possible to affirm unity. The path of evolution crosses threadlike through all the physical and spiritual degrees. Therefore, in the state and in the social order all the cosmic laws could apply toward perfecting of form. On the path to the Fiery World one should be imbued with the power of the unity in the Cosmos.

66. In fitting the affirmation of cosmic law to the state and social order one should keep in mind the law of attraction, repulsion and cohesion. All structures are subject to this same law. And people should be graded according to the composition of their auras. The ray which unifies the manifestation of harmonious auras acquires the strength of augmented attraction, but inharmonious combinations produce repulsion. The results of such combinations can be compared with gases. Just as non-cohesive molecules press against the walls of a vessel, so are inharmonious auras mutually repelled, and the vessel which contains such gases may burst. In governmental and social construction one should have in mind the workings of cosmic laws. Two harmonized auras can create a New World. Two harmonized auras can be a pledge of success, for the reaction from the unification of rays can direct each beginning toward advancement. Let us affirm harmonization and unification of auras. And on the path to the Fiery World let us remember how powerful are the rays of unified auras. Let the co-workers ponder upon the great law of unification. Selfhood, crudity, self-pity, conceit, will produce nothing except a repulsion as of some gaseous substances.

67. The meaning of life is affirmed in the human consciousness when the understanding of man's role in the Cosmos is revealed. The world is then designated by Us as a field for action in the name of the good of humanity. When the spirit apprehends the truth that Macrocosm and microcosm are inseparably bound together, a conscious bond is established, and cooperation with the cosmic energies becomes possible. But how helpless people are when they lead a form of life isolated from cosmic currents! Indeed, life is transformed when the spirit consciously ascends, understanding the leading principle—Hierarchy. Only when the perception of a guiding Hierarchy is consciously affirmed will humanity realize its true role in the Cosmos. Each link is connected with the next link leading upward. How poor is humanity, in whose consciousness the concept of the great cosmic laws is not affirmed! Only the creativeness of the spirit manifest will bring the worlds closer together. On the path to the Fiery World let us remember about the connecting law of Hierarchy.

68. Upon leaving the earthly sphere the spirit is intensified in the consciousness of the achievements which were dominant in that life. The life of a man has, as it were, its leit-motifs, and upon these songs, or laments, the spirit is intensified. The achievements of the spirit lead upward, and departure from the earthly sphere is always a joy for the spirit which has

realized the luminous achievement of Service. Even during physical pains the spirit surmounts all earthly infirmities. In the breaking away from Earth the bond with the Higher Worlds, to which the spirit aspires, is affirmed. The ladder of ascent is built upon the devotion to Hierarchy. But the spirit which dwells within the confines of selfhood has no other path but grief. Breaking away then is frightful, and the spirit is for a long time attached to the earthly sphere. Many hearts which have accepted the power of Service aspire to the Higher Worlds. A ray of help is extended to the devoted disciple. On the path to the Fiery World let us remember about parting from the earthly sphere with the joy of Service to Light.

69. It is right to think about the purging of dogmas which lead away from a just thinking. The concepts of purgatory and hell may be replaced by the concept of affirmation of the life of the Fiery World. There is no mightier purgatory than earthly life, if all the potentialities of the spirit are intensified. Likewise there is no mightier hell than the earthly infections of the spirit. To affirm purgatory on Earth as a beginning leading to the Subtle and Fiery Worlds is a problem of the purification of consciousness. All strivings of humanity for knowledge of the Invisible World should impel the consciousness to take up the thought of purification, which will continue the earthly path to the Fiery World. Only the concept of oneness of the path will impel people to live in beauty, and to depart this life as wayfarers continuing their journey. When the World will apprehend this indissoluble bond with the Subtle World, purgatory will then take its rightful place in Eternal Truth. Therefore it is so important to become affirmed in the realization of the endlessness of life; the continuing, as it were, of the great Wheel of Life.

The manifestation of the accumulation of the "chalice" gives great power to the spirit in the Fiery World; just as the path of darkness imposes its own dark existence. Let us direct thoughts of people to the idea of purgatory on Earth.

70. The consciousness directed through Hiero-inspiration is as a wonderful reflection of the Higher Forces. As a wonderful resonance is the hearing of the heart. The spirit which is affirmed as a true co-worker and helper of the Cosmic Forces should be regarded as a Sacred Source. There are many channels which can reverberate only on one string. We see how one-sided thinking accepts only those currents which are in agreement with the essential nature of the channel. We see how impure channels impose various infections. We see how pages and writings of people become filled with their self-deception. We see how they affirm Cosmic Right as their own. We see the evasion and assaults on the Fiery Right. Along with the scrolls and tablets of the pure spirit there are borne in space vortical rings of destruction. Side by side with fiery hearts We see hordes of self-deluded ones, and because of the Cosmic Law it is impossible to stay the hand of Karma. Each small consciousness first of all ascribes to itself a regal spirit. It is sad to look at the earthly records. Every fiery heart strives to cleanse the records. Thus let us remember on the path to the Fiery World.

71. Among the Fiery Servants of humanity should be particularly noted those who take upon themselves sacrificial labor. The spirit of these servants of humanity is like a fiery torch, for in its potentiality this spirit contains all the qualities which can uplift mankind. Only a powerful consciousness can take upon itself sacrificial labor. Each task of a servant of humanity reflects the quality of his spirit. If the spirit is desig-

nated as a great Servant of Mankind, then in it is contained the whole synthesis. But people know so little about these Fiery Servitors who affirm themselves voluntarily in solitude while serving the great pervading Universal Force. How many powerful manifestations could be observed in each individual achievement! Thus, those who take upon themselves the sacrificial labor know how the Sons of Reason likewise manifest sacrificially their labors. Each manifestation of a Fiery Servant of humanity is creativeness for the good of mankind. One must be affirmed in the understanding of sacrifice. The Fiery Servitor contains within himself each benevolent impulse, each striving for fulfillment of the powerful Will of the Sons of Reason. But it is necessary to conserve the strength of the Fiery Servant.

On the path to the Fiery World let us be affirmed in the understanding of sacrificial labor.

72. Verily, the human spirit is a conductor of all the higher energies. As a strong current, the spirit performs various functions for the affirmation of manifestations of the Higher Will. How else could all the manifestations on different planes be connected? Only the affirmation of the spirit can function as the link. Therefore the heart and hand of the guiding Teacher discern all the factors which are necessary for ascent. Amid fiery concepts the greatness of the link which connects the worlds must be especially sensed. From the hands of the guiding Teacher the disciple receives instruction for his association with the power of Fire. From the heart of the guiding Teacher the co-worker obtains the fiery consciousness. Only the spirit of man can truly bind together the worlds. Thus, on the path to the Fiery World let us manifest a fiery reverence for the earthly Teacher who implants the seed of the Highest.

73. The seed which transmits life to a strong spirit is verily that heritage which is passed on by the Hierarchic Principle. All those who desire to be affirmed in the conception of attainment must undeferrably adhere to the principle of Fiery Guidance. The seed is transmitted as a great fiery approach. The traveller who has realized the destiny of fiery achievement must recognize the law of the cosmic inheritance. Cosmic laws are affirmed in the basis of life, and nothing will be living whose basis is not palpitating with fire. Only he who can aspire to the fiery principle will comprehend the beauty of the fiery receptivity of Fire. Through a realization of unity with the Higher Forces it is possible to trace how the heart absorbs the Rays of Hierarchy. Only the most close ones can resound to the Rays, which affirm a fiery vibration. In transmission and reception one should remember the law that every vibration may be accepted by the spirit which stands on the most fiery step. On the path to the Fiery World one must keep in mind that one's self-manifestation as a transmitter connects one's energies with Hierarchy. Such understanding leads to the unity of spirit, which is one in its essential nature.

74. Among the followers of the Teaching those spirits who take upon themselves responsible missions must be particularly noted. How much more responsible it is to bear the synthesis, in comparison with specialization!

The affirmed guide knows all the joys, all the containments of synthesis, but at the same time he knows the burden of all the manifested and unmanifested fires. This heritage of the ages is precipitated in the "chalice" as fiery strata; therefore those who bear the fire of synthesis are manifested as bearing the burden of centuries. The specialist, having a continuous channel for the outlet of his energies, is rarely burdened, but he who carries the fire of synthesis is a tempestuous ocean of energies. The karma of him who carries the synthesis is so beautiful, but the burden is great. Each inheritance, even if it be unmanifested, lives and palpitates in the spirit. A feeling of dissatisfaction and of striving toward perfectionment distinguishes the bearers of synthesis. Though the path of specialization be outwardly difficult, the path of the bearer of the synthesis surpasses in all ways the path of the specialist. How many quests and selfless achievements does the bearer of the synthesis reveal in the life of every day! Verily, every phase of growth on the path of the synthesis-bearer is an achievement of the spirit. On the path to the Fiery World it is necessary to discern the achievement of the fiery synthesis-bearer. Thus let us remember.

75. The strongest index of achievement is self-renunciation. Indeed, it is necessary to understand this cosmic concept in all its beauty. Not only on the field of battle is the spirit adorned with the power of selflessness. To traverse the path of life impetuously, to cross all lives as upon a wire, to pass over all abysses in song, is possible only for the selfless spirit. All structures which follow the cosmic designation are erected in fiery striving.

Let us look at the life of a hero of the spirit. From early years the spirit knows the Highest Guide. The manifestation of a sacred Guardian is its life's destiny. Physical and spiritual pre-eminence do not cloud the consciousness. Self-education is a manifestation of the synthesis. The realization of one's own superiority has given the spirit firmness and tolerance toward society. All manifested talents have been displayed in inspiration, to the wealthy and the poor, to the seekers and the enlightened ones. The hero of the spirit has known a Higher Protector, therefore he has given strength to others. The Higher Law has directed him to the rudder, and visibly or invisibly he has become a fiery hero. Thus has proceeded the mighty "Lion of the Desert."

Thus has been strengthened the great law of self-renunciation. Striving toward the higher powerful cooperation has given a direct contact with the cosmic forces and with the Highest Fiery Brotherhood. This direct link has been given only through a Higher Designation. When amidst the jungles of life the spirit knows the direction, then truly the worlds resound. On the path to the Fiery World let us manifest understanding of true selflessness.

76. The destruction of many countries is strongly intensified; the entire earthly battle is accompanied by mighty conflicts in the Higher Worlds. All who know the significance of a nation's Karma can realize what is taking place. It is necessary to reflect over those events which are shaking the World. It is easy to see that the dark clouds blanket many horizons. Events in each departing order point to that future which will replace the present. Cosmic magnetism is purifying and assembling new forces. Shadows of darkness hover over the displaced countries. Where the equilibrium is not established within a short space of time, there clouds gather which will decide the fate of the dark countries and their leaders. National Karma is intensified in the West and in the East. From the North comes a New Light. The South is atremble from subterranean fire. Thus is solved the Karma of the nations. On the path to the Fiery World let us remember that national Karma is being solved by powerful events.

77. Not by accident has it been spoken about strange cases of the influence of vital emanations of all

objects surrounding man. The ancient custom of India to construct for each heir a new palace is not without a profound basis. If it were possible to show how many bloody shadows there are around many thrones, how many terrors around ancestral portraits, how many tears upon necklaces, how many ghosts on the wall, humanity would be filled with respect for emanations. For, besides the physical effects of emanations, their psychic energy may be either constructive or destructive. How can a newly chosen ruler proceed by a new path amidst the dark oppression of past emanations! Many misfortunes are caused by these heritages of the past. Not only life beyond the grave was foreseen when in ancient times the personal belongings of the deceased were buried with him. Ancient wisdom was taking measures for the purification of space. Egypt knew the force of the law of emanations. Analyzing events and a succession of historic facts, one may easily become convinced as to how under the influence of emanations destructions have taken place. On the path to the Fiery World one should manifest caution and a profound discernment of emanations. How important it is to conserve each good accumulation!

78. In the idea of traditions, one should be very subtly discriminating. If they are understood as stratifications coming from the ancestors, then indeed we arrive at the same emanations, which came from all the surroundings; the traditions will contain all the imprints of the time. But for evolution a constant renewal and broadening is required. It is correct to think about the spiral, because eternal growth affirms infinity. Creativeness is intensified in continual renovation, and infinity shines truly by the creative power of diversity. Thus traditions cannot be looked upon as a guiding principle. Usually the so-called traditions,

affirmed by people, degenerate into customs. Customs pass into habits. Thus, habits will express all the stratifications of the past. Therefore, having faith in the Fiery World, one should accept all renewal as a movement of mighty time in evolution. Thus, traditions go with the passing time, but the eternal breath of motion leads to Infinity. On the path to the Fiery World let us remember about the saturation of space by great and powerful energies.

79. The forms extant in life are the imprint of the spirit of the people. One may judge the fall or rise of a people not only from historical facts, but also from the accompanying expressions of creativeness. When coarseness and ignorance are in possession of the spirit this will be reflected in the laws and customs of the life. In this unity all the basic features of the time can be traced. Naturally, the set forms of the life give a distinct coloration to various periods of history. By what are distinguished the first three decades of the twentieth century? Wars, terrors, cruelties, coarsening and the most horrible denials! Yet it is possible to discern, amidst all this darkness, forms of Light. It matters not if they be few in number, if they be scattered over the face of the Earth. The equilibrium of Light is not established by quantity, but by potential; not by congestion, but by prowess of the spirit. Thus, on the path to the Fiery World let us be imbued with the significance of great forms, and let us especially esteem the light of the eyes, which bring to humanity the power of beauty.

80. There are many signs by means of which one may form an opinion as to the loyalty of a disciple. One sign is the persistence being exerted by the disciple on all the paths—when a disciple manifests his firmness amid storms and whirlwinds, when amidst plots and showers of stones he is not afraid to continue the designated path. Another sign is the invincibility of his faith, when the path indicated by Hierarchy is the only one. Also, in seeking signs of fidelity one should observe how the mutual relations are developed. One should understand how important is a manifest nucleus of two or three co-workers fortified by a fiery esteem for Hierarchy and for each other. By these signs may a fiery loyalty to Hierarchy be determined. Loyalty between friends, co-workers, is a pledge of devotion to Hierarchy. A nucleus of two or three friends, co-workers, can manifest the strongest support for great works. You have spoken correctly about merited favoritism, which We call the bonds of spirit and heart. Thus is affirmed the chain of loyalty which inevitably leads upward. On the path to the Fiery World one should recognize the beauty of loyalty. This wonderful path excludes that active poison which We call spiritual bribery and spiritual corruption. These ulcers are incomparably worse than physical ulcers. Thus, let us esteem loyalty on the path to the Fiery World.

81. Let us observe how the current of those who have just entered upon the path of Service acts. At first they are impelled toward an invisible, unknown Light, all their expectations are intensified, all quests are stimulated, and the spirit strives aflame. Then the current is affirmed as a personal quest; then follows a swarm of doubts and hopes. But when the spirit is able to overcome all the invasions of the dark ones, then the pledge of aspiration and ascent may become affirmed. Thus must the leaders of spirit remember. Sometimes the obvious enemies are not so dangerous as the aspirants who have approached the Light, because when the terrors of doubt are unconquered, then also is the path of Light unrealized. Indeed, one must be conscious of the full Light, in order to distinguish the voices of the Light from the whisperings of darkness. Each one chooses his way to fight against the enemies; some manifest self-defense, some foresee danger, some carry the fight to the enemy. But the path of those newly approaching Light must be verily directed and watched over, for when the doubts are not fully outlived one must direct the spirit on the path of Light. Verily, as Ur. has said, one should place everything at stake. Thus let us remember on the path to the Fiery World.

82. The Guiding Star is Karma, affirmed by actions of many lives. Each traveller knows how difficult it is to swim across an ocean and to leap over an abyss. The Guiding Star will be that skiff which conveys one to the other shore amid the raging elements. One can investigate how the Guiding Star leads, and where is that shore which will receive the wayfarer. Apparent comfort is not the boat; amid the whirlwinds of life comfort cannot endure, for the affirmation of the Guiding Star takes in all the bases of Karma. The Karmic foundations of life will be affirmed on impregnable principles, and all creative accumulations will manifest their saturated currents. The Guiding Star is kindled by each radiation which is manifested by life. The Guiding Star contains within itself the radiations of the seed of the spirit. The Guiding Star is alive every instant; in it, as it were, is the reflection of all vital energies. The spirit of man reflects in itself its own Guiding Star. On the path to the Fiery World let us remember the path manifested by the Forces of Light. Thus let us remember the Guiding Star.

83. The bridges between Worlds reflect all the energies which saturate the life of the Universe. Along these conductors shuttle all the vital currents, as reciprocal saturations. There where is the intensified activity of the spirit, an exchange of energies is very strongly established. One can take the formula of parallel motion, which premises strong sendings from and to the Earth. Thus, the earthly spheres which have been contaminated by suffocating gases cannot let the fiery currents pass. It can be observed frequently how an earthly zone has been, as it were, left to its own dissolution. This means destruction of the zone by its own gas. The supermundane strata cannot engage in the vital exchange, and, as a result of this, self-destruction takes place. Thus, in the stratifications of the spheres are all the energies of life and death. On the path to the Fiery World let us take into consideration the fact of the exchange of energies.

84. For better assimilation of the higher energies of the supermundane spheres it is necessary to spiritualize the centers. Departing from the earthly sphere, the spirit must be cleansed of lower emanations. Any superfluous husk which the spirit brings along into the Subtle World causes inexpressible pains. In a well-developed consciousness a purification takes place which frees the spirit from the husk. But the spirit which zealously retains its earthly habits experiences in the Subtle World all the infirmities which it was accustomed to undergo on the earthly plane. Going uphill, any superfluous load causes shortness of breath in the Subtle World. It is very distressing to carry things which were not previously overcome, and which in the Subtle World have become a burden. Most painful of all is the perception of one's own coarseness. Even in the lower supermundane strata is felt the weight of one's own crudities. Often there are heard wails from the supermundane strata which are the appeals of the spirits not yet cleansed of this burden. It is reprehensible to litter the Subtle World with the same lightmindedness as the earthly one. And coarse accumulations form, as it were, unerasable layers which are always visible. Thus, spiritualization of the centers is the way of ascent into the Higher Spheres. This reflection is indispensable on the Fiery path.

85. The unification of Worlds must be understood as complementation. Nothing can be given and received without mutual conformity. The supermundane World reflects all earthly emanations. One must not make the error of thinking about a condition of relaxation in the supermundane spheres. There where all is subtle, everything is sensitized. And the law of conformity should be understood as the basis of relations between the Worlds. More subtle and sensitive upward, and more coarse and unreceptive downward. Hence, the formula of intercourse between the Worlds must be understood as complementation. That which the spirit carries with ease in the earthly sphere may be unbearable in the Subtle World. Since in striving the spirit affirms its potentiality, in the Subtle World the spirit is saturated with all subtle energies. Thus, for example, a spirit intensified in a true quest yet finding no application for its pure searching, will find a useful creativeness in the subtle spheres. Thus conformity guides all intensified energies. Deplorable is the existence of those who are possessed by low feelings. Coarseness, egoism and conceit, and certain other noted human traits, bear fruit in the supermundane spheres in the way of frightful Karmic blows. On the path to the Fiery World let us remember complementation as a great law.

86. Fiery Baptism impels the spirit into the spheres which conform to the spirit's requirements. The passing of a man through a fiery transmutation gives him all possibilities for attaining the higher spheres. There where all is intensified by a fiery element, one must be saturated for the assimilation of the higher fire. Thus, one should solemnly accept all steps of the Fiery Baptism. Each step will reveal an opening of the new, supermundane sphere. The Karma of a people may also lead it through a fiery transmutation, manifesting its destined advance. All who follow the Lords are strained in this great Passage. Of course, when the hour of the earthly and supermundane battle will draw near, the Forces of both sides will become joined in flaming tension. The earthly energies and those of beyond are sparks of the One Fire. Thus, each action directed toward Good finds its fiery application in the Subtle World. It is often possible to explain the equilibrium precisely as a unification of the two Worlds. Amidst earthly destructions one may accept the power of the Subtle World as an anchor of salvation sent by the Hierarchy of Good. Let us manifest the understanding of the Fiery Baptism on the path to the Fiery World.

87. Verily, the Invisible World explains everything visible—from the Unmanifested to the manifested, from manifested to the Subtle. Thus, all energies are saturated by the One Fire. Thus, the transmutation of that which is manifested through Fire is the eternal process of evolution of Worlds. Actions invisible upon the Earth are just as vital as earthly processes, and they can affirm the bond between the Worlds. Often those who have approached the Light are perplexed as to why difficult trials do not cease. One may answer that each process invokes in the Invisible World a tension, manifested by the Forces of Light and by the hordes of darkness. Humanity is then made manifest as a useful conductor when the force of the spirit can attract the Power of Light. But it is not easy for a wavering spirit to overcome the hordes of darkness. Thus, let us remember on the Fiery Path that the spirit summons Forces from the Subtle World and from the different spheres.

88. Especially clearly felt on the steps of the Fiery consciousness is the cosmic solitude. When the spirit knows all the infinite joys of the Fiery World, yet dwells amidst earthly storms, it particularly feels the imperfection which clothes the earthly strata. Cosmic solitude is a feeling of the "Lion of the Desert." Breaking away from the Earth in spirit brings in display all the signs of cosmic solitude. Thus, when the Worlds are united in the Fiery consciousness it is difficult to bear all the acute manifestations of the earthly spheres. Rightly has it been said that the spirit can live without a body, because a deformed body can contain a luminous soul, but a body cannot, in spite of all external perfections, contain a spirit which does not conform to the accumulations of the past. It is correct that often illnesses are a blessing, for they unite the spirit with the Subtle World. Thus, each manifestation is based on two principles which respond to the measurements of the Subtle and earthly Worlds. Indeed, these measures often happen to be inversely proportional. On the path to the Fiery World let us remember that the measures of events are in need of subtle understanding.

89. The planetary dates correspond with all the supermundane dates. The dark condition of this planet requires all forces for the affirmation of equilibrium. It is easy to think about the future when the spirit knows the bond of the two Worlds, when the spirit can be successful in its strivings toward the Fiery World. There cannot be an intensification which does not reveal to the spirit the amplitude of the manifest future. In the Subtle World events go on which assist manifestations on the Earth. Especially tensed are the strata which are close to the Earth. Entire armies are being assembled for events. Entire nations are being armed against the forces of destruction. The Supermundane World will not leave the planet helpless. So too, the Mother of the World and the Hierarchy of Good and the Fiery Viceroys are mobilizing their camps. Verily, great is the time solving the earthly destiny—the Heavenly Forces saturate the space. Thus let us remember on the path to the Fiery World.

90. It is difficult to imbue the consciousness of those who think that each one's path can proceed without Higher Guidance. Each one of these petty-minded persons does not accept Hierarchy, because he regards the affirmation of Guidance as a violation of the will. Among these are many confirmed atheists who consider as maleficent a fiery faith in Higher Guidance. One can see how all principles of Hierarchy are being distorted. How is it possible to enlighten the consciousness, when the spirit is isolated from the Light and affirms its own limited life? In a fiery construction one should sense these limited extinguishers of Fires. Consciousness is a manifestation of life, therefore each structure conceived by mind produces its own forms. Actually the Subtle World is created by all the conformities of the Cosmic creativeness. The supermundane spheres clearly reflect the earthly essence. Responsibility before the Cosmos should be affirmed in the consciousness of man. Thus, on the path to the Fiery World let us strive for realization of responsibility for the creation of forms.

91. Daring is the achievement of Beauty which crowns Service. The crown is the revelation of Cosmic Communion. The basis of Cosmic rapprochement can be affirmed as a conjunction of Higher Forces. A great

Crown is ordained for the brow which has been shaped by millenniums of achievements of self-sacrifice. The crown of achievement is molded by the heart, and the winged spirit creates its own ascending Karma. With difficulty do the sparks of creativeness seep through on the path of Karma; and still less is understood the Truth of Karmic action. Not from without comes the proper estimation of Karma. Karma is contained in each cell, and the spirit carries its own attainment and its own armor.

A sunlike Karma contains all flaming achievements. The creative force of such a sunlike heart contains within itself precisely all the pangs and conflicts of the spirit. But the sunlike heart realizes its subjection to the current of the Cosmic Consciousness. The crown of the sunlike heart is verily a flaming achievement.

92. The principles of Good and evil are repeated on all planes with this distinction, that by prolonging the line into the spheres of the Subtle World, all expressions become heightened. Only the principles of constructiveness give to the spirit that resultant force which affirms a conscious striving for good. The servants of darkness will be inevitably attracted to the lower strata. Ancient Scriptures speak of those who dwell in the Kingdom of the Spirit and those who live under the earth. One may be surprised as to why the earthly strata and the Earth itself is inhabited by the forces of evil. Actually, a downward attraction explains these hordes. Each aspiration toward the Fiery World tends to hold the spirit in the Subtle World, but the Spirits who are Bearers of Light, filled with self-sacrifice, rush to the Earth for purpose of salvation. There are whole countries on Earth which are saturated with destroyers. The Earth conforms, with its poisoned emanations, to these spawns of darkness. Therefore, be not astonished that portions of the world are peopled with dark entities.

93. A construction of new fundamentals will be contained in the establishment of equilibrium and of coordination between science, art and life. For an equilibrium is needed based on a survey of all affirmations. Thus, the World is in need of a great manifestation of equilibrium. Coordination is to be affirmed upon a new understanding of all the subtle principles of Hierarchy. One may even foresee how a transmutation of all affirmations will take place; how in science there will be no great division between spirit and matter. Indeed, it will be possible to build on new principles when the spiritual and the physical are united. It will be possible to secure knowledge of the body by means of the coordination of the centers, their functions and qualities. Such a unity of all functions leads to knowledge of life as it actually is. For example, one could study the various precipitations of the kidneys and the functions of the eyes. It is possible to coordinate the functions of all organs which have double branchings. It is possible to compare the organs which act by one channel. It is possible to be convinced of many unities of functions, which are highly indicative. Thus, new structures have their great principles, and a great ascent in the world of knowledge is indicated. Thus the Fiery Bearers of the synthesis bring good and happiness to the World. On the path to the Fiery World let us remember about the great affirmation of equilibrium and coordination.

94. The abyss may be conquered by different paths. Courage in the face of the unfolding abyss is attained precisely when the spirit places everything at stake. It is correct that the spirit can be tempered only in life. The overcoming of life's difficulties will bring the spirit its spark. Spiritual conquests are so difficult. The physical body endures privations in self-satisfaction, but the spirit conquers difficulties. And the fiery spiritual strife can uplift to a great height. Thus, let us aspire to spiritual difficulties. The abyss can unfold itself before the heart. Thus it seems that the path of life proceeds inexorably; but the heart which realizes the abyss is also conscious of the Light. For, when a final boundary has been manifested it is possible to unroll a Fiery Infinity. Only in complete striving can the spirit unfold its wings. On the path to the Fiery World one must be imbued with fearlessness before the abyss. The winged spirit knows this joy of attainment.

95. At the threshold of passage into the Subtle World there occurs a separation of the mental body from the physical. The development of fiery receptivity assists the flight into the Higher Spheres. The separation of the mental body can be clearly realized by the spirit which senses the breaking away from the Earth and aspires into the Higher Spheres; thus takes place a unification of the two Worlds, which liberates the spirit from the physical body. The question of death greatly preoccupies humanity. Precisely it is the transition which frightens people so much. It may be pointed out how wonderfully the spirit which has understood the transitory existence on Earth is impelled into the Subtle World. One should consciously prepare the spirit for the breaking away from Earth. In this manner the affirmed threshold is disclosed to the one newly arrived, in all the Fiery Grandeur. Thus, on the path to the Fiery World one should accustom oneself to the breaking away from Earth.

96. When the fiery spirit plunges into the super-mundane spheres the Subtle Spheres are not foreign to it, because this spirit has known the spatial manifestations. Thus the newcomer can acclimate himself in the strata of the Subtle World. A sensation of joy accompanies the entrance into the Subtle World.

97. One should be very solicitous about the last hours of sojourn on Earth. Often the final striving can predetermine the succeeding life, also the stratum in which the spirit will dwell. Indeed, it is inadmissible to recall the spirit into the earthly spheres when it already has broken away. Tissues which already have been freed from earthly attractions must be strained in a terrific effort in order again to be assimilated into the earthly atmosphere. People should learn to think during someone's departure, as well as during birth, and should be able to ease the processes. As delays are harmful during birth, they are likewise harmful during death. The subtle formation of the new body must be taken into consideration. Wounds caused the departing one must be cured in the Subtle World. A most cruel treatment of the departing ones is often manifested. It may be said that it is not death which torments, but living people. All who are approaching the Fiery Teaching must know about this. On the path to the Fiery World let us remember the law of affirming the last minutes of the crossing.

98. Merit, as it is understood, must be replaced by a more subtle concept. If, instead of external signs, one becomes accustomed to look upon the reality of merit, according to the inner quality of action, then how many subtle signs can be observed! When the spirit learns to coordinate the earthly life with the Higher, then all measurements take on another dimension. Life filled merely with the monotony of the material world correspondingly marks off the merit according to its aspirations. But the consciousness of the two Worlds affirms new measures. The transitory will not be the real impelling factor. Only a striving for fiery

manifestation unites the Worlds, and action will be correspondingly saturated. The consciousness of him who heads into the Fiery World is imbued with the Force emanating from the Hierarchy of Good; but earthly bliss is as quickly dissolved as is the entire transitory World. On the path to the Fiery World let us remember the eternally living energy of the World of Fire.

99. Karma is diffused in all actions, in all Worlds. In the same way as Karma can be hastened, it can be as well prolonged. A deepening of Karma is reflected not only upon the succeeding life. All intermediate states are also affected in an aggravation of Karma. The Subtle World is closely held in bond with the earthly, and it is necessary to intensify thinking in this direction. He who understands the meaning of the connection of the two Worlds, will be careful of his earthly actions. Care toward all energies is of assistance to the striving spirit. A chief impediment is non-understanding of the truth of spatial life; that all is transmuted, all is atoned for. Correctly has it been pointed out about the law of Karma; indeed, about the law of Karma unto infinity. Precisely, aspiration reaches into infinity; and so also do possibilities. On the path to the Fiery World let us affirm a conscious relationship to the law of Karma.

100. The co-participants of Cosmic structure may be called true Regents. Each epoch has its Regents. The Lord, the Man-God, and the Regent of the Forces of Light constitute the great Power. The Hierarchic principle appears as the basis of all constructions, and for a deepening of understanding of Cosmic structure one should become affirmed by the recognition of the manifested law of Hierarchy. The Forces of Hierarchy are joined across two Worlds—the Guiding Principle, and the principle of fulfilling the Great Will are one

Source. Worlds are built upon the two Principles. The Supermundane World is manifested by means of the earthly one. The earthly world aspires into the Fiery World. Eternal life is affirmed in this fiery unity, and the power of life is intensified in fiery structure. For a subtle understanding of the Hierarchic Principle one should delve into the structure of Existence. The Higher Will dictated its Testaments. Manifestation of the Fiery World were assumed by Fiery Spirits; in this manner an exchange unifying the Worlds was taking place. All religions have been affirmed by an exchange of Fiery Forces. This fiery cooperation is the Cosmic structure. On the path to the Fiery World let us manifest understanding of Cosmic structure.

101. Verily, only the heart is able to penetrate into all actions, into all motives, into all entities, manifesting discernment. For penetration into the Fiery World, it is especially necessary to discriminate with the heart. Only that source which strives toward the bases of Truth can provide a concept of the true structure of Cosmos. Only that source which is saturated with the fire of subtle energies can offer a true measure of the judgments. For the affirmation of one's forces in the Higher Spheres it is indispensable to intensify the forces of the heart, for there is no other quality of Fire which can replace these energies. The heart powerfully impels the spirit to the subtle energies. All the Higher Spheres are attained by the tension of the heart. This sacred vessel can reveal all the creative exalted spheres. These heart energies are irreplaceable, truly the Higher Will is reflected in them. The creativeness of the heart may be called sunlike. On the path to the Fiery World let us aspire to an understanding of the heart as a connecting manifestation between the Worlds.

102. The distribution of people according to auras

and to mutual attraction is a scientific truth, but for scientific investigations it is necessary to apply subtle discrimination. Where the cognition of the heart is aglow, there will be discrimination. Where the cognition of the heart is inactive, so also inactive will be the fiery energy. It is necessary to feel how there are gathered around the fiery heart those who have been drawn to it by the striving toward Fiery Service. The attraction of the magnet of the heart acts as a law; it must also be remembered that each life of the heart attracts those who reveal kinship of spirit. Life which is thus begun is extended in the supermundane spheres. Thus can be easily explained each Karmic manifestation. People do not reflect much on this law; and the World does not so much suffer from various calamities as it does from the breaking of this great law by the intrusion of human errors. Intrusion on the harmonious arrangement is always manifested in a derangement of Karmic effects. Many inexplicable misfortunes have been evoked by Karmic violations. In history one can trace how kings have been deprived of their most faithful servants, how generals have lost their troops, and spiritual guides their disciples, through some fearful intrusion into the connecting Karma. Let us deliberate, on the fiery path, about the invulnerability of Karma for the sake of advancement.

103. Transmutation of the centers intensifies the creative energies which are necessary for crossing into the Subtle World. Each spiritual striving produces its sediments, which assume the aspect of subtle energies during the passage into the Subtle World. Thus, it is important to aspire into the Higher Spheres. Ecstasy of spirit and joy of the heart yield those energies which nourish the subtle body. Indeed, only a feeling imbued with higher impulses provides the needed energies.

It must be understood that imperil and gross earthly desires produce their ugly ulcers, which the spirit must heal in the subtle body. Ulcers of the spirit are carried over into the Subtle World if they are not gotten rid of on the Earth. Liberation from the physical vehicle does not mean deliverance from spiritual ulcers. When the spirit, faced with breaking away from the Earth, realizes how it has used its energies, then the consciousness can atone for a great deal; but the consciousness must be impelled toward the thought about the Higher Worlds. Even the most serious criminal can be directed toward the understanding of the burden of Karma, but for this it is necessary to change the social conditions. Thus, on the path to the Fiery World one should become accustomed to the thought about transmutation of the centers, because liberation from the body is not deliverance from spiritual ulcers.

104. Forces manifested for the Service of Light do not invade Karma, as some who are not initiated into the power of Karma think. The Forces of Light observe human actions, giving the direction but not invading life. Many are the examples of this. Messengers appear, warnings are sent, the direction is given and the paths pointed out; but the choice of designated affirmation is determined by the human will. In this way appears the manifestation of cooperation between the two Worlds. Precisely, self-activity of the spirit can bring near a better Karma. Thus it can be explained why the Forces of Light do not stop the spirit from certain actions which violate often that which has been ordained. Often people are perplexed as to why the other paths are not indicated. Likewise they wonder why the Sendings are affirmed through various channels? They wonder why the Forces of Light do not ward off different currents. Let us reply, "The Forces of Light never invade human

Karma." This law must be remembered on the path to the Fiery World.

105. The law of free will often prohibits Us from clarifying a manifestation which appears to be obscure. The very same law indicates Our crossing of paths when the free will directs a heart toward a heart.

106. To be affirmed in the heart upon the Lord is the first condition on the path to the Fiery World. It is impossible to arrive at the ordained Gates without this fiery requirement. Of course, Guidance must be recognized in spirit and heart, for the acceptance of the Hand of the Lord is alone insufficient without devoting the heart to the Lord. One must understand that law which unites the Teacher with the disciple, because without the manifestation of complete attachment to the Lord there can be no bond. A full acceptance of Guidance means a conscious relationship, for one must understand and feel in the heart the warmth which arises from the depths of the spirit. It is especially necessary to feel and to learn to discern that by which the nature of the Lord is linked with that of the disciple. Thus, one must remember that vibrations and Karma are as connecting links on the path to the Fiery World.

107. The spirit is actuated by various levers. Love and striving are the strongest levers. Love for Hierarchy and striving for Service provide the impulse for higher saturations. These powerful levers direct the spirit to perfectionment, not only on the Earth but also in the Subtle World. Even if it were somehow possible to be freed on the Earth from certain manifestations, the supermundane spheres do not permit the spirit so easily to change spheres. The supermundane spheres have their vortices into which the spirit is drawn. These vortices may be called whirlwinds of expiation.

According to the condition of striving or carnate desire the spirit falls into these vortices and may pass into other spheres only by atoning and by transmuting its energies. It is necessary to understand the conditions of the Subtle World. If humanity would reflect upon this inseparable bond with the Subtle World the concept of Karma would become clear. There is no action, no thought, no step which does not impel the spirit into a certain vortex. The fiery spirit is manifested as an inviolate link between the Worlds, for thus all paths are revealed.

108. Indeed, refraining from delving into the existing bond between the Fiery World and the earthly deprives life of its meaning. Each earthly manifestation becomes meaningless. Delving into the Fiery World is indispensable for understanding in life the fact that the unity of two Worlds directs the thought cosmically. Only the unity of each earthly manifestation with its extension into the Fiery World affirms the significance of all earthly processes. It is hard to imagine how difficult it is to direct thoughts if this law is unrealized, or when this law has been distorted by different interpretations. How much more clearly can the spirit grasp the process of life and death when the concept of the Supermundane World lives in one's consciousness! Thus, the whirlwinds of the spheres of subtle tensions impel the spirit during ascent and return. Definitely, the bond of the spirit with Karma is manifested in both Worlds. The understanding of this bond points to the beauty affirmed by the Cosmos. Discrimination of those earthly impulses which in the future will provide conditions for subtle existence, is so very important! For it is impossible to take eternity for the transitory, and the transitory for eternity. Thus does the spirit learn, living in the material world, to appraise the transitory; but Eternity has been ordained in the Cosmos!

109. The bond between Worlds must occupy the thoughts of humanity. How else could one explain certain invisible processes, which nurture life? One may become imbued with that knowledge only when the spirit apprehends in the heart the manifestations of the Invisible World. How else may one explain life and the crossing into the Subtle World, if one is not affirmed upon the Fiery World? Each earthly occurrence assuredly has in the back of it its invisible cause, and it also is a potential cause. It can be easily understood that for fiery receptivity one should first of all affirm thought upon the bond with the supermundane spheres. Happenings in life can be made real only when the spirit senses each higher vibration. Obviously, humanity lives without cognition of the heart, which moves with the force of the Fiery World. For better forms one should look upon life as a union of the two Worlds. Each striving in this direction will be helpful for ascent into the Subtle World. If the perception of higher energies is established as a vital process, one may become aware that earthly life, with all its pangs, is extended into the next World. Thus, let us apprehend the law of atonement on the Earth, in actions and meditations.

110. About the destination of man on the Earth. From times immemorial this question has occupied the minds of people. All religions have noted the affirmation about the destination of man who bears a kinship to Higher Force. Wherein then is revealed a likeness to Higher Force? Only in perfectionment of spirit may man be likened to Higher Force. The destination of man cannot be regarded as something accidental. Likewise it is impossible to regard all forms uniformly, because all spheres have their own forms and very precise correlations. We speak often about the bond between two Worlds, because it is imperative to get out of the vicious circle which has girdled the planet. It is necessary to find the exit. Thinking must be directed to the more subtle principles in order to discover points of contact. Reflecting upon the simplest processes, we shall reach the highest concepts. If we shall discover the subtle bond in all life then indeed a striving toward the Higher World will not delay in coming. Since up to now it has been rather difficult to awaken the consciousness, at present it is necessary to push forward persistently all the foundations of the bond. All events, all affirmations, summon humanity to the achievement of transmutation of the fundamentals of a World outlook. It is especially needed to penetrate into the destination of man.

111. No receptivity is possible without heart aspiration. True, the intellect does perceive, but incomparable is the subtle action of the heart. In fact, when we say that a thought has flashed, it means the heart has revealed a saturated remembrance and perception. Indeed, only subtle energies can be joined to the subtle; therefore, the speediest attainment is through the heart. The bond with the Fiery World is established by the saturated heart, because this vessel alone permits penetration into the Fiery World. To understand the striving of the heart as a symbol of creativeness brings to the spirit affirmation of the Fiery World. The heart bears the burden of the World. The heart liberates from the earthly burden. Thus let us remember on the path to the Fiery World.

112. The protective network is formed out of subtlest energies. All centers participate in the formation of this powerful shield. For a complete circle it is necessary that all the spiritual centers intensify their ener-

gies. From out of the centers of the spirit it is especially necessary to tense the heart, because by its power it can transmute thinking. Right thinking produces stability, which is the first requirement. Steadfastness expels duplicity, fear and doubt. The protective net can defend a man, making him invulnerable. But his shield can only then be affirmed when all subtle energies have been harmonized. The experience of Agni Yoga truly provides this shield, but a most cautious regard for the centers is necessary. The protective net must be continually saturated with the energies from within, as a fiery, eternally ascending spiral. Spiritual centers must nurture this power. The protective net passes on with the spirit into the Subtle World. Woven from the subtlest energies, it can become assimilated into the Fiery World; only the highest strivings may be reflected in it. People who live by means of lower centers have no protective net. Obsessed ones do not have this shield. Therefore, on the Fiery path one should take care of the interweaving of the subtlest energies.

113. The protective net can only then be saturated when the centers have been transmuted. And on the final step, before receiving the Fiery Ray, the protective net is especially taut.

114. The fabric of the protective net is strung by the most diverse energies. Each spiritual center is based upon the collection of precipitations of the subtlest energies into the protective net. All the centers are transmuted and saturated by fire, which weaves the threads of the protective net. Thus, this shield is an affirmation of all cosmic currents, which are refracted in the protective net. Each blow upon the aura may be reflected, as a boomerang, upon its sender. When the protective net can reflect all the Higher Fires, then, indeed, can be fused in this furnace many manifest blows. Each striving consciousness must weave its own protective net. One may deflect many blows and painful stings if the protective net remains impenetrable. The immunity of the spiritual centers may become complete when the protective net is continually nourished by fire from within. Hence, it is so important to be solicitous about the tension of the protective net. Psychic energy, aspiration of the spirit, and fiery transmutation will supply the needed fabric for the protective net. On the path to the Fiery World let us remember the power of this Shield.

115. However diverse the Worlds are in their spiritual properties and functions, nevertheless it is necessary to become accustomed to think about the bridge to the Fiery World. Everything has its connecting energies. Why then not strive to understand the bridge to the Fiery World! As man reflects all the qualities of earthly life, to the same extent must he be concerned as to how to lay a bridge between the Worlds. Just as the abyss of mankind is visible from the supermundane spheres, so should the Higher World be accepted into human consciousness. The bridge between the two Worlds is maintained in the aspiration of thought. Rightly has it been said about the beauty of thought which reveals all Worlds. Indeed, the bridge between the two Worlds can be made real if the actions are filled with beauty. Truly, not words but actions bring all saturations. The bridge between Worlds will be based upon harmonization of the currents of heart and spirit. On the path to the Fiery World let us manifest understanding of the bridge between Worlds.

116. The connection between the life of each Servant of Light and the succeeding step reveals a saturated heart striving. Indeed, people debase the feeling of love and interpret vulgarly the great law. But one must harken subtly to the great law. Thus, verily, the Yoga of the Heart brings one to the mighty summits of consciousness far more strongly and speedily than does the Mind, however refined it may be. Therefore, the great Epoch of Woman will be distinguished by greater refinement of feelings and of consciousness.

117. The bridge between Worlds is based on harmonization of all the subtlest energies. Actually, the majority thinks that transmutation of the centers takes place on the physical plane. This is an error. Such consciousness must be enlightened. Transmutation of centers by Fire is a fusion of all the centers, both physical and spiritual. A spiritualization of the entire being takes place. In fiery transmutation the Fiery World is revealed especially strongly, because a fiery harmonization takes place in one's entire essence, involving acquisition of all the higher tensions. Therefore, one may accept the law of the connection of the Worlds in each process of the refinement of spiritual centers. Accumulation of these energies gives the spirit an impetuousness which carves out the shortest path. Thus one must accept the concept of the bridge between Worlds, and one should remember that no unconscious labor of the centers exists. Conscious harmony of the centers is a great mystery. Thus, on the path to the Fiery World let us manifest understanding of the shortest path.

118. Among the mysteries existing in the Cosmos must be noted that of succession of existences. The rhythms of these existences are just as varied as are the Monads. Some think that it is necessary to spend a great number of lives in palaces; others think that for heroism cavalries are needed; a third group thinks that glory is needed; a fourth that chastisement of spirit and body are necessary, and so on ad infinitum. But We say

achievement of spirit is needed. And this fiery quality is attained only through the inner Fire of the heart. Rightly has it been said that the deeds of the heart are the foundation. Knowledge of the heart affirms the great essence. Therefore, the heart as a magnet is powerful. Of course, a being lives in all potentiality. For a certain cycle of years the potential manifests one form of actions, for another cycle other actions are manifested. Thus, a complete world of actions takes place in a single life. Let us recall how many luminous actions fill the records of the Book of Life. Let us consider each action of Light, for it is especially necessary to realize those powerful energies which fill a being on a great step.

119. The forces of the spirit provide the currents upon which certain energies can proceed. The Hiero-inspiration can be sent only through the currents of the spirit. A power not earthly is carried by the Bearers of these currents. The spirit and heart which are saturated by these currents withstand many attacks. Often have We observed a solitary traveller on the Path of Service repulsing the onslaughts of darkness. The Forces of the Spirit bestow the power of action upon straight-knowledge. Currents of the spirit are the link with the Higher Forces. When the powerful energies saturate a being, then becomes apparent the development of all the higher centers. Hiero-inspiration can be affirmed only in the heart which is aflame with closeness to the Hierarchy of Light. Therefore, on the path to the Fiery World it is so important to distinguish these currents, because it is necessary to apply a conscious relation to everything in order to find the bond with the Invisible World of Fire. Thus, the forces of the spirit can truly conquer Worlds.

120. It is necessary subtly to investigate transfer-

ence of sensitiveness. Transfer of sensitivity, inwardly or outwardly, constitutes a very important branch of science; not only for the investigation of the human organism, but also for the study of reciprocal tension of Macrocosm and microcosm. Up to this point experiments have been carried out between people and objects; further experiments will be made with plants and animals. By broadening the investigations, one can arrive at a study of the exchange of subtle energies. Thus, all animals can serve for the change of currents of diseases. Of course, in this investigation it will be needful to develop an immunity against infection. Magnetism of the Earth and of the roots of trees, as well as Prana, can serve for the purification of emanations. One may reach into the Cosmic Laboratory for all bases for these investigations. Before the experiment of transfer of sensitivity one should study the manifestations of Agni Yoga, for only subtle receptivity will yield a subtle understanding. One must be imbued with currents of the spirit in order to understand all the potency that saturates the Fiery World.

121. The principle of transference of sensitiveness is very clearly indicated in the swelling of the lips. An accumulation of fiery energies in the throat is discharged in another center. Likewise, nasal hemorrhage is a result of a strong transference of fire of a center, outwardly manifested through the third eye. If subtle energies are saturated by Fire, then transmutation of the centers is so strong that a discharge is inevitable. Fires are raging; that is why it is very necessary to guard the health. Tension of the currents of space is strongly reflected on subtle organisms. Spatial currents are very strongly intensified. The vision of the black networks revealed all the blackness of the web which surrounds the planet. A whirlwind is being borne through space. Thus We discharge spatial pressures.

122. The World is plunged into such a dark state that the supermundane spheres are being filled with stifling gases. Various indicated manifestations affirm how black threads envelop the earthly spheres. It is proper to think and to prepare the consciousness for manifestations of fiery shocks. Space is in need of a purification, and a new discharge may occur in the earthly sphere when the spiritual currents will be roused creatively under the tension of new impulses. It is impossible to expect a regeneration on the planet without the affirmation of new principles and of coordination. Only spatial currents are needed for coordination with vital potentials. Thus, on the path to the Fiery World let us strive for ascent through fiery spiritual currents.

123. If one accustoms oneself to penetrate into the depths of the heart, it is possible to evoke vibratory currents of subtle feelings. In the depths of the heart can be awakened the manifestation of the Cosmic Magnet. It is only necessary to recall those moments of life which manifest the resounding of subtle strings. A glance directed into the depths of the heart discovers all the currents of the spirit. It can truly be said that people persist living without pity. First of all it must be understood that in the Subtle World there is nothing more frightful than heartlessness. It casts the spirit down to a step on which the earthly world loses all human likeness. Therefore, magnanimity can follow only after heartlessness has been cast out. Nothing is more frightful than that heartlessness which is in the pretended magnanimity that lives in the heart of egoism. Therefore, the path of Truth manifests a spiritual current which illuminates the searches. A pretended magnanimity is not the foundation of creative coop-eration. Infringement upon the heart of one's dear one is not magnanimity. Thus, let the co-workers espe-cially look into the depths of their hearts, for as Ur. has rightly said—"one should not insinuate oneself into the soul of one's friend; it is better to look into the mirror of one's own spirit." On the path to the Fiery World a pretended magnanimity is a stumbling block.

124. The world suffers from a dismemberment which engulfs all the great beginnings. In place of unity, dismemberment is preached everywhere. There has remained not one principle which people do not distort at its core. Each beginning is affirmed first of all as a part of a great Whole. How could this mat-ter fail to be treated in human searches? The invisible is isolated from the visible World. The Higher is iso-lated from the Earth. Only a striving for unity of con-cepts of magnitudes can establish the necessary link between the Worlds. Without saturation of the heart it is impossible to embrace all the Worlds, for how to affirm a cosmic bond without the acceptance of the Unity of the whole Cosmos? In the small and the great let us manifest understanding of this Great Law. The dismemberment of Worlds leads to a state of savagery. On the path to the Fiery World let us remember about the unity of Worlds.

125. So many distortions, so many inaccuracies have been admitted into the Teachings. Verily, each purification is great Service. Each striving to renew the Truth, as it has been given to humanity, is fiery Service. The black threads seen represent not only the dark-ness of the earthly atmosphere, but also that network which covers the human mind and heart. It is difficult to imagine how many minds have been clouded by various evil interpretations. Each man is full of tension in search of new interpretations, but goes farther and farther away from the Truth. Dismemberment is so vividly affirmed in religions, in science, and in all creativeness. Each World has its correlation to another World. Each Truth emanates from another Truth. Truth is revealed only to the open heart. Thus, the tensed consciousness, which senses the cosmic pulse, passes on its own beat with luminous thoughts. Verily, great is the Fiery Pulse, revealed to the fiery heart.

126. Exactly with fire and sword is the planet being purified. How otherwise will the consciousness be awakened? The aspiration of humanity is drowned in earthly desires. Waves of gross desires impair each zone of light, and each instant reveals oceans of unrestrained lusts. If humanity would compare Light with darkness, the visible World with the Invisible, then it would indeed be possible to affirm the fiery Truth. In the supermundane spheres the spirit grievously atones for its earthly doings. If one imagines vortices of good or evil, which, as it were, are pulling the spirit into their orbits, then one can manifest an understanding of the cosmic currents. Free will engenders a cause of a cosmic current, and the current of evil or the current of good will be chosen by the spirit through free will, expressed by everyday actions. Thus, on the path to the Fiery World, comparison of the currents of good and evil gives the impulse for pure striving.

127. As to how to apply one's qualities in Service, it is not enough to say, "I have come and I wish to serve," for readiness to serve obliges the disciple to acquire discipline of spirit. It is insufficient to say that all indications of the Teaching have been accepted, for only in life is it possible to manifest acceptance of the Indications. If the earthly plane imposes hard and fast rules, the world of the spirit demands the manifestation of striving in life towards acceptance of the Principle of Hierarchy. Firm striving compresses the spirit and tempers it for true Service. One must merit the affirmation of the Call, one must understand the Call, one must free oneself from many burdens; thus, should one understand the truth of approach to the Teaching. One must understand the beauty of giving, for merely earthly givings do not affirm the "chalice." Thus, on the path to the Fiery World let the co-workers apprehend the Call to Service.

128. One can imagine the joy of the spirit which has realized the construction of a New World. If the striving is great, then each form will produce a deepening in perfectionment. The unification of Worlds can advance conscious striving. Let us take the forms of the Subtle World and apply them to the earthly plane. The comparison between psychic energy and mechanical receptions has been rightly applied. Indeed, creativeness can be manifested precisely by the higher energies, but for such subtle perception it is necessary to manifest transmutation of the centers. Only when the spirit feels communion with the Invisible World is it possible to affirm the spatial current. Even simple experiments require complete confidence. How much more strongly affirmed then must be the spirit in full communion with the Invisible World!

Many things which it is customary to consider as phenomena may be explained simply as transmutation of one of the centers. How strongly then does create the spirit of the Agni Yogi whose centers have been kindled by sacred fire! Thus, on the path to the Fiery World it is possible to penetrate into the powerful activity of the Agni Yogi. Let us reverence the Mother of Agni Yoga—I have spoken.

129. In the spirit of each man lives the principle

of good, which can saturate the whole being if these energies of Light are consciously invoked. The constructiveness of the spirit can be intensified by currents manifested by good or evil; it depends upon man to put into action the different levers. Each builder can honestly say to himself what it is that he serves—spirit or matter. Indeed, one can easily be convinced as to the direction in which the forces of the spirit proceed. In its seed each spirit knows the truth manifested by quiet currents; hence, this immersing directs the spirit to right thinking. Certainly, the consciousness of unity can open all the locks which separate man from the Higher Truth. The world of the spirit needs to be understood. Thus, everyone can evoke a most subtle current from the depths of the heart. The best conduit to the Fiery World is the depths of the heart; therein is hidden the Cosmic Fire.

130. The boundary line between the higher and lower spheres must demonstrate that it is possible for their unification to take place. There are many paths for unifying the Worlds. First of all, it is important to accustom the consciousness to the thought that all is possible. Once accepted that all is possible, the spirit can attain the degree of the Fiery Emblem, which bestows an impetuous constructiveness. When the spirit of man becomes accustomed to thought about the Subtle World, the manifestation of many laws of Existence becomes intelligible. A most urgent law directs man to the principle of unity, to the transformation of man by the path of Fire, transmuting all the centers.

Even the dark forces believe in the unity of Worlds. True, in the limited consciousness, the unification of Worlds is expressed by examples which bring the Higher down to the lower; but the aspiring consciousness rises upward from the earthly spheres to the Subtle Worlds. Thus, on the path to the Fiery World let us learn to rise to the spheres affirmed by Fire.

131. When people will learn to respect the Cosmic Laws, then, indeed, the Cosmic Magnet will indicate to them the path to perfection. The subtle understanding of this law can ennoble all humanity. The great law can awaken all good strivings. Pure and great love gives birth to that nobility of spirit which can regenerate man. One can easily imagine how will be manifested all the great feelings engendered by the unified heart.

132. Often the spirit which bears the synthesis affirms its knowledge from within the "chalice," for the accumulated treasures of creativeness are actually tensed by creative vibrations. Often the spirit, as it were, finds its confirmation upon the basis of the unified consciousness. The manifestation of creative vibrations often evokes a thought which has dwelt in the depths of the heart. One must harken to those thoughts which, as if something familiar, live in the spirit. One can find many identical vibrations by subtly examining one's consciousness. The treasures of the "chalice" are not to be regarded as accidental. They constitute the potentiality of the spirit. These creative vibrations open many locks, for the hidden knowledge which lives in the spirit can be revealed. Often the aspiring spirit discovers that vibration which connects it with the Higher Forces. How can one imagine this sacred power which unites the depths of the heart with the Fiery World! The records of space are often available to it, for unity is strongly manifested as the bond between Worlds. On the path to the Fiery World it is needful to remember about the vibration which touches the depths of the heart of the bearer of synthesis.

133. It is difficult even to imagine how infected the planet is! Not one law remains which has not been permeated by the poison of decomposition. Each higher manifestation has been so completely covered by black thought that purification of the earthly and supermundane strata is the most important task. Even the way that the Higher Teaching is being applied only demonstrates that the interpretations of darkness are closer to the spirit. The Fiery Testament will then be affirmed when the human spirit is cleansed of those manifestations which have obscured spirit and heart. Let us investigate how Truth is being affirmed. The Fiery Spirit affirms the Higher Testament. Its successors affirm the given Teaching. The chosen Spirit clarifies the Testament handed down by the Fiery Lawgiver. Thus, for the affirmation of New Testaments the Giving Hand and the receiving one are unified. People think too little about this sacred bond. The unification of the Worlds can take place only in this manner. The Visible World and the Invisible can find a living application only when a bond is affirmed. Therefore, one who takes upon himself the clarification of the Teaching carries a Burden of humanity. Thus, on the path to the Fiery World let us be imbued with respect for the clarification of the Teaching.

134. Therefore, so flamingly beautiful is the task of clarifying the Teaching. It never has happened that the Teaching was affirmed without a fiery clarifier. This task also may be called a sacrificial one. Only a spirit closest in heart can take upon himself this mission. Only a unified consciousness can know the affirmation of Truth. Only a unified consciousness can perceive how to give clarification to the Teaching. We are all, in turn, affirmed as Lawgivers and Clarifiers—this is the Highest Law. The ocean of the Teaching is given only to the nearest one. Humanity suffers so greatly from egoism and self-conceit that it is indispensable to affirm the closest source. Thus, let the heart feel and know in its depths that through the Mother of Agni Yoga is given to the World My Fiery Message. It is essential that the depths of the heart perceive this fiery Truth on all paths.

135. The Living Ethics discerns all the concepts which are the Fundamentals of Life. In order to apply the Living Ethics to life it is first of all needful to find in oneself the quality of true Service to Hierarchy. Precisely all bigots are the first to depart from the Living Ethics. No standing before an Object, symbolizing the Loftiest of Images, can help, if there is no true reverence. We know bigots who can pray with words but are silent in heart. Indeed, these bigots love to talk about a sacred Image hanging near them in a corner or standing close by on a table. The Living Ethics must first of all be expressed in ethics of daily actions. The Living Ethics helps to preserve the image of man. These fiery laws will give the spirit understanding of Hierarchy. Service can be a miraculous bridge between Worlds, for the Subtle World cannot help a spirit to become surrounded with subtle energies if infections of the spirit are not eliminated on the Earth. Useless are all assurances of devotion, useless are professed understandings of the Teacher, useless are honors to the Lord where there is no understanding of the Living Ethics. In the Subtle World one does not depart from one's experiences. As one's own light illumines the surroundings, so too does one's own darkness choke all space. On the path to the Fiery World one must ponder about the threatening consequences if the Living Ethics has not been applied in life.

136. Thus must the Living Ethics enter into everyday life. If the Living Ethics be not accepted, then a series of rigorous consequences will be powerfully manifested.

137. The Living Ethics contains laws for the manifestation of Truth. Life is affirmed in all the higher concepts; thus, the creativeness of the Living Ethics directs thought to the construction of the essential. All strivings in the name of the Living Ethics will direct thought to future constructiveness. Indeed, not by words but by actions will be molded the steps of the future. Each life-giving fire must evoke its own forms. Therefore, the creativeness of the Living Ethics can direct humanity to the Light. The Subtle World affirms its creative power which is manifested for the betterment of Existence. How great is the responsibility of mankind for all the engenderings which have caused such destruction! Each engendering in its turn produces its destruction, and the planet is engulfed in stifling gases. Therefore, it is so important to assume a higher destination of life as a striving toward the true Living Ethics. It is impossible to bring into order the earthly and supermundane spheres without this purification. The present is revealed as the time for introspection and adoption of these great designations, for the battle between Light and darkness is at hand. Thus, on the path to the Fiery World let us intensify our energies in the name of the Living Ethics.

138. Standing before the Lord can be experienced only by the heart. Filling the heart with the Lord propels each quality of the spirit. Only inner comprehension will give subtle understanding. Nothing external can wash the body of Christ. Nothing external replaces the filling of the heart with the Lord. Even small flashes of consciousness indicate that nothing external can be compared with the fire of the spirit and with

pure motive. If the spirit could preserve the memory of the spheres of the Subtle World, then indeed much could have been already established. But it would be impossible to leave behind memory of the experiences, because hard is the path of sensations not yet out-lived. The supermundane spheres have their records, and these direct the efforts of successive lives. Long since have all religions proclaimed this law. Standing before God, standing before the Judge, standing before the Lord, is a single concept. Therefore, on the path to the Fiery World let us remember how vital is standing before the Lord.

139. People do not even suspect how strained the planet is! All these conditions which governments are creating are comparable to a volcano. Each wave of actions is saturated with destruction. There are no such circumstances as would indicate an advancement toward salvation. Yet the more suffocating, the more speedily can the great World Problem be resolved. Supermundane spheres are also agitated. Verily, each spirit striving into the future can sense that "Some-thing," about which only the Lords know. Surely it is imperative to think about the driving clouds which must inevitably destroy the countries going against the Light. A New Dawn is already lighting the way on the dark horizon. Already events are proceeding and new forces are building a better future. Therefore, one must reflect about the appearance of the Fiery Element, for whoever is from Fire, triumphs with Fire.

140. At all turning points in the history of the World it could have been observed how the fiery con-cepts were broadcast in space. Side by side with dying concepts new paths were born. All great changes have been directed by cosmic currents of two poles. Thus, the organization of the World is saturated with the energies of these two poles. The stronger the tension of darkness, the more powerful the creativeness of Light. Fiery energies can be affirmed only in great tension. The explosions of these tensions produce new energies. Viewing the chart of the World, the far-sighted spirits know where is being established the New Magnet of future constructions. One can easily convince oneself as to the procedure of the cosmic energies of the upheaval, as they impetuously drive toward the ultimate battle. All cosmic energies are being assembled for the installation of the fiery foundations. Indeed, this entire great transmutation could have taken place by another path, but, as was said in antiquity, to wish means to have. And this principle is strongly affirmed in life. One must sensitively harken to the approach of the Fiery World.

141. Precisely a Fiery Purification must be affirmed upon Earth. Bodily energies are nurtured with earthly emanations, and the energies of fiery potentials must be just as vitally manifested in the earthly spheres. The path of fiery purifications must reach its mighty limit, because organisms, by exerting their intensities of will, can establish a sacred bond with the Fiery World. Therefore, only saturated spirits can prolong their labors on the refinement of the centers. Without this permeation it is impossible to consolidate the labor of the spirit in the two Worlds. On the path to the Fiery World one must accept the law of Purification by Fire.

142. Resurrection of the spirit—what a sublime concept! It should be understood as the call of Beauty. Resurrection of the spirit can mean not only a succeeding step in the sense of incarnation but also a magnetic transmutation in life. The awakening of the higher Manas can be called a manifestation of the imagination. How necessary it is to strive to those affirmations of the higher emanations which can awaken the higher manifestations of Manas! Man does not study the depths of his heart, whereas so many great and powerful formulas can be found in the depths of the heart! But people dodge each suggestion of introspection, revealing nothing of themselves but the surface, and suppressing such a multitude of accumulations of various spiritual experiences! Resurrection of the spirit must be understood as a most vital law. Certain images of great Spiritual Toilers reveal this great law of resurrection of the spirit. Resurrection of the spirit can manifest its power as a Fiery Call! Thus must one understand the transmuting Fire.

143. Resurrection of the spirit can be manifested in any sphere whatsoever of vital activity. Any step can become the stimulus for this purification. But resurrection of the spirit requires real action. Words or promises or intentions do not cause resurrection of the spirit. Rightly have promises been pointed out which were not intended for fulfillment. Resurrection of the spirit can be affirmed only by true strivings for action. On the path to the Fiery World one must remember how it is possible to attain resurrection of the spirit.

144. Let us speak about fear and foresight. Fear sees its own reflection. Each preconceived opinion is usually a reflection. Fear seeks to destroy each good beginning. Foresight catalyzes the strongest aspirations, and We can point to a cemetery containing fearful records which substantiate this. A preconceived interpretation is a self-justification; therefore, preconception is often death.

145. The composition of the aura is highly complex. Into it enter psychic and physical emanations. Each impulse or thought is reflected in it. Each aspiration produces its obvious emanation. But in studying the aura it will be necessary subtly to distinguish between the two types of emanations which correspond to the two Worlds. During illnesses it is also necessary to study carefully the radiations which may be an effect of the Fiery World. Thus, when We are dealing with auras, it is necessary to take into consideration the subtle body, which sends out rays from the centers to the surface of the surrounding aura. The creativeness of the spirit especially can be reflected on the aura. Indeed, all fluids have their levels, which will be highly indicative for many scientific investigations. Likewise it is very important to investigate the extremities, for the magnet of the extremities, the fingers, feet and the radiations of the eyes can produce a powerful combination for uniting the personal magnetism with that of the earth and of the elements. Thus, on the path to the Fiery World it is important to affirm each unifying of the emanations with Cosmos.

146. Space breathes. Space resounds and creates. As little is known about spatial currents as about the other Higher Worlds. The fiery essence which permeates all that lives is Cosmic Fire, emanating from the Depths of the Cosmos and proceeding into infinite creative manifestation. Rightly have been related the miracles of life. Fiery creativeness is a law of the Cosmos. The impregnation of Cosmic Energy is a law of the Cosmos. In omnipresence it attests its tension. Its omnipresence is expressed in all life. This Fire of space impregnates thought by unification of subtle energies. Space contains subtle forms ready for materialization. One has but to awaken in oneself those energies which can be unified for creative power. Thought and aspiration are the forerunners which can attract spatial fertilization. In ancient times the significance of invocations to the Higher Beings was known. There-

fore, thought-creativeness is a great manifestation in the Cosmos, for the Fire of space assumes forms in the spirit manifested on the planet. Thus, the unification of Worlds is vitally affirmed.

147. To know one's destination means to know that the spirit of man is an expression of Higher Forces. Only he who knows these strivings can understand how it is needful to harken sensitively to the voice of the Higher Forces. What a wonderful concept, that man has been created in the Image of God! Precisely this reveals Infinity, multiplying all forces and aspirations. How is it possible for man to deny Infinity and Immortality when before him is the great comparison of the Image of the Macrocosm with the microcosm? Surely, such an exhortation is a powerful call to perfectionment of the spirit. Reminding about the Prototype of God must lead man into New Paths, for it is impossible to scorn with impunity the higher destiny by an expression of denial. And the ogres who affirm a self-willed sojourn of man on the Earth will perish, together with all the enemies of Light. Thus let us manifest sensitiveness of striving for understanding of our destination.

148. Spiritual foresight is given only when the heart has been opened. Spiritual perspicacity can reveal the mysteries of spirit and matter. Foresight can harken to the Cosmic Forces which affirm life. Indeed, foresight can reveal that which is hidden to the eye. One need not be surprised that the key of knowledge is found in the hands of the Initiates, for spiritual foresight is saturated with Fiery Forces. And use of energies which are elusive to the human reason, discloses a foresight of the spirit, for only a highly integrated consciousness can awaken spiritual foresight. And the Sages of old knew this, for in antiquity subtle receptivity was regarded as a Sign of the Higher Forces. To him who has attained spiritual foresight comes the feeling of the unity of the two Worlds.

149. Foresight of the spirit is also expressed in the transmutation of subtle energies. When the spirit is affirmed as the guiding principle, then its power saturates each manifestation. Therefore, it is often possible to call straight-knowledge spiritual foresight. Let us remember this mighty quality.

150. Verily, thought is infinite. The domains of the Cosmos are revealed to it. There are no limitations where the spirit rules. Is not thought, which pervades all and manifests the beauty of the Cosmos, miraculous? Thought, emanating from the Depths of the Cosmos, revealing all sources, is the most fiery of the manifestations of space. Even if thought does not find its application upon Earth, nevertheless, it fierily saturates space with these creative records. Thought-forms intensify each vital designation, as a fiery impulse of life. The source of creative power is inexhaustible when life is filled with thought. Therefore, to think means to construct life. To think means to affirm the forms of life. The threshold reached by thought always leads to the destined goal, because thought rules with eternal Fire. Thought, which leads to the might of great Cosmic Constructiveness, is not sufficiently studied.

151. Cosmic vibrations direct energies into action. If man would accustom himself to harkening to the cosmic vibrations, he would discover many spatial manifestations. A cosmic vortex, which propels energies through powerful agitations, may be compared with a strong magnet the power of which creates through various actions. Energies which are gathered by a saturated vortex are distributed according to the poles of attraction. The width of application of this law of attraction to the various assignments of man in all the Worlds is immeasurable. Just as man is attracted to certain kindred on the Earth, in the spiritual World he is attracted by a vortex created by his own actions. It is difficult to free oneself from a Cosmic vortex, therefore it is needful to direct the human consciousness to the inexorable laws. Mastery of Karma and of the laws of life requires true understanding of the Cosmic Vortex. Space consists of these vibrations, eternally moving in the spiral of the vortex.

152. Those records which fill space are not contained in a manifested structure. The mind of man has so far withdrawn itself from the higher records. Man is athirst with illusions and more and more draws away from reality. From all the great laws and principles, it is possible to point out distorted crumbs which have beclouded the consciousness. What, then, has remained of all the fiery Teachings? Reason did not subordinate the Universe, but did sink into the terror of its own engendered forms. Therefore, it is so difficult to unify the consciousnesses of the two Worlds.

Fiery energies knock for admission, and there may be observed new forms of creativeness in all domains. But each good affirmation which comes for the unification of the Worlds remains unnoticed. Vortexes which surround humanity bear away all creative fires. Discharges which are bursting around the Earth are a source of terror. Sternly do We speak to the nations, for those peoples which have received true sparks of understanding must bear the responsibility for that created by them.

153. From the small to the great, humanity perverts all Truths. The higher the law, the lower its shattering. The unification of energies affirms so much for conscious strivings, but man has imposed his own

branding mark. Therefore, Fiery Purification comes lawfully. Space is saturated with great records which reveal to mankind the great Truth of Be-ness. A great preparation for a World change, in which the Fiery Forces will participate, is going on. Thus, all the principles of the fiery laws will be given to humanity as a final touchstone. Thus the great Law of integration of the Atom will be that great stimulus. Thus We are prepared for the Great Hour.

154. Discernment, a quality of the spirit, can be exercised in examination of those actions which especially clearly reveal the depths of the heart. Precisely there where humility is lacking will be a place for imposture. There where Hierarchy is not reverenced, will be a place for blasphemy. There where the Decree of the Higher Forces is affirmed only insubordinately, will egoism be hidden. And there where the Fiery Teacher is absent the direction will not be on the side of the Teaching. One cannot realize the great Teaching without the Fiery Teacher, without a striving of the spirit to the World of the Teacher. The manifestation of the Fiery Teacher is the path to the Fiery World. Thus, the records of space are filled with self-styled Teachers, but the Guiding Principle is the Fiery Teacher. One cannot pass without Him, one cannot advance without Him, one cannot attain without Him. Thus let us remember, in creating a better future.

155. Of all the subtle energies the most receptive is the energy arising from the heart. The current which is united with the Fire of space must have radiation from the heart. This concept is deeper and broader than is customarily thought. In speaking about the heart current, it is needful to think about its creative power, for, indeed, when a thought has been felt deeply it can create. Actually, when the heart beats in unison with the Cosmos all currents can be united through Fire. Therefore, nothing compulsory can replace the fiery tremor of the heart. On the path to the Fiery World let us strive for this palpitation which opens the Gates to all attainments.

156. Palpitation of the heart accompanies both joy and pain. How can it not throb, when it knows past and future? How can the fiery heart not ache, when its striving is directed toward creativeness? How can the heart not palpitate, when it knows in its depths the destination of the Cosmos?

157. The regal spirit knows true Service. The man who is striving for the realization of Truth delves into the most basic essence of life. Without this manifestation of delving it is impossible to know the essence of all life. So much indispensable self-control must be manifested in order for man to acquire the necessary humaneness. And so many energies will be manifested before the spirit of man will find its true destination!

The royal spirit of the Hierarch is that power which awakens the consciousness and which manifests the higher conception of Truth on the planet. King of spirit is the Fiery Hierarch! What a power does this great Guardian of Fire manifest! How many great structures are being erected having foundations in the fiery King of the Spirit! Thus, let us remember on the path to the Fiery World about that blessed power which is borne by the King of the Spirit—the Hierarch.

158. It is especially necessary to employ cautiousness for manifestations of cosmic energies. The misuse of energies is a danger connected with every affirmation of cosmic force. Only a conscious and careful attitude can ward off frightful consequences. Forces called up from the Subtle World require a restraint which only a strong spirit can manifest. Otherwise this unbridled force becomes an affirmation of Cosmic Chaos. When fiery dates approach it is very necessary to know this, for vast will be the manifestation of invocations.

159. The protective net contains reflections of the centers. One cannot be affirmed upon any manifestations without touching the protective net. One can imagine these reflections of the centers as their potentials which are inflamed or awakened depending upon this or that feeling, inclination, or action. Even in physical infections one may seek the cause in the unguarded state of the protective net. These processes indicate how important it is to watch the protective net, and how readily possible it is to disturb these radiations of the spirit. True, when the radiation is saturated with higher feelings or strivings, the protective net is strengthened by these energies. But blots, noticeable on the aura, must be studied as indexes of various spiritual ulcers. Therefore, only he who apprehends the whole creativeness of the spirit foresees the advisability of guarding the protective net. In contacting the spatial Fire, it is needful to understand all the processes of the laboratory of the centers. Thus, on the path to the Fiery World one should become affirmed in one's consciousness upon the ruinous effect of selfhood, which causes irritation by manifesting actual poisoning with imperil.

160. Indeed, the Fiery spirit creates powerfully; indeed, strongly does its word resound. Indeed, the Fiery spirit knows no half-wayness. The creativeness of the heart will make manifest all that is designated. Verily, the fiery heart is an invincible force. Thus do We create together. The time is saturated with manifestations of constructions for a great future.

161. Fiery thought knows no limits. As a forerunner of infinite creativeness, thought is impelled into space. It is necessary to accustom the consciousness to this endless manifestation. Measuring all concepts against Infinity, one may arrive at the step of Cosmic constructiveness. Only co-measurement can reveal that great step, which is powerful through fiery Infinity. Fire is manifested as impulse in the heart, as movement of thought, as the great Unifier of Worlds. One must understand creativeness as the unification of various energies manifested by the Fire of space and the spirit of man. Science of the future will reveal the laws of these unions, for it is needed to establish the most subtle cosmic cooperation, so as to accomplish that about which the Fiery Servitors are thinking. All fiery formulas live, awaiting their incarnation. Therefore, science can strive to seek out the spatial energies.

162. The Fiery Servitors can affirm new principles. Before each great Epoch, space is filled with fiery formulas. Thus is fierily affirmed each great beginning. Thus will be fierily affirmed each great manifestation of unification. Cosmic Construction affirms the very highest for the New Epoch. Therefore, on the loftiest principles will be erected the future evolution, for that which was destroyed must enter anew into life, as a great guiding foundation. The manifestation of the law of Cosmic Right sets forth the origin of the New Epoch, the Epoch of Equilibrium, and of Beauty of Existence. A striving for the creation of great new formulas will give to humanity a wonderful new step.

163. The lightning which cleaves space creates purification of the spheres. Each cosmic manifestation transmutes those energies which must be reworked. In the Cosmic Laboratory are many means of spatial discharges. Purification is a necessary process in the Cosmos. Knowing the unity of Macrocosm and microcosm, one must find understanding of each pro-

cess. Who will transmute the spirit of humanity? We say—the lightning of the Spirit of the Bearer of Fire. Who will let fly the cosmic arrow for the destruction of evil? Who will take up the task of cleansing the entrusted Banners? Rightly has been called to mind the Sword of Christ. When cosmic energies are tensed in fiery might, and purifying lightnings are making space atremble, the Fiery Spirit creates correspondingly. The World suffers from half-way measures and suffocates from indulgences—yes, yes, yes! Lightning of the spirit can cleanse space. Lightning of the spirit can make manifest the far-off Worlds. Lightning of the spirit can bestow a wonderful future, for lightning of the spirit saturates space with fiery energies. Who will manifest the prophetic fire of purification? Only the Co-worker of Cosmic forces, only the Co-worker of the Forces of Light. To Her, Co-worker of the Cosmic forces, Fellow-traveler of the Forces of Light, have I ordained the lightning of the spirit. To Her has been given the right to create with the Cosmic Sword. To Her has been given the Fiery Heart—let the Light be of the lightning of Beauty—yes, yes, yes! I have spoken.

164. Cosmic construction is saturated with all powerful energies. Likewise, constructiveness of the spirit manifests its power by the synthesis of all fires. It is possible to create, saturating the surroundings, only when the heart energies have been kindled. Without these sacred fires it is impossible to affirm the Higher Ethics. The Living Ethics can be instituted as the goal of striving in life, but for this it is necessary to know and to aspire to the higher and subtler understanding. Only subtle spirits can manifest the Living Ethics. The application of principles in life is accomplished by directed action. The empty word leaves a corresponding stratum, but action of the fiery heart evokes and sets alight fires in surrounding hearts. Thus creates the true Agni Yogi.

165. The forces of darkness press on by various means, being affirmed in strata which are found to be near to the Light. In the Subtle Spheres this proximity is naturally impossible, but in the earthly strata, where the atmosphere is so thickened with infected gases, the forces of darkness definitely try to come close to the Light. An impulse of destruction impels the forces of darkness to these Torchlights of Truth. The enemies who uplift a sword are not so dangerous as those who penetrate under the mask of Light. There are conscious and unconscious instruments of darkness. At first the unconscious ones create, as it were, in unison with the good, and these bearers of evil infect each pure beginning. But conscious servants of evil enter into the temple with your prayer, and woe to the undiscerning! Dark snares have been laid for them. It is not fitting to admit into the Holy of Holies offenders against the spirit. Djinn can help on the earthly plane, and may even build a temple, but the spiritual plane is inaccessible to them. Thus, on the path to the Fiery World let us remember about the servants of darkness who strive to penetrate into the Holy of Holies.

166. During the reorganization of spatial affirmations, evoked by the accumulation of earthly structures, all measures must be taken for the elimination of dark agglomerations. Each earthly reconstruction appears as a resonance of the super-earthly spheres. Our Fiery Period is saturated with particular energies which must enter into life prior to the designated dates. For the Fiery Period can create fiery manifestations, when that time approaches in which humanity can rise to meet it. Thus must one understand the Fiery Reconstruction which will give inception to the New

Epoch. But one must affirm the spirit in understanding of spatial fires. Because only fiery assimilation can produce the required energy. The manifestation of fiery dates draws near. Let those who can, see, for a Great Time is approaching!

167. Before the great reorganization of the World, a manifestation of all the dark forces is displayed, for a better transmutation. What is taking place in the World cannot be called a step of evolution, but it can indeed be said that what is being manifested is the lowest, the most intense, the most saturated by the forces of darkness. But great is the work which gathers together everything helpful for the great reconstruction. Just as the condensed strata of the earthly spheres are being made ready for battle, so does a manifestation of the Forces of Light stand on guard. The stage which the planet is going through can be compared with a furnace of Cosmic Fire. All dense energies are aflame in tension, and on guard stands the Fiery Right. Fiery creativeness is assembling all fiery energies—thus the World is being reconstructed by the tension of two polarities. It is necessary clearly to discern these turbulent energies.

168. A fiery epoch has begun. As at present physical manifestations are being studied, so will be studied the fiery manifestations of the centers. Agni Yoga is being manifested as a forerunner of the Great Epoch—yes, yes, yes!

169. Everyone must think about the reconstruction of the World, for when we apprehend what is taking place, we grasp the approach of the future. Each thought directed to the construction of the New Epoch will produce its own forms. Thought-forms manifest the trend of the future; hence it is needful to understand the chain of saturated strivings. Creativeness of the spirit is as a fiery lever in space, as a powerfully impelled fiery creator, as a ruler in space, as a great saturating Fire. Thus, one who thinks about preeminence and about the great future molds an affirmation of constructiveness. Space must be cemented with fiery formulas and fertilized by the manifest fire of the spirit. On the path to the Fiery World let us manifest striving for understanding of the reconstruction of the World.

170. Spatial Fire shivers during earthly shocks. The subtle bond which exists between spheres and between Worlds is so strong that there is no manifestation the further effect of which is not recorded. The subtle bond is unmistakably expressed in the conformity of Macrocosm with microcosm. The condition of the spirit so often reflects manifestations on different spheres. The appearance of Spatial Fire often serves as a discharging agent for the purification of the atmosphere. Indeed, it would be possible to make use of these energies consciously, but for this the organism must be refined. It can be observed that the fiery spirit must bridle its subtle energies because the lack of correlation between the fire of the centers and the planetary conditions is so great that it is impossible to manifest full labor without injury.

The ecstasy of Saint Catherine could be made manifest because the Saints lived in a world apart. The pattern of life when such forms were being manifested is so unlike Armageddon! Never before have such spatial battles raged. The tension of all spheres is fiery. On the path to the Fiery World one must be especially conscious of the bond between spheres.

171. Yes, the heart of the Arhat is like the Heart of the Cosmos. But wherein is contained the sunlike quality of the heart of the Arhat? We say—in love, but

not in that aspect of love to which humanity likes to limit it; nor yet in that benevolent love which people ascribe to a Patriarch. No, the sunlike heart of the Arhat propels into achievement and smites everything corrupting. The Heart of the Arhat contends with darkness and affirms fiery striving.

With what, then, is the Heart of the Arhat fed? We say—with love. Only this Source knows how to saturate the fiery heart. The great Mother of the World knows this Source. Each pure heart knows this Source. How, then, are the hearts commerged? We say—with love, that powerful source which converts life into a manifestation of beauty, that source which contains all the subtle energies of the heart. The Heart of the Arhat is a secret stronghold, which guards the sacred gift of the Cosmos. And not outside of life but in the very depths of life is forged the Heart of the Arhat. Let us say, by love. Yes, yes, yes, thus saith the Lord of Shambhala.

172. The most difficult of all for humanity to understand is the beauty of achievement. Verily, achievement in life is a great motive power, for what can better awaken the consciousness than the beauty of achievement? What, then, can produce a striving upwards, and tear one away from the lower strata if not the spirit impelled to achievement? The direction of humanity manifestly is exactly the opposite, and is affirmed in the spheres which hold the spirit to the Earth for long periods of time. Therefore, each exalted feeling takes on such monstrous interpretations. Verily, life summons to fiery achievement, to great fiery Beauty. But man is torn away from his everyday life with such difficulty! Thus, on the path to the Fiery World let us strive for the achievement of Beauty.

173. There exists many different means for the rar-

efaction of the dense body. Indeed, each fine thought must be regarded as a fiery manifestation, therefore it is necessary to accustom oneself to think fierily. Rarefaction of the dense physical body must also be understood from the spiritual point of view, because, while dwelling in a dense body, it is still possible not to manifest coarseness. The Agni Yogi, who has passed through fiery baptism and fiery transmutation, no longer dwells in a dense body, because when the body admits the fiery currents, its whole substance is changed. The basis of this experience of fiery transmutation of the centers is this rarefaction. True, only to the subtle is the subtle accessible, and science of the future will study the subtle body. The ever-increasing fiery manifestations, while directing the spirit into the Higher Worlds, make the earthly spheres burdensome. Let us remember that the subtle is accessible only to the subtle, and let us reverence the Mother of Agni Yoga.

174. A fiery current can be assimilated only by a refined organism. Only the fiery heart can adjoin the Heart of the Cosmos.

175. Each Epoch leaves its impress in Eternity. These manifested remains of time are just as vital as life itself. Each Epoch leaves its echo, as a repetition of spatial records. But never do the records manifest a repetition, because to them are added always new energies and new decisions. An identicalness of time can be affirmed, but the reconstruction of the planet has its own new levers, and into the change go new energies. Thus Babylon fell, thus Rome fell, thus sands have covered civilizations, and waters engulfed empires. But for the change of our Cycle there approaches the most fiery, and the greatest, destruction and construction. Space is saturated with fiery energies for reorganization. Extraordinary is the time; the Fire is raging! On the path to the Fiery World let us manifest understanding of the approaching Fiery Cycle.

176. It is idle thought to imagine that the Forces of Light endure with ease the conflict with the forces of darkness. If the forces of darkness receive burns from contact with the Forces of Light, it must be understood also how hard it is to be in contact with the dark spheres. The battle, earthly and super-earthly, burns the dark ones, and purifies space. But at the same time, contact with the dark spheres produces tensions and pains. On the higher plane as on the earthly, knights of the spirit feel pain from the contact with dark weapons. True, the protective net insures against defeat, for Light overcomes darkness, but rebounding blows and shocks to the aura and the protective net are real and are felt. Therefore, it is necessary sensitively to harken to the affirmations of the battles of Light with darkness. Those who realize this fiery conflict know all the manifestations of spatial tensions. Those who are conscious of fiery pain in the heart know Our tensions.

177. The infirmities of humanity are connected with psychic conditions. Each human imperfection of the spirit also poisons the physical world. Be not astonished that there are spirit and body plagues which are just as infectious as the spatial plagues. Indeed, the atmosphere surrounding the planet is saturated with wails of imperfection. And the auras of mankind are so physically and spiritually infected that only a fiery cleansing can give salvation. Half-way measures bring no purification, therefore one must become accustomed to the thought of a powerful cleansing, for the firmament is in need of severe measures. Rightly has Ur. said that a pure manifestation sometimes has to be covered partly with a dirty cloak, just so the sparks can catch. Thus, humanity must atone for all its engenderings and all outrages which have taken root so deeply in the consciousness. On the path to the Fiery World let us remember the law of fiery purification.

178. What heart, then, has taken up the enormous Burden? The all-encompassing Heart which knows the Cosmic Burden. Who, then, bears the load of the ages? The One Heart which knows the manifestation of Infinity. Who, then, strives in fiery achievement? The One Heart which knows Cosmic Right. Verily, thus is the World saturated by the One Heart. Humanity suffers more from the spirit than from matter, and only when the spirit adheres to the law of Cosmic Right will humanity overcome its spiritual infirmities. The planet has lost sight of its great and pure destination. Matter has been so steeped in density that it must be refined. When the great Tidings of the Unified Heart will saturate the spirit with pure striving, then will life be truly transformed. Who, then, will give to the World the Tidings about fiery Unity? We say—the all-encompassing Heart, the Heart manifested by eternal Fire—yes, yes, yes! That which has been put together by Cosmic Right and by strong aspiration of the will is immutable law. That which is from the Cosmos will dwell with the Beauty of the Cosmos—thus saith the Lord of Shambhala.

179. Fluids of the fiery heart and spirit nourish the protective net. The fiery centers are a most powerful panacea. The Agni Yogi, being affirmed in the might of fiery energy, possesses the power of the Light; therefore, let us not be surprised if the heart saturated with higher Fire knows nothing of whisperings and temptations. The fluids of such a heart act as purifying energies in space. Currents of the subtle fluids saturate at enormous distances, serving as powerful discharging agents. For example, when the solar plexus is tense, the heart is sending to a far distant point its purifying energies. For example, if absentation is noticed, it means that divisibility of the spirit is in creative process. Pulsations in the extremities and in the heart denote sendings of fiery projectiles. Let us subtly refer to the different manifestations of the spatial creativeness of the powerful Agni Yogi. These cosmic sendings are affirmed by Our Tara, who has taken upon herself the whole achievement of Beauty and Fire.

180. The earthly firmament is infected, and is to be purified by humanity itself. Each vital manifestation leaves its precipitations on all space. All must be transmuted, all must be lived through. Thus, each stratum represents a sphere saturated with human lusts, survivals, and aspirations. The fluids of heart and spirit, which saturate space with pure fires, refine the spatial strata. Only in this way can equilibrium be established, because energies are hurtling through space and mankind is surrounded, as it were, by explosive projectiles. These fluids are accumulated and exploded in all spheres. So, too, the chain of effects is being affirmed by the saturated actions of humanity. On the path to the Fiery World let us be reminded about the spatial projectiles.

181. As the Fiery Guards stand on watch, so do powerful Dischargers purify space. All Cosmic Battles are saturated with forces proceeding from all the Centers of the Cosmos. The Centers, flamingly intensified, are building all cosmic affirmations. When We speak about fiery Centers of the Cosmos, one must have in mind those fiery strivings which are radiated by the centers of the great manifested Arhats in the distant and the earthly spheres. Without these fiery centers of the Saviours of Mankind it would be impossible to hold back events until the designated date. Verily, great is this labor in the defense of humanity!

182. Yes, yes, yes! great is the labor of the fiery centers. The Dischargers of the spheres are the most powerful Servitors of the Cosmos. Most subtle threads hold in unity these great Servants of the Cosmos. But this work also takes place only during fiery unification. Fiery equilibrium can save the planet. Only fiery might can at the last moment bestow new life. Creativeness of the unified heart will effect the salvation of the planet and affirm a New Cycle. Therefore, Our Heart is so tensed in unison with the impetuous current of Fire—thus the essence of life manifests its Fiery Right. The tension is great; in the World a great World Mystery is being made manifest. I affirm Great Cosmic Truth. This Mystery is Be-ness itself.

183. The construction of new beginnings can be affirmed upon great principles only when humanity will apprehend all the Higher Origins. Without this it is impossible to manifest the Beauty of Existence, for the manifestations of life proceed in conformity with the thinking of humanity. The creator of thought creates forms. But how frightful are those movements in the World which arise out of decomposing sources! These sources infect the atmosphere surrounding the planet. It is necessary to purify the strata for the reception of new energies. So many powerful forces are awaiting reception and application, but to perceive them means already to manifest them. But is it possible at this time to reveal these energies to a destroyer? Certainly the planet is passing through Armageddon, and all its affirmations are sharply divided into the camps of Light and darkness. Therefore, the great discharge leads to fiery purification. Then it will be possible to bestow the affirmed Beauty of Existence. Verily,

the time draws near. On the path to the Fiery World let us remember the great principle of Beauty.

184. Each epoch has its own distinctions. Each peculiarity of time is an imprint of consciousness. These manifestations of peculiarities can be magnified by the will of humanity. The peculiarities of the epoch, in the same way as evocations, have their roots in the consciousness. Those visions and conditions which filled life and thought several centuries past were engendered in the spirit of the servants of religion in response to popular demand. Long ago was it enjoined, "Seek and ye shall find." In this evolutionary and incessant turn of the spiral, man will find the Truth. The affirmation of Truth is purified of all distortions, because the rubbish and accumulated dust is transitory. But Truth is manifested in Infinity. And though human darkening be prolonged, yet from under the dark strata will be exhumed the affirmations of the Light. Thus, that which is ordained enters in awesome immensity.

185. Thus everything great enters imperceptibly and powerfully into life. The manifestation of Cosmic Right likewise enters fierily into life. Invisibly is space saturated; thus powerfully are the fiery threads stretched forth. But when the hour of entrance comes, fiery might will flash out with all the manifested rays of Beauty. Therefore I affirm how vitally necessary it is to understand the power of that great fiery force which is incarnated in the Mother of Agni Yoga. In awesome immensity the threshold draws near; thus a great Mystery enters into life.

186. Verily, resurrection of the spirit will produce a new Epoch. What, then, can be compared with the power of the spirit? There is no other lever which could intensify the fires of the centers. Each creative force which will be saturated by the resurrection of the spirit can be a pledge of a great Epoch. Each construction which will be based on the resurrection of the spirit can be a pledge of ascent. Spiritual advancement can begin only when there comes an understanding of the regeneration of spirit. It is impossible to dwell in the old distortions. It is impossible to create the great Kingdom of the Spirit without realization of the affirmation of the pure, fiery understanding of achievement. Thus, only regeneration of the spirit provides a firm foundation for the new construction. In it humanity will find its great destination and its place in the Cosmos. Verily, resurrection of the spirit will be the creative force of the New Epoch.

187. Resounding on the cosmic note can be transmitted spatially to the spirit which perceives the subtle currents. Among the subtle manifestations of such reverberations of the spirit must be especially noticed those which are audible to the fiery spirit. How vital it is to harken to that apparently inaudible tone which can transmit to the spirit spatial joy or anguish. The manifestation of inexplicable anguish can derive from the sounding of a spatial tone. The subtle organism of this bearer of Fires shudders from these notes of space. The physical ear cannot hear it, but the subtle hearing detects that which is inaudible to the ear and receives it in the heart. Therefore, the striving spirit is a creator in unison with the Cosmos, and knows the cosmic soundings which intensify space. In them is contained summons or call; in them is victory or battle; in them is sorrow or joy. Verily, he who knows these soundings and experiences the joy and anguish of communion with space, may be called a great Fire-bearer. To this the fiery heart of the Mother of Agni Yoga bears witness. Thus let us remember the great unified Heart.

188. The cosmic note fierily saturates space. It can commune directly with the heart; that is why these currents act on the heart. We, too, receive those soundings which are transmitted in the beginning to the heart, and We seek their source. Thus, the anguish and joy of the World are transmitted to Us also by these spatial notes.

189. Contemplation of the World will yield an understanding of the shortcomings and the lack of balance which is proven as a harmful manifestation. First of all, it must be understood how that influx of new unaccepted energies acts on the planet. Evolutionary movement is not affirmed so long as correlation between spheres is not established. For, when the Higher World is striving upward and mankind propels itself downward, then indeed the cosmic current cannot be affirmed. Therefore, a manifested disharmony rules in the World. Not without reason has been recalled what was said about Buddha. Not idly has been recalled—"let the dead bury the dead." Indeed, a world concept can be affirmed if only the fiery striving is victorious.

190. The trampling of laws by humanity must rouse the consciousness, since pure foundations have been affirmed as the guiding principle. Loss of the bond between the higher principles and actual life has taken humanity far from the sacred origins, which alone can restore the disturbed equilibrium. Among the fundamentals may be named the affirmation of most vital principles which have been mutilated beyond all recognition. Purification of the Bases of life and of the great Teachings may be called the most fiery creativeness. Thus the Bearer of fires saturates space with manifestations affirming the equilibrium of life. On the path to the Fiery World let us direct a call into

107

space for the purifying of the Fundamentals of the Teaching.

191. The different Epochs enter as succeeding steps in the evolutionary ascent of humanity, and it is necessary to understand how each Epoch has developed. A determination of the subtle currents which saturated the Epoch will give the key to understanding of its essential nature. If spiritual achievement has imbued the national spirit, it means the ascent of that Epoch was affirmed. But never before has the World been so in need of the sword of the spirit! Always, at the time when energies have manifested their potentialities in movement, the wavering magnetic needle has indicated the agitation of the cosmic magnetic poles. Thus, the Epoch of the Sword of the Spirit brings out flamingly the Highest Principle. Therefore, the Cosmic scales are weighing the very highest Fiery Right. The Epoch of the Sword of the Spirit will affirm that Principle which has been proclaimed for evolution to the Higher Worlds. Space is saturated with the fire of the Cosmic Magnet. Thus, at the threshold of the Epoch of Fiery Right, the Sword of the Spirit stands on guard.

192. Truly, mankind is unable to get out of the charmed circle of effects. How, then, can humanity overcome all the malignant energies which saturate life? Only fundamental manifestations can give the true direction; but the charmed circle, which is affirmed by humanity, will be cloven only when the sword of the spirit pierces the web woven by darkness. Struggling with effects does not lead to the designated manifestation which must bring near the great future. Rightly has it been stated that the Leader knows the cause of cosmic manifestations. Therefore, on the path to the Fiery World let us follow the Hierarch of Light who knows those causes and effects. Thus let us remember when the great Epoch of Fire draws near.

193. The fundamentals of Life can be affirmed through resurrection of the spirit. Purification of the foundations must be affirmed, for without this it is impossible to manifest the New World. The degeneration of the foundations is ruinous; and pure energies cannot be attracted to the earthly plane without transmutation of the accumulations which are stifling the planet. How, then, to affirm the New World? As has been said—with fire and sword! To abolish the old there will be a new purification, which will give the great Fundamentals of Existence. The fiery sword of the spirit will smite the corruption of the planet. Those who are looking into the future are not afraid of the fiery sword, for the tempered spirit knows the true creativeness of the sword of the spirit. Fiery creativeness can be affirmed as the great transmutation of darkness into Light. On the path to the Fiery World let us manifest understanding of the Fiery Sword of the Spirit.

194. Indeed, if humanity would not violate the manifestation of the First Causes, the foundations of Existence would retain that basis which manifests the beauty of life. Cosmic Right brings understanding of the fact that a one-sided administration of the planet is plunging it into an abyss. Cosmic Right offers to humanity that Principle which can pierce the darkness. Cosmic Right reveals to the planet the unity of Principles which guides the entire Universe. Cosmic Right reveals the Feminine Principle as a manifested power. Cosmic Right reveals the greatness of the Feminine Principle, which manifests self-renunciation, and before which verily the great Arhats bow themselves. Verily, We reverence the great Feminine Principle. Verily, We reverence the giving Principle which bestows the life of Beauty and of the Heart.

195. Humanity must be prepared for upheavals and for the reconstruction of engendered conditions. It is impossible to accept that which exists on the planet as a lawful affirmation, because all evil engenderings must be exterminated and atoned for. Each apostasy from the great laws produces grievous consequences. The creativeness of the Cosmos determines another destiny of life; therefore, atonement is inevitable, because fiery purification gives a new direction to the stream of Karma. In space are manifested energies prepared for the transmutation of all existing accumulations. Verily, humanity must be prepared for fiery purification. He who does not fear the fiery element will truly go along with the Cosmic Fire. On the path to the Fiery World let us remember about the elemental events which will cleanse the space.

196. When the Forces of Light are tensed, of course, the darkness gathers together its own forces, but the Light is the stronger. Thus do We create manifestations. Events are drawing near, the time is grave and saturated. Thus shall We be victorious.

197. In the Cosmic Battle let us defend that which is sacred. In the Cosmic Battle let us affirm that basis on which Existence itself is upheld. In the Cosmic Battle let us manifest that by which life of the future is constructed. The World will have in its fiery foundation those great laws which We defend in the Cosmic Battle. Humanity affirms its ordained destination in the Cosmic Battle. Just as earthquakes cast out from the depths of the Earth onto the surface different accumulations, and swallow subtler energies from the supermundane spheres, so, too, does the spiritual reconstruction involve the darkest accumulations.

Verily, when the highest and the lowest meet in the Cosmic Battle, one may be impelled to the attainment of the great Fiery Purification. Thus, during the great reconstruction of our planet We saturate the human spirit with the realization of imperfection of engendered forms, and with the ordained beauty of manifested forms of life. In the Cosmic Battle is affirmed the principle of the New World. On the path to the Fiery World let us remember about the Cosmic Battle.

198. Certainly, the Initiates of ancient Egypt knew the great law which rules the whole Universe. The Pyramid itself presents a symbol of the mountain with a broad foundation and narrow summit. Indeed, the significance of the Chamber of the manifested King and Queen is that a crowning perfection is to be expected at the approach of all Cosmic Fiery dates. It is well to remember these manifested dates. It is well to remember these ancient indications and calculations. Thus is it possible to trace how from the most ancient times cosmic dates have been affirmed. One must also pay attention to the fact that those calculations lead up to our date and time. Thus immutable is Fiery Right, which has been inscribed on all the tablets, and which has been written by the great life of the eternal Magnet.

199. In the Cosmos Cycles have their definite significance. One may trace how in substance each is affirmed by certain energies which preordain entire epochs. One can observe how each Cycle particularly manifests and expresses the essence of cosmic strivings. But above all Cycles is the one Cosmic Right, which is intensified by all the energies of the World. Thus, the entire structure of the Cosmos leads to that principle which has been established in Existence. Let us affirm the Cycle of Cycles, and the predestined will take place. In the Cosmic Battle is being forged the crowning completion. In the Cosmic Battle is being tempered each law, but the great Fiery Right is being saturated with cosmic tension. Thus the Cycle of Cycles is manifested as the victory of the Cosmos.

200. In the furnace of life many concepts must be transmuted. So many layers have been deposited upon the loftiest conceptions, that Fiery Baptism must truly be administered to the planet. Around the concepts of the Fiery Images have been gathered those imaginings which are close to a low spirit. Not thus taught the Great Teachers. Not thus lived the Great Teachers. Not thus walked the Great Teachers. Verily not thus, as people insist. The Fiery Images must take shape in a form appropriate and adequate for Them; therefore spreading of the Teaching must go flamingly side by side with a clarifying of the Great Figures. The creativeness of true strivings will grant those new steps which will give to the World resurrection of the spirit. On the path to the Fiery World let us remember that it is vital to bathe the Teaching of Beauty in achievement and with service.

201. Such grandeur is ahead! Such a great step awaits its fiery affirmation! Our Teaching and the affirmation of the Higher Principles will reveal so much that is great to humanity! A great period is drawing near. Thus do We create together.

202. The creativeness of Light affirms its power precisely by manifesting all tensions and potentials. It must not be thought that the Forces of Light do not admit great tension. It is right to imagine the Forces of Light in that cosmic measuring scale which can be used only for the structure of the Cosmos. Verily, only the affirmation of the most powerful energies will produce manifestations of this mighty construction. That is why space is saturated with the necessary energies.

The Forces of Light propel all the fiery centers. The Constructiveness of the Cosmos proceeds in the propelling of all the needed energies. In this construction let us strain all our forces with a fiery heart and the sword of the spirit. Thus do We build a great future. Thus the great manifested law will proclaim the future!

203. Bridges of the spirit thrown across all difficulties, over all abysses, built on the path of striving, will manifest those constructive energies in the Cosmos. Verily, the spirit can unify the different centers. Humanity is straining toward a visible construction, and is not inspired by higher strivings for cosmic construction. Each bridge of the spirit, indeed, affirms conscious construction which manifests the cosmic connection between structures. Thus, in the Fiery Epoch it is especially needful to devote oneself to subtle, conscious activity of the spirit. Only the bridge of the spirit can close that abyss which yawns before humanity. The bridge of the Spirit is a bridge of Beauty. With these concepts of achievement of the spirit will we ascend the great Summit which unifies theWorlds.

204. The saturation of space with formulas which clarify the Teaching, will result in great effects. Thus do We affirm the manifestation of the New World. Thus is the manifestation of the Predestined being brought about.

205. Beginning with the Epoch which proclaimed the Fiery Right, there has been a great magnetization, with continuously directed force. Since then, whenever the human spirit has assumed a course which leads it away from the path of Truth, with each Lord the World has received the fiery Truth. Thus has the cosmic magnetization proceeded. The Cosmic Magnet directs the spirit to a search which leads to realization of the great Fiery Right. Since every thought is a mag-

net, each striving quest is a powerful magnet. These magnetic fluids are stratified in space, and form manifestations of magnetic poles. Since the physical plane manifests the power of magnetism, it is evident how very powerful must be the direction of the Cosmic Magnet. Verily, magnetization of the spirit can create powerful strata which will attract all the great energies. Therefore, quests of the spirit lead to Fiery Right. Verily, the whole World seeks that Cosmic Truth. The Great Epoch of Fiery Right will bestow the key to a higher existence.

206. The strongest Source of fiery energies, the heart, still has not been investigated as a manifestation of impelling force and of creative power. One must penetrate into the nature of creativeness in order to understand how invincible the heart is when all the fires are aflame. One must know that only a true source of powerful energies can create. Therefore, cultivation of the heart must be understood as the kindling of all fires. Each truly lofty manifestation of the heart depends upon the tension of the higher energies. The fiery heart saturates the subtle bodies with subtle energies. Those vibrations which establish the sacred bond between the Subtle World and the World of Fire are the fiery vibrations of the heart. Verily, on the path to the Fiery World it is necessary to strive for the creation of these sacred vibrations of the heart. Thus, the Sun of Suns is the Heart.

207. All manifestations of energies are creatively saturated when the impulse which moves them issues from the source of the heart. That which in the Cosmos is considered to be the true impelling force, in the laboratory of the heart is called striving. That which in the Cosmos is called the Source of Truth, in life is called sincerity. That which in the Cosmos assembles and creates, that which has been fierily affirmed in life, is the flame of the heart. In the spatial unitings of bodies is it possible to affirm the flaming, pure stimulus of the heart. In the Fiery World the force of unification is the stimulus of the heart; only fire can kindle all fires. No meditation but heart-feeling results in the revelation of the spirit. Only that which has been lived through can be rooted out. Only the heart which has been kindled by all fires can cognize the beauty of the higher life. The future leads to realization of these higher unities. On the path to the Fiery World let us strive to the cognition of the Higher Laws of Existence.

208. How, then, can the heart realize all the beauty of Existence if it has not penetrated into all the joys and sorrows of life? Thus it is that often, reading the Book of Lives, the heart trembles, but then the tear of suffering is transmuted into a pearl. The more fiery the heart, the greater the joys and the sufferings. The law of Fiery Right is forged in life. The Higher Command is affirmed by passing through all the vital steps with the heart. Creative impulses must be saturated in the heart, therefore each life issues its own radiations of the heart. Fiery Right is certainly not that phantom of perfectionment about which humanity has become accustomed to think, but is the fiery kindling of all the vital fires of the heart. Not in a placid existence is the heart saturated with fiery love.

209. Verily, both spirit and heart must hearken to the subtle and invisible manifestations. The unknown achievement must enter into life. Indeed, the higher principle of Fire is affirmed in Cosmic Creativeness as the main stimulus. It is with good purpose that there have been pointed out those subtle physical manifestations which affirm the essential nature of the invisible and fiery energies, and which must awaken and broaden the consciousness of humanity. Indeed, the subtle realization of the Cosmos discloses each new step. That which cannot be apprehended today will be audible in the future, and the Subtle World will become visible. When spirit and heart are filled with striving, when humanity apprehends the law of existence of the Worlds, then will it be possible to begin to broaden the consciousness. Man himself unifies the Worlds with his consciousness. Thus the great time approaches for the replacement of the narrow horizon. Thus Our affirmation of great Fiery Right will result in the great Fiery Epoch. This Great Epoch must transform the face of the planet—thus do I affirm!

210. The ray of the Higher Consciousness is united with the rays of the closer consciousnesses through fiery striving. When, in the creation of good, the spirit is tensed in a fiery transport, the spirit is always unified with the Higher Consciousness. The fiery law manifests its might on the Earth, therefore is it so necessary to manifest understanding of the Subtle World. Each action can acquire a double force by the unification of the rays. The unified consciousness is the most immutable shield. In full striving and fiery understanding the rays will always create by manifesting a single power. The ray can pierce the consciousness, but We call the unification of the rays of the consciousness Hiero-inspiration. The rays of creativeness of the heart manifest the most fiery labor in Cosmos, but the heart must actually be saturated with the striving of achievement. Certainly the Sun of Suns will conquer all obstacles and create new beginnings. The Fiery World honors the creativeness of the heart.

211. Precisely as Ur. has said—the fulfillment of one's own duty. Precisely the distribution of assignments in the Cosmos upholds the foundations, and the Hierarchic Chain maintains equilibrium. There is in the Cosmos one great action which admits of a unified Karma, but inasmuch as this is held secret in the Cosmos, the confluence of Karma is a solution of Higher Forces. The fiery consciousness and heart can coalesce and bear that Burden of the World, and this will be consecration for the new construction which has been ordained in the Cosmos. The manifestation of the Cosmic Magnet must be saturated with the creativeness of spirit and heart. Thus is affirmed a joint Karma. This must be understood as a Higher Token. But when the law of higher significance is applied to daily conditions, this is contrary to Cosmic Ordination. Therefore, on the path to the Fiery World let us be imbued with the significance of the higher uniting of Karma.

212. Tension of all the energies of the spirit is manifested during the collision of forces. Actually, only a spirit impelled to creativeness can be conscious of that power which is contained in counteraction. How, then, to affirm fiery kindling, and to intensify each channel of fire? The attraction of all conformities takes place when all fiery currents are aflame. It is necessary to accept the law of counteraction as a stimulus of creativeness; the stimulus which intensifies each construction. Attraction of spirit is developed precisely by the fiery tension of all forces. In fact, each inscription in space can enter into life as magnetic opposition to the forces of darkness. Ascending on the path to the Fiery World, let us remember about striving in the higher tension of spirit, when on the brink of the abyss, when on the summit, when before a dark wall. Thus let us tense all forces.

213. All nations are intensifying their forces. All is tensed toward transmutation. Great and rigorous is the time—thus is the great future being affirmed. I affirm a great saturation of space.

214. Cycles which are shaped by the Cosmic Magnet have in their foundation the affirmation of the Higher Forces. These fiery Cycles appear as the foundations of planetary life. The Cosmic Magnet builds commensurately with spatial power. The Spirit of the Builder of the Cycle must be that Power which corresponds to the designation of the Cycle. The whole synthesis of the Cycle must be saturated in the Spirit manifested for Cosmic Synthesis. At the fiery change of the Cycle there is given a Fiery Principle for the purification of the planet. So few spirits understand the fundamentals of Fiery Existence! So few spirits understand Who stands at the Helm! The beauty of the Cycle can enlighten only the consciousness which can understand the Power of the First Causes. The helm of the planet's life and the foundations of Existence are affirmed by Fiery Right. Thus, on the path to the Fiery World let us manifest understanding of the Basis of Cycles.

215. The depictions of Cosmic Cycles are affirmed by whole millenniums; in them the Higher Will is united in the Chosen Spirit Who by His own fiery tension creates that preordained Epoch. By its spirit and will each fiery spirit creates also a certain Cycle around its strivings. These creations of Cycles are strongly outlined in the cementing of space. Each fiery striving can already be a pledge of a new link in the affirmation of the Cycle. If the consciousness would become affirmed in the fact of the structure of Cycles, then indeed, would cosmic construction clothe the World with beauty. Verily, a world understanding can be manifested with every thought projected. Thus, on the path to the Fiery World let us consciously create links in the World Cycles.

216. Realization of responsibility for the spirit and for religion has been put by humanity in the last place. The tribunal of regulated society is concerned with preserving the physical body, making mangling of the body liable to prosecution. But existing laws and temples do not concern themselves with the millions who have been mangled in spirit. With justice has Ur. pointed out the stern responsibility which religions must bear. The uniting function of religion truly has not been awakened on the planet. That sacred power of the Earth, instead of uplifting, has been turned by mankind into production of that obvious disunity which is as a cleaving sword. And priests, and brahmins, and temple servitors all have distorted the cosmic ordainment. Verily, only affirmation of the true designation will impel the spirit to the higher understanding of the great Cosmic Right. Thus let us strive for the great responsibility for the spirit and for religion. So much must be purified in the Teachings of the World! The labor of strivingly purifying religions will result in a new consciousness. On the path to the Fiery World let us affirm the Bearers of Fiery Purification.

217. Of all the depraved traits of humanity one must subtly note faint-heartedness. This quality borders on many other dark traits. Nearest of all is treachery. Faint-heartedness borders on fear, cowardice, and selfhood. And in the Fiery World there is no place for faint-heartedness. And the crown of courage can be placed only on the head which is adorned with self-sacrifice. Yes, let the lone warrior fight single-handed. Let the arrows of hypocrites pierce his breast. Let each manifest aspiration be met with rejection. Yet will his armor be studded with courage. Who, then, knows the fiery striving of the warrior? Who knows the truth of the aspiring heart? Only the manifested fiery heart. The subtle consciousness will illumine the manifestation of courage. Faint-heartedness is contempt for the higher Ego. Faint-heartedness is slavery of the spirit. Only the head which bows not in faint-heartedness will be adorned with the great crown. And the disdain from slaves of the spirit is an attainment for the warrior who walks the fiery path. And alone, the courageous warrior, scorned by faint-heartedness, finds the Fiery Gates to the Hierarchy of Light. Verily, faint-heartedness and self-deception are sisters of darkness!

218. Concentrations of crystals of psychic energy grow during each heightening of aspiration. Each tension of power of the spirit multiplies the crystals of psychic energy. Sediments of precipitated crystals, consisting of subtle energies which have been chemically transformed in the organism, feed those organs which are in special need during the expenditure of energy. Crystals of psychic energy melt down substances harmful for the organism. Through conscious tension one can actually promote this dissolving process, which is of service as a counteracting factor. Conscious sendings of psychic energy to infected or injured organs can produce a healing effect. Conscious tension of the will causes an intense reaction of the crystals. Thus, thoughts about psychic energy crystals can bring needed assistance for the injuries of internal organs. On the path to the Fiery World it is necessary to realize those fiery batteries which are contained in man.

219. The center of the solar plexus is a focus of fire radiation. It must be imagined how fire acts. As all the higher functions of the Cosmos act from within, so too, the fire of the solar plexus is intensified in its own seed. The center of the solar plexus gives equilibrium to all the bodies, and its radiations saturate also the ethereal body which feeds the astral body. The interweaving of all the centers and all the bodies is comparable to the rings of a spiral, centered, as it were, in the solar plexus. Each planet, each fiery center, has its solar plexus and Divine Fire of life. If the consciousness is broadened in the understanding of these manifested conformities, then the bond of Macrocosm with microcosm becomes a fiery Truth. The waves of currents are infinite in their diversity. Over these waves the fiery spirit is in communication with space and with the other Worlds. Just as in antiquity the sun was depicted with its rays, so too, is it possible to represent the solar plexus, which has its own particular radiations issuing out of the seed and extending throughout the entire protective network. These powerful currents bring to the heart all the reflections of space.

220. Therefore, when cosmic manifestations are intensified the solar plexus trembles. It is difficult for the fiery heart when in the center of the solar plexus waves are breaking, bringing all the spatial resonances. The manifestation of rays is affirmed as a manifestation of the protective net, and in fact each current resounds with its own fire. Thus is the solar plexus tensed by so many fiery rays! The appearance of fatigue on the part of the Mother of Agni Yoga is of cosmic significance. The dark forces cast on the scales all their stakes. We send rays which shatter their machinations. The center of the solar plexus feels these fluctuations of the scales. It is necessary to tense Cosmic power in the direction of the Light. Thus the fiery heart knows the affirmation of this Battle.

221. At the start of a physical illness the ethereal body is naturally quite enfeebled, and only within the

fiery centers does it remain strong. This explains why people who manifest life of the lower centers only are so afraid of death. The fiery spirit manifests joy, repulsing the dark manifestations with fire. Lower spirits feel their separation from the astral due to the injury of the ethereal body.

222. The magnetic attraction of the aura greatly varies depending upon the combination of manifestations of different tensions. The consciousness sets aflame the power of the aura. When the consciousness is saturated with higher strivings, when it is directed to higher creativeness, the magnet of the aura increases a thousandfold. When the spirit aspires to the Higher Source the magnet of the aura is affirmed in its might. Each lofty striving produces a sediment, manifesting its saturation for each action. Each fiery transport gives to the aura a strong particular attraction which is irrevocably affirmed as the basis of higher action. The attraction of magnetic waves exerts its influence at great distances, and sendings of the spirit can especially be attracted to the closest auras. The creativeness of the spirit acts by means of these fiery magnets. On the path to the Fiery World one must affirm one's own magnetic attractions.

223. Rotation of the solar plexus can have many other causes besides all the cosmic ones. It is necessary to examine the functions of the center of the solar plexus in connection with the organism and the sendings of energy at great distances. Rotation of the center of the solar plexus occurs under compression of psychic energy. The radiations of the solar plexus pass through all the centers, and by this rotation these rays penetrate all the centers, bringing to them nourishment and unification through fiery energy. Rotation of the center of the solar plexus can also coordinate different energies by compressing, as it were, any one center which is in special need of saturation or of strengthening. The radiations of the solar plexus then reach, as it were, the outer circumference of the protective net. During the sendings of energy into a determined place, all radiations are gathered into a seeming conical spiral, and all the projectiles go into space spirally. Thus the functions of the solar plexus are as numerous as are its radiations, since it is also a powerful regulator of the energies emanating from all the centers. Absorbing cosmic fiery energies, the center of the solar plexus distributes the latter according to the respective tensions which are inherent in the centers.

224. It is necessary to observe carefully the manifestation of cosmic subterranean fires through tension in the solar plexus. One can notice such exact coincidences. A path of tension of subterranean fire is always reflected in the accompaniment of red flame. Thus is it possible to affirm the fiery seismograph.

225. If only it were possible to see with the naked eye the processes which, during various transmutations and functions of the centers, take place upon the aura surrounding man! Each vibration of inner fires saturates the space roundabout with fire. Each vibration fills the space either with purifying discharges or with discharges of creative sparks. Unmanifested energies are attracted to these discharges. Fiery radiations of the centers saturate and intensify all contiguous spheres. During sendings of fiery energy the spirit transmutes also the whole space in its path. Let us give our attention to the great laboratory of the spirit which creates subtle energies. Only subtle attainment can penetrate into the Subtle World. All achievements within these subtle boundaries will result in attainment of the Fiery World.

226. So tense is the time! The Cosmic Magnet is displacing and regenerating the manifestation of human actions. Thus I affirm the New Epoch. Thus do dates draw near, and events are approaching.

227. The consciousness contains within itself all the traces of past lives, impressions of each manifestation as well as each thought and striving for revealing of a broad horizon. The consciousness is fed by the "chalice" and the heart, and each compressed energy is deposited in the consciousness, unbreakably connected with the spirit. The spirit, upon becoming separated from the body, preserves the whole aggregate of higher and lower energies. Certainly, the Teacher leads wisely in pointing out the affirmation of vital transmutation. Indeed, through the immortality of the spirit there are preserved all manifestations of vital energies. As are the deposits, so will be the future crystals. And thought, and heart, and creativeness, and all the other manifestations collect this energy. The whole fiery potential of the spirit consists of radiations of vital energies. Therefore, speaking about spirit and consciousness, one must take the spirit as the crystal of all higher manifestations. The ancients knew about the crystalline quality of the spirit, and the spirit was revealed as fire or flame in all the higher manifestations. Therefore, it is so important to understand the true significance of fiery transmutation. Verily, spirit and matter are refined in one impulse toward attainment of the higher fiery consciousness.

228. The Divine Fire manifests its sparks in all Existence. Concealed are the potentials of these sparks, and, even though they are invisible, yet they must be accepted as the basis of all manifestations. One must accept this spark as a link in each center of the organism. Taking this Truth as a basis, one can imagine how the centers are unified by functions. Each divine spark inhales and exhales fire, which serves as a unifying agent. All forces of the spirit's potential are intensified in this continuous exchange. The potential of each center is a link to immortality, therefore great is the error which stresses physical exercises. Certainly not from without but from within is the spark of Divine Fire set aflame. Under the guidance of the Teacher's Ray the spark can surely take fire, but also the spirit must be prepared by independent search. The Teaching of Zoroaster about Divine Fire, Love and Beauty, brought to the World the affirmation of Higher Law.

229. Divine Fire impels each cosmic manifestation to creativeness. Each lofty potential is saturated with this Divine Fire. Each spark of life bears within itself this Divine Fire. Let us apply to all vital manifestations the significance of Divine Fire. In each center of life is this Fire affirmed. Human actions, indeed, bear in themselves these divine sparks. If one regards human fires as creative centers, then one can observe how bodies unified by Fire have their conformities in the different planes. It is correct to think that essence is distributed upon the planes affirmed by subtle energies. Therefore, when We speak about the Fiery World one must be able to imagine how bodies are unified by a vortex of Fire. Thus the one Divine Fire appears as the unifier of all energies.

230. The laws of cosmic Equilibrium govern the planet. In the cosmic laws can be included the law of Karma, for the law of Equilibrium contains all the other manifestations of life. Equilibrium is revealed as the creative action of each manifestation. Just as chiaroscuro creates and saturates an action, so is the law of Equilibrium affirmed in correspondence with the development of the will. Cosmic Scales affirm correspondingly the growth of national Karma. The scales of man's Karma affirm their measurement of free will. Therefore it is so important to affirm an understanding of striving for perfectionment, because a desire projected into space can always attract what is desired, and according to the quality of the desire is Equilibrium determined. Thus, let us make a wish which can be fulfilled—a wish for those energies which can be applied to life. Equilibrium can only then manifest its affirmation when the free will chooses the path of the General Good.

231. The cosmic laws of Equilibrium are applicable to all dates on the planet. Spatial solutions are attracted to the designated dates and can be manifested in all the affirmations of life. Equilibrium is saturated with these spatial solutions. Therefore designated dates must be subtly calculated. One may study the map of the World in different epochs and perceive how the Cosmic Scales have manifested great Equilibrium. The Command has affirmed its manifested actions as Cosmic Equilibrium. Dates are attracted according to these spirals of Cosmic Ordinances. Thus menacing epochs have been displaced by creative ones, and destructive epochs by constructive ones. According to the spirals of creativeness one can observe on-coming cosmic displacements. On the path to the Fiery World let us manifest understanding of displacement, affirmed by the dates of Cosmic Equilibrium.

232. Dates are approaching. Displacement is being affirmed in the very depths of the planet, in the very depths of nations, in the very depths of life. The cycle affirms displacement and the arrival of new principles. Thus do We create together the New Epoch.

233. The distribution of different manifestations depends upon Equilibrium, on which life is built. For example, a spirit which is athirst for certain external affirmations can attract them (by its will and depending upon its strivings), and the law of Equilibrium either saturates the spirit with or deprives it of some quality or another. The law of Equilibrium anticipates each unrelated manifestation. The World is suffering from these imbalances. The spirit of man has so turned away from the desires which are favorable to Equilibrium that each human manifestation produces a force of destruction. On the path to the Fiery World one must remember these laws which saturate Cosmic Equilibrium.

234. These laws of Equilibrium likewise govern the inner lives that underlie every existence. Thus each spirit attracts its own creations. But even in the highest laws Equilibrium proceeds through vital manifestations. Therefore life, which leads to the sacred Mystery of Crowning, is filled with the most fiery experiences.

235. Strivings of the spirit can be affirmed on the Earth as a pledge of vital ascents. Strivings of the spirit can transform the life of the Cosmos. Strivings of the spirit can disclose new paths to the spatial treasures. But each spirit must discover within himself that stimulus which points out the path to transformation. In the cosmic conflict, in creativeness, in the quest of achievement, in beauty, in striving, the spirit finds that stimulus which transforms life. But woe to those who insist on denial and imbalance, for the Cosmic Scales are agitated, and in the reconstruction of the World there is unprecedented tension which cannot hold imbalance and those who manifest destruction. Thus, on the path to the Fiery World let us strive toward the basis of Equilibrium.

236. The reconstruction of the world is being intensified. In space new energies are being assembled;

new beginnings are being affirmed. Thus is being created the New Epoch.

237. The will which is directed toward unity with the Higher Will acquires the power of a magnet. Among creative affirmations must be observed each manifestation of the will. This strong magnet can indicate in advance and affirm life. It can attract all needed energies. Certainly the divine spark can burst into flame from striving of the will. The confluence of the Higher Will with the human one results in an elemental unity. Creativeness is saturated by these energies. Cooperation with cosmic energies is manifested in a corresponding spatial confluence. Thus the aspiration of a saturated will produces new cosmic combinations. On the path to the Fiery World let us be affirmed upon the union of the will with the higher manifested Energy.

238. As long as humanity does not learn to control its own energies, does not learn to govern its own qualities, by transmuting its heavy human traits, so long will each cosmic energy be dangerous. We see how humanity deals with the energies given! Each force which reveals a new possibility for the Common Good also manifests cosmically a channel for other revelations. But each revelation meets with the same reception as does everything else manifested to mankind. Not going along with the Cosmic Magnet, humanity goes against it. Even at best, inceptions of construction are affirmed in a most personal manner. While the Cosmic Magnet is now gathering together its parts, so too the Magnet itself is responding to cosmic movement; and thus the parts of the Magnet draw near to the great task. On the path to the Fiery World let us remember the law of the Cosmic Magnet.

239. A great horizon of shifting can be taken in by

the consciousness which is saturated by the Cosmic Magnet. When joy for the future lives in the heart, then each impediment is merely a step for ascent. Therefore it is so important to cultivate the heart in this striving for the creation of a mighty future. The impetuousness of the current of shifting does not frighten the spirit which has been tempered in battle. Thus, when old, out-worn energies are being displaced by new ones, the fiery hearts know the full significance of the great time. The shifting of energies saturates space. On the path to the Fiery World let us affirm the law of shifting of energies, and of the creation of great new paths.

240. The Equilibrium of the World rests upon the foundation of Being. So powerfully is life affirmed when the higher manifestation is kept in the consciousness. Each lofty thought will be a pledge of the spirit's striving. And in an endless chain of action and thought can be expressed all new trends of evolution. Space affirms its tensions which conform to the actions and thoughts engendered on the Earth. The more responsible is humanity for all its engenderings, for the Subtle World is thus held back in its development, just as is the whole chain of evolution on the Earth. Therefore thought about spirituality must enter into life, but as a true understanding of the Fundamentals of Existence. The Equilibrium of the World cannot be established without true understanding of the First Causes. Thus, each fiery word of the heart proceeding towards purification of the Teaching is a fiery stimulus which will give impetus to the consciousness. Therefore, let us be affirmed in the consciousness upon the power of Equilibrium, as the stimulus of Existence, of the First Causes, and of Beauty.

241. Hence it is so indispensable to affirm in the spirit the Feminine Principle. For the Banner of the great Equilibrium of the World has been given to woman to uplift. Thus the time has come when woman must fight for the right that was taken away from her and that she did voluntarily give up. How many powerful records fill space with the attainments of the Feminine Principle! As the Teacher creates through the disciples, so does woman create through the masculine principle. Therefore woman flamingly uplifts man. Hence also degeneration, because without true knighthood the spirit cannot rise.

242. On the Cosmic Scales the destinies of countries are being weighed. Those going with the Cosmic Magnet will stand before the Light of the Future, but those going against all the illumined beginnings will realize the full weight of Karma. Certainly the battle of Light and darkness saturates all space. So many manifestations are being weighed on the Cosmic Scales! Each hour brings a new cosmic wave, and on the Cosmic Scales are new fluctuations being affirmed hourly. Space resounds with the new conditions which lead to the Fiery World. In the cosmic tension new fiery conditions are being created. On the path to the Fiery World let us apprehend the law of the Cosmic Magnet in each action and each aspiration.

243. The imbalance has so greatly increased that the time has come when humanity must investigate its nature. Every appraisal of life and its levers has been so distorted that man lives in his own engenderings. But no one knows about the true levers, beginning with the fundamentals of Existence, and extending to each lever of life in the World created by men. The True World differs as greatly from the one which has been engendered as does Light from darkness. Verily, space is in need of the unification of the existing great Foundations. Therefore, the World cannot be reborn with-

out the affirmation of Equilibrium and the eradication of the essence of imbalance. And in this determination is the wavering of the Cosmic Scales. The Fiery World is being affirmed on this great law.

244. Free will impels the affirmation for the unifying of circumstances that create the chain of actions. It is so important to create a current of intensified action and conscious direction, for in this unifying of inner impulses with external energies is contained the centralization of all the actions that are being created as Karma. In conscious, tensed striving of the will it is possible to attract the cosmic energies that are indispensable for the construction of Good. Therefore, the consciousness which is united with the Higher Will produces that mighty force which can resist all the tensions of darkness. Discernment of good and evil is already a pledge of the cognition of the true path. Transformation of the spirit is affirmed by the striving of transmutation and by the unification of the will with the Light. On the path to the Fiery World let us strive for the linking of our will with the Higher Light.

245. Cosmic laws manifest in their potentials that power which can best of all direct life. Difficulties which have arisen for the planet in the coordination of cosmic laws, are produced not from unadaptability of cosmic laws, but from the severance from the Higher Worlds. In the entire structure of the Cosmos there has been manifested fiery goal-fitness. Therefore it is impossible to regard cosmic laws as inadmissible. Long since has Unity in Cosmos been spoken about. In all the old Teachings this magnetic Unity was indicated. How many spatial records have failed to impress, albeit they carry sacred affirmations of Unity! How many spatial records there are which point out the engendering of severance! As it has been necessary to remind the planet for thousands of years about eternal Unity, likewise one is precisely obliged to indicate the effects of disconnection upon the planet.

246. The correspondence between Worlds is manifested by the action of affirmation of the firm foundations. Violation of this conformity produces an effect in every direction. By placing the emphasis upon the visible World, humanity has rejected the Invisible Worlds. Living in an external World, man has edged aside from the inner strivings which intensify the spirit in its quest. The separation of the Worlds is thus affirmed by each act of man! The manifestation of disconnection penetrates all the foundations and acts reciprocally, because negation is a confirmation of the force of destruction. The Invisible Worlds manifest all the powerful energies. How, then, to affirm the Kingdom of Divine Fire? How to reestablish the law of Existence? How to affirm conscious striving for the manifestation of unification? The World trembles from violation of the Foundations, and their reestablishment and unification is required. On the path to the Fiery World let us accept the law of Conformity of Worlds.

247. Life is brought into balance only through spiritual attainment. Spiritual ascent is the only way to individual attainment and to attainment of the Common Good. When humanity is engulfed in its desires and its engenderings, how can one attract energies out of the Subtle World and reconcile them with human actions and aspirations! An impetus toward attainment does not result in an accumulation of energies if the will does not act in affirmation of the initiatives of Good. It was spoken with reason about the distorted mirror. Precisely humanity distorts each great initiative in its warped mirror. Purification of consciousness and of the Teaching is the greatest task of our time. Thus, on the path to the Fiery World let us remember the necessity of restoring the equilibrium of vital initiatives.

248. The law of correspondence must attract the spirit toward fiery realization. The creativeness of the spirit reveals all the possibilities for communion with the Subtle Worlds. Overcoming coagulated thought will give the tension which will correspond to the formula of the Subtle World. Just as the spirit can refine a densified thought-form, so can it densify subtle forms. Each concept will actually sound conformably to these refinements or densifications. The spirit can rule its refined aspirations. At first it is necessary to become accustomed to the refinement of one's feelings, in order to saturate the spirit with necessary attraction to the World of Beauty. Thus the conception of conventional standards will be replaced by the true concept of Beauty. The revelation of refinement of feelings must certainly be introduced into life.

249. Penetration into spatial depths reveals new forms. It is possible to create with a densified thought-form a great many affirmations admissible for our life. Each thought-form is in need of spiritualization by the human spirit. Contact with different concepts of the Subtle World bestows the possibility of spiritualizing these forms. Thus, each striving for refinement of feelings will produce fiery manifestations of beauty. One can accept the law of fiery striving for the refinement and the densification of thought-forms. Construction on the earthly and the super-earthly planes can be unified in these manifested aspirations. Broadening of the horizon and of the boundaries of creativeness will be the pledge of new forms and new steps. On the path to the Fiery World let us exert a fiery striving for the refinement of feelings and the densification of thought-forms.

250. A conscious regard for spatial records will provide an approach to different higher energies. The harmonization of various vibrations will institute perfect physical relationships between thought-forms and energies, which will assist in densifying thought-forms. The essence of the relationship will be affirmed as a correspondence between the Subtle World and the Earthly. Refinement of forms depends upon striving for beauty; therefore each more refined concept of a form draws beauty nearer. Therefore they are right who affirm that the path to the Fiery World lies through the heart and beauty. Therefore Cosmic Construction is being refined by manifestation of spirit-cognition.

251. The process of building of the New World is confirmed by fiery means. The energies being generated are introduced and gathered together under a manifestation of particular rays which direct those domains which are to be creatively intensified. The creators of the planet fierily propel these energies, and, indeed, they will possess the power of densification and refinement.

252. The realization that the spirit contains in its seed that quality of the Light which can become aflame in striving, can verily serve as the eternal motive for ascent. Each spirit must sense this unity with the Light, which lives fierily in the seed. Why, then, not strive for that force which can awaken the best impulses in the spirit! Each spirit manifests its possibilities by partaking of the Fiery Source. Only separation from the Light leads the spirit away from the fiery path. When this higher concept is awakened will the spirit be directed to the fiery quest. Spatial Fire summons man to the attainment of higher energies. On the path to the Fiery

World let us cognize with the heart the power of the seed of the spirit.

253. The essential nature of man can be transmuted by the invocation of better vibrations. Only such a reminder will give man access to a higher status. At the present time humanity is found to be continually in the vibrations of the lower spheres; therefore the lower Manas motivates life. The contact of the Ray of the higher spheres will truly give that vibration which will rouse the consciousness. Perception of the spark of Divine Fire in the seed of the spirit will lay the foundation for a new humanity. Precisely it is necessary to establish in the spiritual structure that in which religion has not succeeded, and to apply to each affirmed manifestation the law of attraction. For realization of the Light in the heart will propel toward the Light, but darkness will dwell in darkness. Thus let us remember on the path to the Fiery World.

254. The will of a warrior spirit can direct an entire army to the good. The will of the warrior spirit can direct an entire militant world. The will of the warrior spirit can affirm new channels by which constructiveness can proceed. Therefore any and every wall can be destroyed under pressure of the warrior spirit. The warrior spirit which discloses the fiery horizon is the spirit which affirms the Higher Power. The warrior spirit can saturate each manifestation proceeding along with the Cosmic Magnet. The warrior spirit can overcome many tensions. The warrior spirit creates and constructs new possibilities. Thus let all who are on the way to the Light apprehend the significance of the directing warrior Will, because those who follow the warrior Will are following Fire. Thus let us manifest understanding toward the fiery bearers of Our Will.

255. An external appearance of striving toward the

Teaching of Good does not advance the consciousness, does not broaden thought, does not open a wide horizon. Actually only a penetration into the very essence of the life of the spirit will result in the needed force of upliftment to the Higher Image. Each striving inwards produces a new manifestation of the penetration of the spirit into the light of Beauty. The forces of the spirit are saturated with Cosmic Fire. The consciousness can actually bring the Fiery World and the Subtle nearer to itself. The significance of aspiration into the Worlds lies in the understanding of the depths of spirit and heart. Thus, on the path to the Fiery World let us be conscious of striving for the regeneration of spirit and consciousness.

256. When the consciousness stands still, its condition can be likened to petrifaction. In such a state people resemble stone idols. These idols of spirit affirm the perdition of the planet. On all paths are encountered these idols of spirit. Judging by what is obvious, one may affirm the manifestation, as it were, of life, but no life surrounds the idols of the spirit—verily, only death and dissolution. Who, then, will assert that such ossification can give the planet its needed equilibrium! Verily, idols of the spirit engender cataclysms and catastrophes. This ossification infects the atmosphere just as does the most frightful epidemic. That is why it is so necessary to purify the space and each affirmation of life. Only purification will help save the planet. Seldom is understood the manifestation of the fiery Bearer of the Sword of the Spirit. But the "Lion of the Desert," the Sun Spirit, travels the way of the great Light, and with him go We.

257. The principle of life has been cultivated in all the higher Principles and is contained in life as has been preordained by Existence. The application of all the higher Principles is the very basis of life, for each higher Principle is affirmed as the very breath and movement of life. A higher principle is space itself, and the force of all vital manifestation. Each affirmed principle can bestow its attainment, preordained by Beauty. Therefore it is necessary to become familiar with the application of the higher Principles. Demarcation of the Principles does not produce equilibrium. Verily, the principle of creativeness produces that greatness which is predestined for the planet, but the choice is in the hands of humanity. Light or darkness, construction or destruction, this is to be decided by mankind itself. On the path to the Fiery World let us carry with us a striving toward Fire and the principle of Beauty.

258. The cleansing of space is reaching into all undertakings. The time has come to make evident the forces marching with the Light and those marching with darkness. Indeed, the temptation of the Prince of darkness is therein that he promises repose, but We say—it is the last hour! Only an accelerated purification will make possible the salvation of the planet; indeed, this is not a matter of eons, nor even of many years. Actually fiery explosion will save the planet. Fiery explosion must be displayed in every manifestation. Only the cleansing of space, only the purification of the consciousness, only the purification of the Teachings, will produce the manifestation of purified explosions of the spirit. True, the darkness is becoming dense, but when the tension of the forces of darkness reaches its limit, then will the Forces of Light affirm Their might. Thus one should be prepared for the acceptance of great tension. Light conquers darkness!

259. The awakening in the seed of the spirit is roused by fiery flashes, which can be variously manifested. The saturated consciousness can evoke the flashes of true accumulations of the "chalice." The fiery heart awakens striving by its tension. The foundation of manifest fires awakens the seed of the spirit by establishing new potentials. Therefore one must study vibrations and apply them to life, for each manifestation can serve as a bond between the spirit and spatial Fire. One must accustom oneself to sense the seed of the spirit. Thus, by straining the forces of the spirit, let us be affirmed in the higher quests.

260. One should study the network of circumstances. There is a sort of surrounding network of subtle currents which, according to the necessity, leads to that current which furnishes the best magnetic force. One should know how to assure each undertaking. According to the given seed it is possible to determine the effects in everything. If man would take the great seed of the task in its potential, then indeed the World would be a great reflection of the Higher Will. Therefore it can be affirmed that the Higher Will purposes but man disposes, and thus perish the best sprouts. There is only one path of success—when the spirit realizes in all its might the affirmed seed of the task. But instead, people re-cut everything to their own pattern, and only pitiful remnants remain. Thus, it is necessary to strive in all fiery beginnings and to understand how to accept the seed bestowed by the Sovereign. Once uplifted to the Highest, we may also dwell with the Highest. On the path to the Fiery World let us cognize the Higher Forces.

261. When constructing, one must remember about great correlation. Those who have adhered to the Source of Light must understand that burning of the spirit is beauty and shield in the service of Good. But only those bringing beauty know all the great-

ness of Service. Therefore it is necessary to note those who defame the manifestation of the Teaching. Many more slanderers of the Teaching can be found among those who have adhered to the Path than among the open enemies. You have pointed out with reason the misunderstandings that inflict blows upon the Shield. Actually it is an application of unfit manifestations. Who will be a follower, if the Teaching is merely an abstraction? It is possible to trace each deplorable consequence precisely as a neglect of understanding of the Living Ethics. Fiery is the heart which knows the affirmation of Service with the Teaching. I manifest as My Will the installation of the Living Ethics and the purification of the Teaching. Without this there is no path to the Fiery World. The greatest task is to affirm a new subtle consciousness. My Will transmits to the Tara My Teaching.

262. Regeneration of thinking must be affirmed as the basis of a better Epoch. Thinking is a pledge of success, a pledge of new construction, a pledge of a mighty future. The transformation of life is indeed affirmed by transmutation of thinking. In each manifestation one can trace how thinking undergoes either evolution or involution. Besides inspired thinking, there acts the impulse of kindling the thought. Therefore the law of striving produces that conformity which brings the Worlds closer through a saturation with creative fire. To ponder over the trend of thinking already helps to shift the consciousness. Thus, on the path to the Fiery World let us direct our thinking toward a better future.

263. The construction of the future will manifest the needed turn of consciousness. Regeneration of thinking produces its own fruits. Thus, construction of the future takes place by the saturation of space. Great is the time, and formidable.

264. In this time of world obstruction there is only the one path of regeneration of thinking. Precisely it is important to awaken the consciousness. Indeed, when the spirit can look back and know that yesterday's thinking has already passed, then takes place the transmutation bringing discernment. Indeed the expiring time can indicate to the spirit how all energies pass on and are reworked. But woe to those who wish to encounter the future by looking backward! For the spirit overburdened with yesterday's remains is laden with a massive weight. With such a burden one cannot ascend the Mountain, one cannot pass through the Gates of Light, one cannot become associated with the luminous Future. Thus, if the Church Fathers summon into the past, the Servants of Light summon into the future. Awakening of consciousness, clarification of the Teaching, and summons into the future will result in a great regeneration of thinking. On the path to the Fiery World, My Guiding Hand shifts energies.

265. Vibrations can evoke in the heart a great many subtle sensations. If man would understand how to make use of affirmed vibrations in order to draw forth subtle feelings from the depths of his heart, it would be possible to avert many evil actions. Science certainly must occupy itself with the investigation of a means of evoking these vibrations. Indeed, sound, color and odor can provide an entire synthesis for the higher sensations. When gross methods of the spirit are replaced by subtle ones, the spirit will possess sensitiveness of perception. Contact with more subtle energies will result in a refinement of the entire way of life. When space begins to resound with subtle energies, one will have to know how to apply them vitally. Therefore it is possible to resort to contact with hardened criminals in the search for new ways for regeneration of the spirit. It is necessary to find new means for vibrations. On the path to the Fiery World let us ponder on how to purify the spirit of humanity.

266. Humanity attaches significance only to those concepts which are stored away in a consciousness of mediocrity, for it arrays correspondingly each form in its consciousness. Why, then, have all the Higher Concepts not been inculcated? Why so many distortions? Why so many belittlements? Because, in truth, the essence of human quests and strivings has been turned downward. But the task of the New World is to rouse the consciousness and to restore to the World the predestined Image of Beauty. Creativeness of the spirit must indeed be intensified in ascent. Precisely, not to lower the Higher but to allow It to rise. Therefore the first requisite will be to create the Divine Image according to Divinity. When the human consciousness will cease to depict Divinity in a human way, then the attainments of the spirit will be fiery.

267. The paths of earthly forces hold snares there where the dark forces perceive instability; but each plan of the dark forces can easily be destroyed by freeing oneself from those who are non-resistant to evil. Paths of the dark ones will follow those of Light, but where there is open access to the Light, thither the darkness cannot penetrate. For those refined, fiery strata are inaccessible to the dark ones. Paths of partial revelations do not lead to attainments. Forces of Light, directed to world construction, must therefore so flamingly arm themselves against the dark forces which attempt to penetrate into the stronghold with the formula—by thy God. On the path to the Fiery World it is necessary to repeat about these dangers, because many are the attempts to penetrate into the stronghold of Light. Thus, let us remember all the masks behind which the scratching ones are hiding.

268. Fohat, as actually omnipresent Fire, is hardly understood. Equally little understood is the Laboratory of the Universe. The great Inhaling and Exhaling of the Cosmos must be applied to all manifestations. In fact, hardly pondered over is the exchange of forces being projected and returned into the treasury of the Cosmos. Thus, the role of humanity does not consist in borrowing only; there must be included a process of returning the forces with which it has been saturated during communion with the Fire of space. Thus, taking this communion as the Truth, it is possible to reveal why, in fact, there is such a difference between the giving and the returning. The extent of this difference is just the measure of that which on the Cosmic Scales represents the Karma of humanity. The ignorant are astonished that the Subtle World can be chaotic; but one should ponder as to how sparks of Fohat remain not fecundated, and how many forces remain either unapplied or distorted. On the path to the Fiery World one must deeply absorb the understanding of the chaos of humanity's consciousness.

269. Indeed, the very loftiest consciousness strives toward the Fiery Principle, while the lower one creates the Higher Image in its own likeness. The capacity of the small consciousness will determine the created Image, hence so many obvious distortions! How is it possible to fill a small consciousness with a Universal Concept, when all-comprehensiveness leads the spirit into a frenzy. I say—distressing, grievous is human thinking! A spatial horizon is accessible only to him who knows the Universality of the Principle, for the kingly spirit can merge with the Higher Principle precisely as the microcosm merges with Macrocosm.

Hence, a small spirit cannot merge with the Fiery Principle. Fiery power reveals the entire Furnace, manifested to him who senses the pulse of the Fiery World. This life-giving Principle builds life upon Fohat. Thus, let us remember that only a small consciousness denies, but the fiery spirit is all-comprehending. On the path to the Fiery World let us remember about the great Principle.

270. Spatial Fire contains within itself those sparks of Fohat which are attracted to all vital manifestations in the Cosmos. Thus, these sparks nurture each life, and, according to the potentiality of the being, these sparks are multiplied in their impellent attraction. Their rarefaction is connected with the pressure or accumulation in space, hence one can investigate where is taking place construction for good or destruction. One can interlay the strata of space with thought about the fiery energies and with strivings of the spirit. On the path to the Fiery World let us affirm thinking about the impellent thought of Fire.

271. It is affirmed that it is possible to draw blood out of every single thing in Nature. The World holds such vast potential powers that one must penetrate into and absorb the meaning of this great formula. Being accustomed to physical definitions, man applies all formulas physically; but what is needed is to correct this distortion and renew the truth, returning to a conscious employment of higher concepts. It is not blood that can be squeezed out of a stone, but a spark of Fohat, which lives in and animates everything in Nature. And in the spiritual World is the same law. But with the gradual growth of conscious cooperation with the Cosmic Magnet, the spirit acquires that fiery magnetism which corresponds to sparks of Fohat. Nothing of physical psychism has anything in common with this spiritual magnetism. Indeed, the lofty experience of Agni Yoga results in this spiritual magnetism. So powerful is the action of such magnetism that the thought of such an Agni Yogi, by attracting sparks of Fohat out of space, creates through the Will of the Sender. On the path to the Fiery World the attraction of the spirit is a great creative power.

272. People do not reflect upon acts of disintegration and their consequences. How to remove frightful emanations, once having determined that the infection is actually spread by these emanations? It means that for each disintegrative action there must be found an antidote. One should be affirmed in the search for those fiery energies which can resist these poisonous emanations. The aspiring to a Higher Image will give equilibrium to the spirit. Purification of concepts, aspiration to the higher quest, will provide antidote for decomposition of thinking. Thus, each dark dissolution must be removed through quests of good. Spatial fires can dissolve the fluids of darkness. On the path to the Fiery World let us strive for the purification of Space.

273. Fohat penetrates all the manifestations with which life is saturated. Precisely into the spiritual manifestations are sparks of Fohat drawn, for the Cosmic Fire saturates all identical affirmations. Therefore contiguity with the current of the Cosmic Magnet attracts sparks of Fohat. These fiery assistants affirm each protective action. Just as the protective network acts around the body, so also acts the Fohatic net. The bond between the protective network and the Fohatic consists of the same fiery spirals which emanate from the depths of the centers. Indeed, the Fohatic network is that magnetic body which the spirit, through powerful striving and tension, weaves around all mani-

festations which it wishes to guard. Thus is the space being cemented with each tense action which goes along with the Cosmic Magnet.

274. Therefore, the flaming heart can affirm each manifestation. For the revealed magnet of the heart attracts sparks of Fohat. Hence the heart, which creates in the name of Cosmic Right, has that powerful force, and gathers together sparks of Fohat and arrays with them those manifestations which are intensified for creativeness. This magnet of the fused heart creates on all planes. Therefore Our Heart creates so fierily. It is the heart which can contain each affirmed degree of Fire. Such a heart can be affirmed only by Cosmic Right. The Heart which realizes Cosmic Right has all the Fires.

275. Indeed, if the consciousness be affirmed in the fact that only through equilibrium is it possible to develop any swiftness whatsoever, then humanity will become accustomed to thought about the transference of all magnitudes, for each construction is developed through equilibrium. Every consciousness can attain this systematic constructiveness through intensified search for that with which to adorn the treasure of life. Through equilibrium speed increases creatively, and the focus can affirm its own radiation for a corresponding constructiveness. Thus is it important in cosmic reorganization to accept equilibrium as a basic principle. The power of growth of the structure is affirmed in the proportions upon which equilibrium is established. On the path to the Fiery World let us strive for equilibrium.

276. The sparks of Fohat line up into various extended threads and channels of transmission upon which subtle energies can be directed into space. Sparks of Fohat influenced by the fiery consciousness

respond and collect together, for they are thus saturated with the fiery emanations of spirit and heart. These currents can resist all spatial assaults, for they are intensified by a fiery will. It has been said, "He who raises the sword perishes by the sword." Precisely, not the sword of the spirit, but the destructive sword whose name is the malign striving of selfhood. Truly, the sparks of Fohat can resist this sword. Where there is the crude physical sword, there is also disaster. But lofty and invincible is the sword of the spirit, for with it abide the Heavenly Forces.

277. When hostile forces disclose an assault, it is needful to think about foresight. The servitors of Light must realize that actually not only do the hostile forces breed treachery, but the menace of treachery and destruction lies precisely in omissions and in slumber. Rightly has she who guides under the Star of the Mother of the World spoken about the fact that a leader values truth, for on the field of battle it is important to know which swords have been sharpened. Only selfhood impels the spirit to the suppressing of truth. But an irresponsible warrior can cast each beautiful beginning into destruction. Not to conceal but to reveal is a most primary duty of the servant of Light. Verily, when truth is concealed, the servant of darkness can act through a servant of Light. But is it likely to be so with the Rule given to the servant of Light? Is it ordained thus by the Hierarchy of Light? Has it thus been set forth, that the forces of the Hierarchy of Light must be expended in fiery currents of help in order that a servant of Light betray not, through his irresponsibility, selfhood and untruth? Thus, let him who inflicts so many blows upon the Shield of the Hierarchy of Light remember.

278. To affirm that the World can continue on in a

state of happy comfort is equivalent to an affirmation that existence can be prolonged without a regeneration of the spirit. Indeed, only the obscurity of dissolution can affirm that dissolution does not exist. But the Forces of Light, standing on guard for evolution, affirm precisely the danger of destruction. The trend of the World's Karma is revealed in all events. On the path to the Fiery World the consciousness must be saturated with a fiery understanding of purification through the path of spiritual regeneration.

279. There is no evil to equal the offense of faint-heartedness. In it is hidden treachery; in it is concealed a fraudulent magnanimity; in it is secreted a ruinous half-wayness; its master is Satan; its motive power is selfhood; its actions include construction with the one hand and destruction with the other; its face displays aspiration but its reality manifests egoism; its domain is a manifestation of selfhood; its affirmation is selfhood; its evidence is compromise, and each of its manifestations for good is a self-affirmation and justification of obvious destruction. The pledge of selfhood lies in the foundation of faint-heartedness.

280. The consciousness which is impelled to affirmation of regeneration of the spirit can vanquish each will which leads to conflict against the spirit. But the dark forces and ignorant deniers will not adhere to this affirmation. One must aspire to those currents which proceed with the Cosmic Magnet, for there are so many destructions around the sources which engulf the spirit in their whirlpools. The spiral of the whirlpool carries away into the depths, but the spiral of spiritual ascent propels upward. Thus, one must manifest a conscious attitude toward present occurrences, for there is much of significance accompanying the spiritual regenerations. On the path to the Fiery World let us follow the spiral of spirit and heart.

281. The Heart of the World can manifest its forms in each conjunction of energies. Each new combination of forms affirmed with a new energy is actually an expression of the Heart of the World. Indeed, cosmic creativeness can be used to define the action of the Heart of the World. In fact, to all the manifestations of the Cosmos, in which the magnet intensifies all attractions, one can apply this concept. For indeed, the power which collects all suitable energies, acts consciously. Spatial fires are subject to the law of attraction of the Heart of the World. Subtle is the world of manifested attractions, and each wave of attraction assembles new combinations from the energies propelled toward union. Therefore the Heart of the World creates quick conjunctions. There are so many fiery attractions in the Cosmos!

282. The Heart of the World contains all the properties of cosmic energies. Each force of attraction acts according to the law of the Heart of the World. Each form and the process of concerted actions create according to the great fiery command of the Heart of the World. A manifestation of fiery conjunctions has its own power of unification which gathers together cosmic energies. Verily, all human actions can be saturated by the Heart of the World. But for this great action it is necessary to feel the pulse of the Fiery World. In this fiery creative power it is verily possible to regenerate the consciousness of humanity. On the path to the Fiery World let us strive for creativeness in unison with the Heart of the World.

283. Each cosmic combination leads into a succeeding action; becoming, as it were, a nucleus for a new regeneration. Out of this movement grows a spiral, and the Heart of the World attracts all the spirals of creativeness. Thus, the spiral refers to the sphere of activity of man, to group Karma, to the formation of states, to the conceptions of epochs, to the attraction of particles of atoms, and to all the creations of the Cosmos. Therefore each thing born in the Cosmos brings its own spiral movement, which, in its turn, tenses the adjacent spheres. Thus, currents of Cosmic Fire are distributed by the Heart of the World. The Fiery World consists of these fiery spirals.

284. So, too, does creativeness proceed according to the spiral, and each vital attraction or repulsion creates its own spiral. That is also why spirals of the Masculine and Feminine Principles proceed in such divergent directions. The Masculine Principle strives for seizure, regardless of the heart of man. The Masculine Principle makes bridges for its achievements by stepping upon hearts and heads. The issue is not brain power, for potentially the Feminine Principle contains the same fires. But the Feminine Principle is in need of freedom for heart expression. When it becomes customary to allow the Feminine Principle to live and develop its potentiality toward regeneration through its feeling of continuous giving, then will the Feminine Principle outdistance the Masculine in all directions.

285. The World is covered with the ulcers of human vices and defective engenderings. Incalculable are the human diseases of the spirit which infect the planet. One of the greatest ulcers is untruthfulness. When the World is crumbling away soap bubbles are no shield. When it is necessary to act in defense of such great affirmations as the Banner of the Lords, then it is inadmissible to resemble warriors carrying paper shields. It behooves us to give credit to the dark ones for their speedy actions and foresight, for each day can be considered the Day of Eternity. Therefore, in the days of the destruction and reconstruction of the World, it is important to affirm the principles of true constructiveness. Therefore, each damaging distortion will be considered as an obvious blow upon the Shield. Indeed, faint-heartedness and selfhood are the brothers of distortion. The practice of untruthfulness becomes a habit, and egoism displays its harmful effects. Therefore, when the World is crumbling, it is well to ponder how to destroy all distortions.

286. The Heart of the World manifests its affirmation to all Existence. Each World, each atom has its heart; and the power of attraction conforms to each designation. The center of the planet may be considered as that reflection which issues from the Heart of the World. Each ray propelled from the Heart of the World already unites other worlds; thus life is saturated with rays emanating from the Heart of the World. And these fiery energies are intertwined, being reciprocally tensed in the process of creativeness. The law of fiery spirals is affirmed by the Heart of the World. On the path to the Fiery World let us be affirmed upon the realization of the Fiery Heart of the World.

287. The sunlike quality of the heart is manifested in courage; when the heart knows no terror; when the self-sacrifice of the Agni Yogi carries the spirit away into different spheres above the earth and below the earth; when the spirit untiringly creates with all the fires of the heart; when sensory perceptions manifest resonance to all cosmic manifestations. Verily the spirit knows the Heart of the World and it also knows how invulnerable is the Shield of Hierarchy. The sunlike heart of the Agni Yogi knows that full chalice of the World which is produced by the coming of the great Ray; for the unification of the Worlds is the highest creativeness for the Agni Yogi. Thus, each sphere of Fire is a creative power for the striving Agni Yogi. The Macrocosm, in palpitation, evokes in its microcosm identical vibrations. Hence equilibrium is established when fiery energies are united in space. Just as projectiles of destructive energies, emanating from one center, fly in different directions, so does the sunlike heart of the Agni Yogi absorb into itself all cosmic energies by concentrating them in space. On the path to the Fiery World let us remember the sunlike heart of the Agni Yogi.

288. Hence, each of Ur.'s centers is so sensitive to catastrophes. Hence the heart absorbs all energies as in a spatial funnel, feeling each vibration. Therefore the sunlike heart helps in the purification of space. The impetuous heart goes to meet each fiery energy half-way. Such impetuousness is possible only through fiery self-activity, which is attained on a highest step of fiery transmutation. Therefore each cosmic vibration is felt so sharply. When We indicate earthquakes, one should not always expect external manifestations. One must first of all bear in mind those tremors which take place in the depths. Therefore those pangs which are felt so deeply by the centers, have a relationship to the depths of the Earth. Thus, the sunlike heart senses all fiery manifestations.

289. The power of the spirit and the will can create cosmically then when the potential is sunlike; for to have an effect upon another aura it is indispensable that the source itself be one of higher energies. Therefore, all experiments in this direction must be conditioned by a higher, subtler energy. Each source intensifying its currents of will along with the higher energy affirms a cosmic influence. But each spirit which heightens its currents in order to saturate another aura with them must be especially careful in affirming the sending, for there is no more subtle process than that of the fiery sendings. Therefore, in the treatment of illness through such sendings one may make use of only the higher energies and pure fluids. One may develop these sources if one's spiritual development has been attained through the transmutation of the centers. Thus, the concept of spiritual sendings must enter life as a higher manifestation. On the path to the Fiery World let us remember this fiery requirement.

290. The Heart of the World raises all manifested energies toward constructiveness, which rules the Universe. Cosmic striving holds in its tension each energy of spatial Fire. But the cohesion of all cosmic creative forces, as well as the directing of them, is subject to the Heart of the World. The unification of Worlds also depends upon this supreme Principle which kindles all lives. Thus, the cause of all primary causes is the Heart of the World. Each torch of life is set aflame by the Heart of the World. The consciousness which acquires the fiery vibration of the Cosmic Ray, senses the vibration of the Heart of the World.

291. If science would penetrate deeper, and go into research of the fiery atoms, which serve as life givers for every manifestation, then it would be possible to discover a great many basic causes. But a constant requisite is that the search be most vigorously pursued, for the propelled quests must actually go as far as the fiery atom. Studying only the external traces of various reactions, it is impossible to reach the fiery solutions. So much has been said about the fiery essence of the World; therefore thorough study of the manifest vibrations of all the subtle currents and energies and their interaction must be made. The spiral which unites the fiery atom with the Universe must be investigated in all its powerful manifestations. On the path to the Fiery World let us be affirmed in the conception of fiery interactions in the Cosmos.

292. Interactions between bodies should be investigated, because as the condition of the physical body acts on the condition of the astral body, likewise the astral body reacts on the physical. A sickly state of the organism is reflected on the astral, and a spiritual indisposition of the astral body is reflected on the physical. All spiritual experiences have their influence on the astral body as well as on the physical. But these manifestations must be analyzed with subtlety. Each experience on the astral plane does not leave its impression immediately on the coarsely healthy body. True, when the subtle body collects around itself all the poisonous fluids which infect the astral body, then an infection also breaks out in the healthy gross body. In the infected astral body there results the affirmation of interaction. The astral body easily absorbs all the fluids of the physical body; therefore, each violation of equilibrium is first reflected on the subtle body. Hence, it is so important for the physician to know the spiritual state of the patient. During illnesses and the fight against them, one should have in mind the concordance of the bodies and the indissoluble bond between them. Such sensitive relationship must be acquired on the path to the Fiery World.

293. When subterranean and supermundane fires are raging, it is indeed necessary to manifest great caution. The Center of the Earth is so intensified, because the attraction of different strata acts reciprocally. The tension of creative centers is affirmed by spatial Fires. Congestion of the blood can confirm the state of cosmic tension. Therefore it is so necessary to guard the centers. Spatial Fires are raging.

294. The causes of diseases lie in the root of the bond between the physical and astral worlds. The body reflects all the effects from affirmations taking place in all the strata and recesses of the Cosmos. It seems to be clear as to what an indissoluble correlation exists between Macrocosm and microcosm, but, except for the enlightened consciousnesses, this concept is not taken into consideration and does not advance scientific investigations further. If it were known how atmospheric pressure influences the organism, would one not strive for realization of this link, the power of which saturates each cell of life with its Fire? The bond between the bodies and the interaction of currents must be investigated, for it is impossible to determine precisely the condition of the organism and its ailments without establishing the fiery correspondence. Sensitive investigation of the spiritual and physical states will provide the possibility of discovering the fluids of dissolution.

295. Study of the centers and their reaction to spatial Fires will disclose to humanity the approach to the Fiery Cosmos. Indeed, the heart most of all demonstrates conformity and correlation. Heartache reflects cosmic manifestations, and this fiery condition must be subtly noted, for it is a reflection of the reaction of the subtle body. The physical heart cannot but record this fiery state. Thus, for example, one with an ailing heart cannot but observe this correlation, and a so-called neurosis of the heart is nothing else but a subtle condition of the heart which resounds with the Cosmos. Therefore it is highly important to observe carefully the heart in connection with cosmic manifestations.

296. The liberated spirit always aspires into the higher spheres, but the spirit attached to Earth remains for a long time enchained in the lower strata of the Astral World. The bond between the physical body and the astral is not easily broken during earthly consciousness. The occurrence of a rupture between the bodies recoils painfully on those spirits which manifest earthly attractions. During ascent of the spirit, of course, the liberation is affirmed at the point of breaking away from the Earth. The cosmic law of attraction stands behind this attachment, which is intensified by the energy of the consciousness. Let us imagine a sphere filled with the gases of base desires. Such spheres do engulf spirits which have not as yet been liberated from earthly burdens. The spirit impelled to the Fiery World manifests its own attraction by pressing itself upon all fiery energies. On the path to the Fiery World, saturation of the consciousness by the Higher World produces its spiral which draws the spirit away into the Higher Spheres.

297. The bond between the physical and astral centers is saturated by intensified transmutation during life. Functions on both planes manifest unity, the distinction being merely in that independent activity which is manifested by the centers on each plane. The transmuted centers intensify the centers of the subtle body. But at the same time, while the centers are laboring in fiery tension on the earthly plane, the astral centers have an opportunity to propel the subtle body into the Fiery World. A sensation of pains is manifested on the astral plane and on the mental, but only at the beginning of the ascent. After that, each center, while preserving its connection with the physical body, can function by being intensified in other spheres. There follows a separation of the bodies, freeing the subtle body from pains. The physical pains then correspond to the creative tension of the astral centers. Thus do the

155

Worlds act in mutual intensification. On the path to the Fiery World let us be affirmed in fiery transmutation.

298. At the threshold into the Subtle World striving plays the decisive role. Striving into the higher spheres gives the spirit the strength to break away from the Earth. The greatest task is to teach every living being to aspire. In the construction of life, the breaking away and the attraction to all vital manifestations must be equally cultivated in the heart, for such spiritual equilibrium will reveal many hidden aspirations. Surely, an open window into the Fiery World and a striving in the heart for the fulfillment of life's laws impel the spirit to broad constructiveness. Actually a conscious attitude of an earthly being toward the World being traversed by it, and a fiery realization of Infinity, disclose the World of higher existence. The liberated spirit knows the breaking away from Earth and all the joy of creativeness of Beauty. On the path to the Fiery World the fiery spirit strives for eternal construction.

299. Exchange of energies can be accomplished by the human will. Observations upon the organism can yield results in this direction. However, for the attainment of results, it is necessary to know the condition and the consonance of the centers. First of all one should study the tension of the centers, for this tension is a powerful accumulator. Exchange of energies must bring about a disclosure of each aspiration. The manifestation of fiery energies conforms to cosmic upheavals. And each epoch has its manifest signs of accord between Macrocosm and microcosm. Indeed, the receptivity toward subtle energies reacts on the consciousness and on the entire organism. In fact, this exchange of energies has in its basis the fiery consciousness, which acts as link and magnet. Fiery thought is the first requirement for perception and ascent. The heart knows when the Cosmic Fire, attracted to the fiery exchange of energies which are propelled to the organism, compresses the centers; and the spirit can create together with the Cosmos. The free will serves as a magnet which attracts the Cosmic Heart to the Fire of the centers. This connecting magnet is the creative power of the Agni Yogi. On the path to the Fiery World let us especially affirm this connecting power.

300. This exchange of energies extends into all the functions of the organism. This regulator saturates the organism and distributes the cosmic energies. Sensations during earthquakes are not merely echoes of Cosmic Fire but are precisely an exchange of energies. The creativeness of the fiery centers affirms a most powerful cooperation. Therefore, tension, anguish, and also absence, indicate an exchange of creative energies. Space is filled just now with various processes of constructiveness. It is difficult even to imagine how the fiery thought of the Agni Yogi penetrates into the spatial strata. Verily, the fiery heart builds by the most fiery means. Thus, the saturated heart gives rise to fiery construction.

301. Equilibrium in the distribution of energies in the organism is brought about through knowledge as to how to allocate consciously the forces flowing in. Currents can intensify this or that center in which there is an influx of energies which in turn can propel a fiery vortex into the region of the center which is in need of saturation. The breathing serves as such a regulator, through a subtle manipulation of the fluids of Prana. The application of regulation in the organism must be regarded as one of the principal requirements for equilibrium. Thus, through exchange of energies is affirmed the necessary regulation of fluids and vibrations.

302. The World is in need of reconstruction. Manifestation of purification is indispensable. The fire of the spirit and heart affirms a new principle. Thus let us build. A miracle is at the door.

303. Spirit and Matter are united in space. While being unified they begin their existence in their sphere of germination. In this unity forms of life are created, and they pass through their circles of perfectionment. Being unified with matter, the spirit can be liberated only by the path of perfectionment; for, from the moment of realization of the act of liberation, the breaking away is accomplished. In the Cosmic Laboratory these two principles—unification and liberation—are the fundamentals of creativeness. Only impetuousness of the spirit leads to deliverance, which reflects upon consciousness and heart. Striving of the spirit creates a most subtle vibration. Thus, the liberated spirit knows the cosmic fiery vibration. The manifestation of spirit and matter must be sought in each affirmation of life. On the path to the Fiery World let us strive for deliverance from matter.

304. When we speak about Spirit and Matter, we should have in mind the higher meaning of Matter. But speaking about the liberation of Spirit, we refer to those manifestations which can be called material life units. It must be known that in speaking about these unifications under various forms a downfall of the spirit is understood. For the spirit, being made manifest in matter, must aspire to the higher functions together with matter. Matter is impelled to creativeness which gives rise to forms of life. And the spirit must know specifically how sacred is the sojourn in matter. The cosmic concept of the Feminine Principle as Matter is so lofty—the Truth is so far above the worldly understanding! Only a pure and elevated consciousness can appreciate this comparison. It is difficult to dissociate Spirit from Matter.

305. The Subtle World has been so isolated from the human consciousness that only enhanced transmutation can disclose the path to refinement and to unification of the Worlds. There has actually occurred an ossification of consciousness, and man has become so dissociated from the Subtle World that the tension of subtle energies is inaccessible to him. Only the cooperation of the bodies on the different planes will bring the needed transmutation. It has been said, with reason, that only a miracle will save the World. Verily, the earthly aspiration is not in the direction of that transformation. The creativeness of the New Epoch requires a spiritual realization. The course of events on the Subtle Plane does not correspond to the course of events on the earthly. Verily, a striving will, emanating from the fiery heart, creates a karmic wave which produces a vortex drawing in the corresponding energies. These waves are disclosed in cosmic reconstruction as the basis of creativeness, and also as the energies which sustain the planet. Only on these energies is it possible for the World to build its future. Thus, on the path to the Fiery World let us be conscious of the power of great constructiveness.

306. The consciousness which is impelled to the Higher Worlds, is able to draw from the treasury of the Cosmos. Those who affirm that man has a limited capacity for revelation shut out by this all possibilities. The fiery consciousness affirms measures which make for the evolution of the Cosmos. The attraction of energies from Space is the basis of creative power, for records and manifested energies can be mutually intensified through conscious attraction. Man is a source of knowledge and is the most powerful transformer of cosmic forces. The symbol of the transmuter must live in the heart. On the path to the Fiery World let us strive for the attraction and transformation of spatial energies.

307. The condition of the spirit during the crossing into the Subtle World is subject to the state of the consciousness. Withdrawing from life with the most subtle striving, the spirit is unable to harmonize its vibrations, and thus for a time remains within earthly limits. Yet not only does the sojourn in the earthly state place a burden on the spirit, but, indeed, the conflict between physical emanations and flashes of the higher magnet makes the dwelling of the spirit in the lower strata very burdensome. The feeling of hopelessness which man so sharply senses gives rise to many torturing experiences. Indeed, hopelessness becomes the lot of him who lacks refined aspirations. While on the earthly plane man can atone for his Karma, but in the Subtle World man is dependent upon his aspiration. Space is filled with ones who have not expiated their Karma on the earthly plane. Thus, the exalted spirit knows not these fiery torments. Refinement of the spirit is the key to the Gates of the Fiery World.

308. Fiery energies, being drawn into tension by some center, can often cause enhanced actions of the energies of this center. Partial action of energies gives a center the power to manifest partially. These tensions lead to those partial manifestations which bring into error consciousnesses of small discrimination. With reason has Ur. pointed out those manifestations, evoked by the tension of one center, which lead to psychism. Truly, each opening, saturation or irritation of the centers gives a sharp direction to the fiery energy; but only conformity between the state of the organism and the spiritual awakening produces, as an inevitable

effect, the opening of the centers in highest tension. A partial pressure will produce a partial attainment which may prove to be a very dangerous manifestation. On the path to the Fiery World let us strive to realize the higher tension of fiery energy.

309. Much has already been said about psychism, nevertheless this scourge of humanity is insufficiently understood. Psychism blunts each aspiration, and higher attainment remains inaccessible. The sphere of activity of a man engulfed by psychism is limited within a charmed circle in which all the energies which retard growth of the spirit find their fitting place. Psychism embraces the manifestation of the lowest energies, and the fires of the centers are extinguished by these precipitations. With psychism there is inevitably to be found disorder of the nervous system. In addition, the breaking away from vital functions closes the path to self-perfectionment. Creativeness is blunted, and there is established a passive state which makes a man an instrument for the influx of all kinds of forces. By reason of relaxation of the will, control is weakened, and by this the attraction of various lower entities is increased. He who wishes to approach the Fiery World must battle with these forces of evil.

310. The accumulations of countries are being weighed on the Cosmic Scales. The preponderance of the forces of destruction is unquestionable, but transmutation of the spirit and purification of space and of humanity will afford a new destiny. The reconstruction of the planet will touch upon all values, spiritual and material. Each center, manifesting its Karma, will produce a new tension. Humanity passes through a fiery cleansing. A new affirmation will be revealed upon the horizon of the planet. In truth, a fiery purgatory will reach all the ends of the World. On the Cosmic Scales, for the good of the Universe, are found both the sword and fiery transmutation. Thus, for the planet's good the Fiery World draws near.

311. Each great reconstruction summons from space great energies. Nets of constructiveness are cast far beyond the limits of the earthly spheres. But together with all the pressure of the Forces of Light, there are intensified also the forces of darkness. As one substance manifests a reaction against contact, another, likewise, reacts to each dislocation. During cosmic transformation space reacts to each vibration. Indeed, events are being compressed, as is a substance through chemical reaction. Spatial Fire begins to assemble new forces, but subterranean fire seeks to break through. So, too, the forces of the spirit are expanding, manifesting their strivings subject to their accumulations. A great transmutation draws near and the Fiery World awaits an affirmation.

312. Least of all does humanity understand the indissolubility of Karma, whereas this cosmic law is applicable to every manifestation. Actually, man is not only a monad concluding its evolutionary path; he is a part of the Monad of the Cosmos. All the monads which are conceived in the one Monad of the Cosmos carry responsibility for the existence of the entire Universe. The bond between man and the manifestations of the Universe is mutually nurtured, and thus it is important to recognize how one generator of evil retards all advancement. The course of events indicates to what an extent history repeats itself. At the root of this lies the manifestation of the same monads. Indeed, the Karma of great construction points out the indissolubility of the bond between the prince of darkness and humanity. The fall of powerful foundations is inevitably reflected on mankind. But the resurrection of the spirit can mean resurrection of every manifestation of life, including even the fallen Angel. On the path to the Fiery World one must reflect upon the indissolubility of the paths of the monads with that of the Cosmos.

313. For affirmation of actions and of progress it is indispensable to be imbued with the essence of the acting manifestation. When action premises a great goal, each step must conform to the destination. One cannot mix the great with the insignificant. One cannot mix treachery with the higher destination, or a lower impulse with a higher goal. Such a confusion inevitably causes a sharp reaction. Each higher destination is in need of fiery saturation and non-resistance to spatial designations. Besides higher vigilance, a conscious discernment of the forces of Light and darkness is indispensable. Only steadfastness and conscious fearlessness will bring victory.

314. The condition of the planet is so catastrophic that only the most intensive action will hold people back from savagery. Those who assume the Fiery Vigil of cosmic events can only keep guard over this saturation in unparalleled tension. In the defense of humanity it is necessary to contend with manifestations of imperfection, faint-heartedness and fear. The Karma of humanity consists of a mosaic of the most terrible atonements. Only the fiery guard of Hierarchy will save humanity. On the path to the Fiery World let us assemble all the best swords of the spirit.

315. The consciousness which has been illumined with an understanding of the immutability of achievement, can welcome the New World. Such a consciousness will adopt a striving toward the conflict against darkness, and will know how to oppose all the progeny of hell. Many worldly pronouncements may be said to be hell-born. For the sphere which surrounds humanity is saturated with the products of the actions of mankind's Karma. The concept of achievement within one's heart will reveal all paths to it. The fiery battle fills all spheres. A manifestation of creativeness speedily intensifies new energies. On the path to the Fiery World let us imbue the spirit with consciousness of achievement.

316. The essential nature of one's striving depends upon the potential of the spirit. The urge for confluence with the Cosmos directs the spirit to the significance of unity throughout the Universe. The realization that the spirit is manifested as the engenderer of all that exists, and as the bearer of what has been engendered, will compel man to understand all Karmic ties. All the existing laws of Cosmic Construction indicate this unbreakable unity. How otherwise could the events of the world be explained?

All Light-bearers manifest vigilance for this unity. Nourished by the unity of Cosmic Fire, each spirit compares equally with a spark of Fohat. On the path to the Fiery World let us strive with regenerated consciousness for union with the Cosmos.

317. One must also meditate about the quality of good, for this concept is much abused, when every expression of weakness and foolishness is taken for good. Rightly has it been said that one should defend Truth and fight evil. The quality of good is a great saturation of action by justice and by the heart. Through higher justice the fiery consciousness manifests its own attraction toward the creation of better Karma. Attraction of the heart is always saturated with fiery energies. The quality of good must be understood in all the higher measurements. Let us strive for the improvement of the concept of the quality of good.

318. The present condition of the World corresponds to the stratified sedimentations accumulated by humanity. The manifestation of the conformity can affirm those cycles which are ensuing; in them will be reflected all the expiations of Karma, and each cycle will introduce its new step. Speaking about cycles, let us keep in mind the transference of cosmic conformity. Truly, let us look upon expiation as fiery construction. These cycles will be instituted by three causes—the transmutation of old accumulations, purification of space, and the molding of a great future. The transmutation has begun. And as monsters rise from the bottom of the seas, so is all rubbish rising from the depths of the rabble. In the Furnace of the Cosmos much is being melted down for the useful construction. The efforts at transmutation will attract each Karmic action. The condition of the planet creates an inevitable Karma, woven by the engenderings of humanity. But on the path to the Fiery World it must be kept in mind that the purification of space will bring a great future.

319. Action depends upon the tension of that sphere in which the spirit abides. As intensity of striving affirms the power of action, so does resistance saturate action with the essence of the consciousness. The different planes require different measurements in the expenditure of energies. Where the dense World requires exertions, the Subtle World not only does not require them but allows easy locomotion. The dense World affirms that force which overcomes all resistances. But in the Subtle World the principal lever is the accumulation of spiritual aspiration. To overcome opposition in the Subtle World is possible only through spirituality. It is wrong to think that the Fiery World is merely a reflection of the Earthly World. For, while the strata of the Subtle World represent the reflections of the earthly strata, in the Fiery World there are strata which preserve earthly spheres in their evolutionary growth. In these strata are marked out all the currents of evolution. They are not only the Treasury of the records of space but are also the Cosmic Laboratory. Such strata occupy the loftiest spheres. The ascent of man depends upon his attraction to these spheres.

320. In the consciousness are contained both power and all the weapons of victory. The directed consciousness can move huge masses, but the consciousness must surmount all obstacles, as only the fiery paths lead to Us. Therefore, on the path to the Fiery World it is so important to be conscious of the goal and its attainment. The attraction of the spirit toward the goal creates the shortest path, and can reveal every possibility for attainment. Indeed, creativeness of the spirit leads to the destination of fiery achievement. Let us accept each affirmation of the great Hierarchy of Good. On the path to the Fiery World let us remember that achievement is the corner-stone upon which is being constructed the great future.

321. Of all the destructive energies one should mark the vibration of fear, because fear can destroy each creative vibration. If it were possible to relate all the occurrences engendered by fear, humanity would be terrified by these forms. Fear recalls that frightful Gehenna, which creates such encumbrances on the earthly plane that the path to the higher spheres is cut off. But in addition, fear intensifies dark forces by giving them an impulse for evil actions. But even by the simplest examples of life one may become convinced as to what an extent fear destroys the most affirmed destination. Furthermore, each action of fear on the subtle plane destroys innumerable possibilities. The manifestation of fear is a barrier against each under-taking. Indeed, the power of perfection bestows purification against fear. On the path to the Fiery World one must eradicate fear, for its products are destructive.

322. Standing before the Lord means to comprehend the Guiding Image. Standing before the Lord means to devote oneself to the Lord. Standing before the Lord means to turn one's gaze to the Highest. Standing before the Lord means to deliver one's heart to the Lord. Standing before the Lord means to serve the Hierarchy of Good. Standing before the Lord means to manifest understanding of the Service of Light in space. In sending thoughts of good beforehand, we already create those channels through which energies of Good can be collected and brought together. When the great reconstruction of the World is going on we must direct our affirmations to the assistance of the constructions of Light. Thus are new bridges created. On the path to the Fiery World let us stand before the Lord of Light.

323. The order of life has become so disconnected from the Cosmic Magnet that all human products tend toward monstrous forms. The development of forces has proceeded by a channel directed to destruction. Thus millions of dark souls are being incarnated; souls which have lost the bond with the spirit. For many centuries multitudes of souls have striven toward a way of life rather than being; and life has been directed by these desires. Each action is reflected in the Karma of the World, and the salvation of humanity can come only from inner realization. For this alone it is necessary to awaken the best energies, for Cosmic Justice is manifested there where there is attraction. There is no escaping Karma; there is no transmutation of energies without tension of the will. On the path to the Fiery

World let us strive for realization of the immutability of the law of Karma.

324. The transformation of the World always evokes tension of all the energies of the Cosmos; and spiritual possibilities appear as saturated impulses of the new paths. Regeneration of the planet inevitably evokes all creative aspirations on all planes. Contact with the currents of space is intensified and becomes very painful; for all strata are permeated by gases from the dissolute actions of mankind. Be not astonished when you sense this spatial load. Regeneration of the World has roused all energies. And the transmutation produces its consequences. On the path to the Fiery World, understanding of the spatial conflict is indispensable; thus let us be affirmed in the victory of the Fiery World.

325. The sunlike heart of the Hierarch illumines the existing tension of things as a result of cosmic reconstruction. The beclouded consciousness of humanity does not know the cause of the disintegration which is taking place. People speak about the Wrath of God, they voice their fears when faced with floods of misfortunes, but they speak not about the Hand which retaliates for that which the hands of men have put together. Cosmic Justice brings not reward but merited action. Thus must humanity understand that which is created by Karma. Spatial Fire is raging, saturated with the affirmations of Light and darkness. The Cosmic Scales know the Higher Justice. A Cosmic Ordinance draws near. The sunlike heart of the Hierarch is impelled to creativeness by Fiery Command.

326. Humanity, in the position of an obvious mutilator of cosmic laws, produces those effects which are being reflected in all events. Indeed, for centuries the idea of perfectionment has departed from mankind;

and the spirit which imbues the multitudes is precisely that of rushing to the creation of a cul-de-sac. The whirlpool in which mankind has sown its desires has created that disunity which has violated cosmic laws. Human qualities attract some spirits which incarnate without having any spiritual aspirations. The condensation of such strata above the earth forms a solidly compressed sphere. This sphere is so filled with the display of concupiscences that rays piercing these strata must be increased three-fold. The creative power of rays is especially intense when affirming new possibilities. On the path to the Fiery World let us affirm the consciousness in the necessity for purifying space.

327. The World is atremble from the tension. Events are being compressed. On all planes the energies of Light consist of all strivings to create a better future and to preserve the World from destruction. The forces of darkness creep in under many masks of Light, trying to destroy that created by the Light, and, where possible, to destroy the foundation of constructiveness. In this grave epoch of Armageddon, it is especially necessary to be conscious of the forces which set in motion the actions of each day, of each event, of each manifestation; for the time of choosing has come and there is no middle course on the path to the Fiery World.

328. The condition of the supermundane planes moves events onward at an accelerated pace. The supermundane strata are being, as it were, shifted because striving toward the Earth rouses many dormant spirits. Before great events the supermundane strata are always awakened. A testing is begun, as it were, for the spirits, which may choose their path. Consciousnesses which are ruled by low impulses can be impelled only to the lower levels. But there, in the

same way as on the earthly plane, the servitors of Light stand on guard, and the final Call can summon the spirits to the choice. These Calls resound on all planes. On the path to the Fiery World let us remind about the Final Call.

329. The World is experiencing a most tense time, and the layers close to the planet are saturated with energies which strive for transmutation of the supermundane strata. The condition of the planet is so acute that every supermundane affirmation is intensified in creative efforts, for it is needful to create a powerful counterbalance to darkness. Spirits which are found on the earthly plane in ignorance of the fiery transmutation taking place, may be burnt in the Great Battle, because the mighty conflict requires evidence of one's belonging to the element of Fire. Impetuousness of choice affirms for the spirit a place in the Cosmic Battle and in the Cosmic Victory. Knowledge of the paths to the Light is a task ordained in the Fiery World.

330. Fanaticism pertains to the most violent manifestations of cruelty. Other manifestations in the Cosmos which appear so destructive cannot be compared to fanaticism, for this feeling destroys the heart, it destroys all exalted feelings. Verily, Satan himself saturates the world with fanaticism. Truly, the crimes of destroyers do not compare with the frightful blasphemies of fanatics. The actions of fanatics contribute to the dissolution of each higher Teaching; for the Karma of these godless ones, under the mask of faith, affirms the most horrible destruction. The conditions of life reveal the process through which such Karma creates. Truly, these fanaticisms cause streams of blood to flow. The construction of the New World requires regeneration of the consciousness.

331. Those vibrations which saturate the World

respond to the qualities of lower manifestations. Improvement of the planetary vibrations can take place only through the tension of humanity. The center of all manifestations is mankind, which reflects all strata. Vibrations are so disharmonious that it is difficult to establish a connection with the Higher Worlds. Vibrations which contribute to disunity have the lowest quality. Therefore the lower strata can admit the infiltration of low vibrations, while higher radiations do not reach the Earth. The saturated World awaits the great epoch of Regeneration of the Spirit. The permeation of space with vibrations which assist the establishment of higher radiations is the task on the path to the Fiery World.

332. Man represents in himself a magnet, the qualities of which are quite multiform. Best of all, it is possible to reveal that influence which either the Higher Forces or the dark enslavers exert on man. When the centers and consciousness are correspondingly developed the force of the magnet becomes invulnerable, because this magnetism becomes a conformer to the Higher Force. But the spirit which is saturated with low currents cannot attract. Magnetic currents are directed only by forces which attract them. By losing attraction, it becomes impossible to respond to a vibration. Man is the magnet—thus let us remember on the path to the Fiery World.

333. How, then, is it possible to expect successful results, when the seeds, laid into the foundation, bear within themselves a potential of dissolution? The process of planting the seeds is, indeed, that fundamental on which is molded the main foundation. The stones of which the foundation is composed must be used with the most exact perspective of the entire structure; a breach in them can wreck the entire building. The process of planting the seed must be looked upon as the potential of all the following consequences. Thus the husbandman is solicitous about seeds. But woe to the plougher who is ashamed of his field! The seeds which are planted too deeply may come up too late for the harvest. Deep planting of the seeds exposes the earth to suffocating brambles. The process of planting seeds is a most important one. Creativeness of the potential works by invisible effects for him who is stupid and blind, but the essential nature of the field reveals a frightful aspect of consequences for him who does not harken to the Voice of Justice. Woe to the plougher who did not estimate correctly the planted seeds. Only the great is suitable for the great. Only from the luminous germinates the luminous. On the path to the Fiery World one must remember the great significance of the process of planting the seeds.

334. The most frightful bane of humanity is its narrow world outlook. The best people think that the adoption of their horizon is the principal key to the salvation of the World, but their world outlook goes no farther than the boundaries of the physical world. Representatives of the church promise people salvation of the soul, but beyond the physical world they do not go. National leaders direct the thinking of their peoples toward reorganization, but further than the lower spheres they do not lead. Thus one can enumerate all the degrees of human leadership, and become horrified at the blind alley into which humanity has entered. Verily, only the reconstruction of the World and the regeneration of consciousness can awaken the energies needed for the maintenance of the planet. We untiringly repeat about the vital necessity of purifying the consciousness, for the last hour has come for the cleansing of that which has been created by mankind.

Let us apprehend in the heart the Fiery Command to assist the reconstruction of the World.

335. The consciousness of humanity is so distorted that for construction one is obliged to make use of even such stones as contain barely a spark of aspiration. In the Laboratory of Nature one is obliged to extract one substance from a mass of substances and discard all else. The laboratory work of the human structure reminds one of this reworking. In view of the existing human terrors can it be expected that the direction of the Cosmic Magnet will be taken? If this seemingly harmonious existence were to be exposed, every spirit would be terrified at the disintegration of the fundamentals. A harvest of hatred has taken root in the consciousness and must be eradicated. We cannot name even one religion which, while praising the Lord, does not give utterance to blasphemy. Distortion of the Teachings has produced an ever-living terror. Precisely, the Teachings have been reduced to the human level, and the temples of man are not temples of the Lord. And the word of the Lords is not affirmed by humanity, because the Teaching of Light has been lost in the obscurity of the human consciousness. Only the heart tempered in battle and knowing the complexity of life can understand all the darkness of humanity. One can say that the World will be saved by regenerating the consciousness.

336. The equilibrium of the World has been violated to the very limit. Spiritual striving proceeds apart from matter, and instead of unity there is derived a frightful disunity and dissolution. All unapplied energies remain in the earthly strata, and instead of finding employment they are borne into a chaotic vortex. The spiritual quest is also carried into a chaotic vortex because the isolation of mankind severs the cur-

rents from the Higher Spheres. Equilibrium does not come about without the participation of all spatial and human radiations. On the path to the Fiery World, the basis of equilibrium is affirmation of the beginning of the Enlightened Epoch of the World.

337. Human intolerance toward everything high has converted people into degenerates. Upon all concepts and principles man has imposed his stigma. In each higher affirmation man has displayed his blasphemy. Not the World is cruel, but man. Not the World affirms injustice, but man; for man's choice of the path of isolation and selfhood has brought on a most threatening destiny. Intolerance toward everything high and enlightened has become the disgrace of humanity. The purification of the consciousness is the great task on the path to the Fiery World.

338. If people would only understand the whole power of the magnet contained in the heart! Of all the fiery energies this constitutes the greatest potential power. For the magnet of the heart no obstacles exist, because the sunlike heart knows how to affirm great action. The sunlike heart creates the Cosmic Ordinances and guards the Teachings over an extent of thousands of years. If people would understand that all impediments yield before the powerful fire of the heart! Thus the magnet of the heart creates, and there is no power like this Sun of Suns. Thus let us remember on the path to the Fiery World.

339. The process of the creation of a pure atmosphere parallels the creation of a channel for the reception of fiery energies. Each manifestation of life is filled with poison created by human society. This poisoning is equal to the most terrible hotbed of diseases. Often people are amazed as to why there are so many difficulties; why so many misfortunes and miseries. The

human mind does not grasp the fact that dissolution is far more powerful on the spiritual plane than on the physical. The physical world has its visible symptoms, but the infection on the spiritual plane is so strong that often it indicates how the processes of existing evil are maturing. Therefore, traitors and agitators and doers of dark deeds are most frightful violators of Cosmic Equilibrium. Therefore, on the path to the Fiery World let us develop within ourselves discernment of faces, and let us strive for the establishment of Equilibrium.

340. The consciousness of humanity has become so saturated with the dust of usualness that it is necessary to break through this wall. A single kindling of a consciousness is ineffectual before that terror which darkens the consciousnesses. A completely fallen consciousness can arise more quickly than that one which hides itself under various manlike masks. Take a consciousness imbued with self-conceit and with its own great importance in the world structure; when this consciousness destroys the construction of Good, it is hopeless. It is important to know about such a consciousness on the path to the Fiery World.

341. Even a little foresight should whisper to man how much the World is atremble, how tense are all spheres, in preparation for spatial and earthly battles. Even a small consciousness can be imbued with thought about that reconstruction for which the whole World is getting ready. Even those who are unwilling to understand whither human engenderings are leading, must realize that inevitable Karma which leads on all paths to a great Reconstruction. One can only be amazed at the extent to which humanity dwells in a state of mirages. Clear understanding must be striven for on the path to the Fiery World.

342. The Cosmic Will directs consciousnesses to

understanding of the necessity of equilibrium; indeed, of that equilibrium on the spiritual and the earthly plane without which the different spheres cannot be unified. The spiritual plane appears as something so strange to the majority of humanity! Above the limits of the very lowest spheres mankind does not penetrate, and the lowest psychism is the result. That toward which man is striving becomes his manifest tyrant and his scourge. The subordination of humanity is, indeed, affirmed by these concupiscences. The Cosmic Will summons to regeneration of the consciousness. On the path to the Fiery World let us strive for the realization of equilibrium.

343. The structure of the earthly atmosphere and of supermundane spheres is mutually tensed. The composition of the earthly strata is saturated by all the emanations arising from all the actions, thoughts and vices of humanity. One need not be astonished at the quality of the manifest interaction, for the currents are intermingled and the composition of the atmosphere becomes a reflection of what is taking place on the Earth. The equilibrium of the World can only then ensue when humanity shall manifest higher radiations, because all the spheres surrounding the planet are infected by the emanations from earthly actions. Only purifying radiations produce those gases which rarefy the condensed strata; thus each good cleansing produces its own channels. On the path to the Fiery World the purification of space is the great task.

344. There are so many energies manifested that it is necessary to understand what kinds of ingredients make up the planet's atmosphere. A study of its chemism can easily reveal those stratifications which surround the Earth. If we speak about earthly evaporations, then how much more important are the evaporations emanating from spiritual actions! The time is coming when the atmosphere of assemblies will be analyzed. It will be possible to determine the strata saturating different living quarters. Since earthly strata attract supermundane entities, it will be possible to determine the composition of the atmosphere within a wide radius. The study of human radiations will reveal vast horizons. On the path to the Fiery World one must become aware of the need to know the composition of the atmosphere.

345. Tension of the higher energies of the spirit is one of the most powerful creative channels. Tension of the spirit concerns the subtlest energies in the depths of be-ness. It is impossible to let such potent creativeness escape with impunity, for only in the depths of be-ness is it possible to be in contact with the most direct energies. Through contact with the depths are revealed all the qualities which govern all creative origins. Therefore humanity has lost its fiery receptivity because it has clung only to the external manifestations of space. When tension of the spirit will lead mankind to a conscious realization of the creative depths, then it will be possible to affirm the principle of the Fiery World in beauty and in the subtlest creativeness. One should develop this aspiration on the path to the Fiery World.

346. Spiritual development must inevitably open the eyes of man to those frightful errors which are roots of evil. Inadmissible are discussions about the stronger or the weaker principle, for such discussions lead to lack of co-measurement. Cosmic Equilibrium is not maintenance of stronger and weaker principles. In fact, this human division is what has brought the Cosmic Scales to such a condition. And only atonement by humanity for the violated law will result in new constructiveness; for it is possible to divide mankind only according to established potential. Often man does not even understand what has affirmed the equilibrium on Earth. Cosmic Laws must be looked upon as prophetic Commands. Therefore humanity must learn to adapt the small to the great. In the reconstruction of the World a most important care will be the establishment of the cosmic laws, precisely by the Cosmic Will, not by the earthly. Thus, on the path to the Fiery World only equilibrium reveals the Gates.

347. In the future reconstruction of the World, on the higher spheres there will not be access for those who do not understand equilibrium. Long incarnations will be necessary, to study how to create cosmic equilibrium. Indeed, empires have fallen, nations have fallen, countries have been destroyed, all because the greatest question, that of equilibrium, has been reduced to nothing. Therefore it is so important to affirm the significance of the feminine principle. Precisely, not in the household measuring scale, but in that of the state. If the planet is retained, then future countries will flourish only through equilibrium. We will even admit a preponderance on the side of the feminine principle, because the conflict will be very intense. Indeed, Councils of Ministers will have to include women. Woman, who gives life to a people, must also have a voice in the making of its destiny. Woman must have the right of voice. If woman were accepted, as was ordained, the World would be quite differently impregnated. Thus, only affirmation of the law of Existence can restore the order of man.

348. Humanity has so far departed from a true contemplation of the World, that all that exists becomes illusory. Do, indeed, people wish to know those roots of evil which destroy constructiveness? Closing the eyes to the existence of evil and its source abases man to a

still lower level. The fact that the evil principle exists as opposition to Light is long since known. Just as good is manifested in limitless ways and aspects, so also is darkness. True, mankind prefers the way of unmanifested evil. Indeed, such darkness is very attractive to the small consciousness because it is not necessary to expiate flamingly its actions; and the personifications of evil assume such an attractive application! The consciousness of mankind is truly deprived of co-measurement! Therefore only the purified consciousness can accept Light and its antithesis—darkness.

349. A horizon which takes in only limited concepts always isolates man from the Higher Principles of the Cosmos. The unity of the Cosmos can direct the spirit toward the contemplation of Fire. The consciousness turned to the Principle of Unity can understand the chain which unites all the higher concepts. It can be affirmed that dissolution is manifested as the result of those actions which disunite all the fiery principles, because, throughout the multiformity of cosmic manifestations, in the basis of all structures lies Fiery Unity. Thus, for the institution of Beauty and of the Higher Principles, one must fierily comprehend the magnitude of Unity.

350. The planet is completing a cycle which leads everything to summation. The time is coming when each principle must manifest its entire potential. These rings are looked upon in history as downfall or renascence. But these rhythms must be regarded as the triumph of Light or darkness. The time has come when the planet is drawing near to such a circle of summation, and only the most saturated tension of the potential will result in victory. The circle of summation awakens all energies, for in the final battle all the forces of Light and darkness will take part, from the very Highest down to the dregs. Sensitive spirits know why there is being manifested so much of the Higher, side by side with the guilty and the inert. In the conflict, before the circle of summation there will be contentions of all spatial, earthly and supermundane Forces. On the path to the Fiery World the co-workers must remember the Ordinance of the Cosmos.

351. The circle of summation is the Highest Ordination. The circle of summation manifests its Will also for the Fiery Right. The circle of summation is manifested as the highest creativeness of the Cosmic Magnet. Therefore all Commands and events are led down to the present time. Thus, in the Luminous Ordinance the might of the prince of this World likewise intensifies all its forces. Therefore Cosmic Right enters into life. Realization of the circle of summation reveals many structures which saturate the World with Light and darkness.

352. The World is living through those stages by which have been signalized all the decisive moments in the history of mankind. Stages of destruction precede construction. Creativeness, having been tensed, calls all energies to life. That epoch into which humanity has entered will inevitably manifest all the potentials of forces, for this epoch is a decisive one, and a turning point in history is approaching. Surely, the condition of the planet has not come about by accident, and each tension bears witness to that current which is engulfing all spheres. If the conflict is inexorable, so will the victory be decisive. For all forces and spheres participate in this Cosmic Battle. On the path to the Fiery World one must take up the Sword of Light for building the New Epoch.

353. Waves which engulf nations arise out of the national Karma. In Cosmic Construction each epoch leaves its waves in space. When the date draws near for magnetic attraction, all waves begin to act—thus Karma is unavoidable. When in ancient Scriptures it was said—"All is from the Heavenly Father," by that precisely the law of Karma was voiced. All is created according to these waves, which depart into space and preserve an everlasting bond with the planet. The bond between Worlds, supermundane and earthly, is conditioned by these waves. The records of space consist of these waves, and nations create their own historical redemptions. The realization that everything passes into the waves of space can awaken best aspirations. On the path to the Fiery World let us manifest a striving for the betterment of the national Karma.

354. The magnetic tension is very fiery. Each energy is manifested in its most powerful form. One must regard current events as the expression of all potentials. The most inalienable tension reigns in the World, for the epoch of regeneration of the spirit propels all energies to higher transmutation. Therefore both Light and darkness manifest so grimly their potentials. Beautiful is the time when all events are signalizing an ensuing great reconstruction. Saturated space carries out the will of the Cosmic Magnet. The Fiery World is revealed before fiery consciousness.

355. Bodies are transmuted each according to its essential nature. Just as the physical body transmutes and refines blood to an evolutionary extent, so does the subtle body transmute its corresponding essence. The bond between these processes is especially important to observe, because in the process of transmutation of bodies there is attained a correlation which so fierily cooperates with space. While at the beginning of the process of transmutation the physical body strains the centers of the subtle body, after saturation of the cen-

ters by fire the subtle body holds power over the physical. This fiery process transfuses psychic energy from body to body. The power of the subtle body represents a panacea on the physical plane. Indeed, the feeling of transmutation differs on the physical and subtle planes, because the sensations depend upon the tension of the spheres. The purification of matter and spirit likewise takes place only through the fiery energies and centers, strained in spatial atonement. The Fiery World is thus accessible to the consciousness which knows the bond with spatial Fire.

356. The earthly and supermundane centers display corresponding tensions when events are being propelled toward reconstruction. There is no affirmation on the planet which is not intensified by the fire of construction or by the force of destruction. Soldiers of Good manifest the preponderance in the Cosmic Construction, and each manifestation of the Light has inherent supremacy. For, even notwithstanding the apparent triumph of darkness, cosmic creative power is being saturated with fiery Justice. Therefore, the spiral of creativeness of spatial Fire leads events to its fiery triumph. Thus, on the path to the Fiery World let us remember that the Subtle World manifests a conformity with the earthly.

357. It is possible to trace how events are being crowded, how clouds are piling up, how all the centers of the planet reveal their sharpened trends. Even limited minds can see that the chart of the World is being altered. Verily, not much time remains before the great events. Reconstruction of the World is going on in all quarters, and apparently affirmed comfort is only a mirage, for each energy is found to be in a state of transmutation. It is not difficult to confirm the fact that the Cosmic Scales are oscillating. Thus, on the

path to the Fiery World let us strive for saturation by the Cosmic Magnet.

358. If people would only understand with what foundations it is possible to build a better world! If humanity would only reflect upon the concepts which permeate life! So many higher impulses could become awakened in the consciousness, so many dormant energies could act, if humanity would only accept the Principle of Service, inasmuch as this has been affirmed by all the Higher Forces! All the fiery qualities of Service are precisely based on devotion. Verily, this quality is the basis of constructiveness. On the path to the Fiery World it will be necessary to affirm this foundation.

359. A strengthening of the subtle body accompanies each exalted transport. The subtle body contains all the spiritual centers; conscious nurturing of it can produce great possibilities. The essential nature of the subtle body depends upon these spiritual saturations. The usefulness of these nurtures can be great for the physical body. Each transport of the spirit strengthens the centers of the subtle body; contrarywise, each center of the physical body, which is saturated with lower energies, acts destructively on the fiery centers. The subtle body is in need of spiritual nourishment. The constant bond between bodies can thus affirm a conscious exchange of energies. On the path to the Fiery World let us cognize the reality of the bond between the bodies.

360. Human construction is in need of true foundations. The way construction is proceeding at present, the World is threatened with destruction. All Cosmic Reconstructions require higher foundations, for the creating spiral is affirmed in ascent. But, the foundations of humanity are found to be in a state of intense dissolution. All cosmic processes manifest transmutation upward, but the will of mankind has steered into a blind alley, for the circle of selfhood is reaping its harvests. Therefore, cosmic fire is not being utilized in transmutation by humanity, and instead of evolution involution is the result.

361. Transmutation is inevitable, in the whole Cosmic Plan. Only fiery reconstruction will yield new creative energies. The Cosmic Magnet creates and intensifies all that exists, for dates are approaching which will compel everyone and everything to participate in the Cosmic Battle. Space is in need of a discharge. The Cosmic Scales affirm the process of agitations; throughout all space resounds the call to a final tension. I affirm that the transmutation of energies will produce new steps in evolution. Therefore one must strive with heart and spirit toward the Fiery World.

362. One may picture how the Cosmic Scales are fluctuating when there are placed on one of the cups of the Scales all the historical events which have preceded the present time. And if the future World be gazed upon, one may see how the battle is growing. One may be convinced as to how spatial fires are spreading. One may observe how the Heavenly Forces are being equipped with fiery armor, and how earthly forces condense each spatial manifestation. It is important to think about this, because Fiery Reconstruction must meet with the consciousness manifesting understanding of what is taking place. The fiery fluctuation of the Scales creates vortexes which are a danger to unstable ones but which uplift to the Higher Worlds those who are flamingly aspirant. Amidst the oscillations of the Cosmic Scales humanity cannot choose a middle path, for only Light or darkness will be contending for the victory. On the path to the Fiery World let us keep in mind the Cosmic Scales.

363. If the consciousness of humanity could compare the eternal with the transitory, then would be made manifest flashes of understanding of the Cosmos, because all the values of mankind are based on an eternal foundation. But humanity has been so imbued with respect for the transitory that it has forgotten about the Eternal. Whereas, it is demonstrable that form changes, disappears, and is replaced by the new. Transitoriness is so obvious, and each example of the transitory points to eternal life. Spirit is the creator of each form, yet it is rejected by humanity. When the fact is grasped that the spirit is eternal, then, too, will infinity and immortality enter into life. Thus, it is imperative to direct the spirit of peoples to the understanding of the Higher Principles. Mankind is engulfed in effects, but the root and principle of everything is creativeness—and it has been forgotten. When the spirit shall be reverenced as sacred Fire, then will be confirmed the great ascent.

364. If we but ponder upon just what suppresses the higher concepts, we inevitably arrive at a consciousness which compares everything with the lower manifestations. Bringing everything down to compare with the lowest is a labor of the dark ones, and humanity is indeed subject to these tendencies. Every one instinctively has recourse to this destructive action. Therefore the condition of the consciousness is the best indicator of all epochs and all human directions. Whither leads such error as the losing of connection with the Fiery World? Purification of consciousness will indeed give access to the higher energies. On the path to the Fiery World one must contend with the dark consciousnesses.

365. The destruction of the contact with the higher energies actually isolates humanity from the Cosmos. How is it possible to exist in the Cosmos without any comprehension of world evolution? Thus, a conscious relationship to world evolution includes indirectly an understanding of Hierarchy as a life-giving Principle. Precisely, psychism and mediumism turn man away from the Higher Spheres, for the subtle body becomes thus so saturated with lower emanations that the entire being is altered. In reality a most difficult process is contained in purification of consciousness. Man does not precisely differentiate between the fiery state of spirituality and psychism. Thus, we must overcome the terrors of psychism. Actually, the ranks of those instruments are filled by the servants of darkness. Thus, on the path to the Fiery World one must contend with psychism.

366. Just as the consciousness can be a pledge of fruition, so can it be manifested as dissolution. Limited thought can prove to be a conduit for all dark manifestations. Therefore, thought can be developed into a great vital beginning or it can destroy each origin. Limited thinking shatters all possibilities, because the process of constructiveness is based upon the growth of consciousness. How can one aspire to the Highest Ideal without broadening the consciousness! Surely the Higher Image can be realized by the fiery and fearless consciousness, because there are no limits to a fiery consciousness. Thus, on the path to the Fiery World one must strain all one's forces for broadening of consciousness.

367. The condition of the planet is becoming worse because of the consciousness of humanity. The forces of the spirit are expended on the affirmation of destruction. A faint-hearted cowardice toward all concepts which do not correspond to the present consciousness, is leading humanity to the borderland of destruction. The forces of the spirit can bring mankind out of the rut if mankind will purify its thinking. Each great principle is that prime mover which uplifts the spirit. A search for the higher principles is the primary task. The Existence of the World is affirmed by fiery principles. Therefore, aspiring to the Highest should be a most essential task. Humanity must ponder upon a reformation in its actions. The Karma of atonement draws near. Each striving must be directed toward the Source of Light. On the path to the Fiery World let us manifest in action the achievement of great realization.

368. When understanding of the Fundamentals of Being burns clearly in the spirit, then the abyss of life ceases to appear impassable. When the realization of achievement burns in the heart, then the day of the future appears near. The horizon, which takes in the World in all its structure, embraces all transitoriness and apparent Maya. Thus space is saturated with the creative power of Fire and with future construction. Knowledge of transitoriness results in a feeling of breaking away from the Earth and impels the spirit to those planes where man verily dwells in his fiery essence. On the path to the Fiery World let us manifest aspiration towards the spatial energies which aid the spirit in passing over the abyss of incomprehension.

369. Indeed, the abyss of incomprehension is the path by which humanity is now proceeding. Verily, contemporary thinking is the proscriber of psychic investigations. Yet, so much farther and deeper is it possible to go by knowing the division and the connection between the three bodies. Because, if the physical body is already formed, the astral body has been almost formed, and the most subtle, mental, body has been formed only by the chosen ones. But those who have been initiated into higher fiery energies, and who know the fiery transmutation of the centers, can affirm fiery manifestations. All other manifestations must be divided into two categories. The first, when the spirit cannot pass over the abyss because the mental body has not yet been sufficiently formed, so that the spirit cannot appear beyond the limits of the lower strata; the other category, when one center is manifested partially. It must also be remembered that the Fiery World is inaccessible to a spirit so long as the higher centers have not begun to be transmuted. But above all stands the spirit which kindles its own spiritual Fires, for its mental body creates correspondingly. On the path to the Fiery World one must sensitively discriminate in psychic manifestations.

370. Advancing the consciousness is as difficult as moving a mountain. The most immovable consciousnesses are, indeed, the old and ossified ones. This refers to all those who proceed looking backward and not into the future. I affirm that the ossified consciousnesses require powerful measures, just as do those who do not develop beyond the limits of childhood, for co-measurement is needed in appraisal of events. Ossification and backwardness can destroy the most immense possibilities. Therefore it is most important during construction to remember that the grave time requires fiery measures. On the path to the Fiery World let us manifest understanding of the power in the uplifting of the Fiery Sword.

371. Measurement of the degrees of consciousness over the extent of the last centuries places man now near the zero point. And so many gates have been opened before the horizon of humanity! So many beacons have been placed everywhere, so many sum-

mations shown to be possible! But uplifting of the veil must impel the spirit to true fiery attainment. To what, then, are we to be held as witnesses, during this saturated giving, when the World is atremble at the Battle of Armageddon? The ponderous power of creation can be turned into a festival of the spirit, which will reveal to the World a resplendent future. But the extended Hand must not remain rejected by human lack of understanding of the path of Light. On the path to the Fiery World, one must understand the urgency of striving toward the Light Origin.

372. How little do people reflect upon those fundamentals which are shown to be the foundations of construction, whereas this process is a most essential one. Into the foundation of construction is laid a most substantial and steadfast affirmation. Of all the supports the most fiery one is the magnet of the heart. To exclude it means to leave the structure without a soul, for the magnet of the heart contains all the cosmic saturations. The magnet of the heart is the synthesis of all subtle energies. The magnet of the heart consists of the accumulations of thousands of years; in it is expressed Karma and attraction. Just as it is impossible to replace the sun, so also does the heart remain a powerful creator. Thus on the path to the Fiery World it must be especially remembered that the fiery magnet of the heart is the basis of construction.

373. Karma is creating its effects throughout the World. A conscious attitude toward world reconstruction can establish a basis for the New World. The present trend has so widely deviated from the manifest Cosmic Magnet, that, truly, all the Forces of Light are assembling to assist humanity. Constructiveness is being intensified on all planes. Amid Armageddon can one possibly imagine any sort of security in

those regions of the World which are subjected to reconstruction? The array of Spiritual Forces will lead humanity out of its blind alley. The period of transmutation will bring higher energies to the World. On the path to the Fiery World let us apply all our forces for the new construction.

374. The consciousness of the majority of people does not penetrate into the depths of the cosmic structures. Not reflecting upon the significance of principles, people become isolated from the Fiery World. All creative abilities are in need of this cosmic association, for this association affirms the co-measurement which humanity has lost. Man, who has been predestined by the Cosmos to be a builder and co-creator, has turned himself away from this crown. Completing his circle of actions, man has not adopted the cosmic principles as a basis; therefore the Fiery World differs from the world created by man. Everything is refracted in the consciousness in non-conformity with the laws of the Cosmos. On the path to the Fiery World one must manifest realization of adherence to cosmic laws.

375. The attraction of the magnet of the heart acts powerfully at a distance. These currents awaken resonances in conformity with the force of the sending. Indeed, one must resound correspondingly to the extended thread. The creative power of the heart is unlimited and immeasurable in its might. Aspiration toward the awakening of energies refers to the most essential principle of the development of creativeness. The development of this lever requires a fiery consciousness. Thus one must understand the urgency of such development of the heart. On the path to the Fiery World let us be affirmed upon the understanding of the lever of the Fiery Heart.

376. The strata which humanity creates, surround-

ing the planet with them, become more and more congested, because that life which has been instituted on the Earth hinders not only spiritual discharge but also the physical. The conformity between the Worlds in Space thus depends upon the saturation of these strata. In cosmic space each manifestation calls up an entire chain of effects. And the atmosphere of the Earth forms, as it were, a crust, spotted with dark stains. Knowing how much the Worlds are in need of nourishment by the higher energies, one can imagine the effects of such isolation! Those who stand on Eternal Watch direct the rays of Light, straining all their forces. On the path to the Fiery World let us manifest understanding of this tension in which the Forces of Light are saving the planet.

377. The Cosmic Battle which overtaxes space encompasses the entire Cosmos. In this battle are being solved many problems, and these solutions will be turning points in history and will affirm new principles. Each energy is being transmuted by these fiery conflicts. The turning will be sharp, but the fearless consciousness knows the joy of the spirit. For only daring can turn the spirit to the new future. Only the knowledge of this Cosmic Battle reveals understanding of the current events, for Karma is crowding everything together. Fiery fearlessness will lift the veil of tomorrow and will affirm the cause which is taxing the space. Therefore search for the cause will reveal the effect. Thus the Fiery World will be affirmed as accessible to humanity. Thus let us turn in heart to the Fiery World.

378. The manifest Battle summons to a discernment of the paths which lead to Light and to darkness. During the cosmic tension of all forces, this discernment is indispensable, for space is saturated with fiery

arrows. Every consciousness must be imbued with affirmation of the fiery Battle. Verily, during such fiery tension of manifested arrows humanity must straightway accept that direction of salvation which has been indicated to it by the Forces of Light. To the assistance of the planet are sent fiery currents; they must be received with spirit and heart. On the path to the Fiery World it is especially important to realize the power extended for the salvation of mankind.

379. On the path to Service it is important to remember the necessity for honesty, for this is the first requirement in building. Distortion of facts is distortion of the structure. Only self-deceit impels the spirit to distortion. The Karmic mirror reflects these distortions, and the spirit which manifests a Karmic evil-interpretation, inflicts injury to the entire structure. Why, then, has humanity so enwrapped the planet with false emanations? Distortion of truth, distortion of the Teaching, distortion of principles leads to destruction. In this blind alley dwells the spirit of man who lives by egoism. One is obliged to sweep away the dust, and crevices yawn in the littered structure. Verily, ulcers of the spirit hinder the erection of the building. One must sensitively distinguish tolerance and moveability from those qualities which are so chaotically revealed in experimentation with people who turn about where neither conscience nor honesty nor truth call to the spirit. On the path to the Fiery World the first requirement is honesty. Thus let us remember.

380. The accumulations around the planet are a most condensed mass. If that mass were to be investigated, it would be possible to discover many useful things. Precisely, this atmosphere contains substances which attract to the Earth corresponding energies. If these substances were investigated from the point of view of subtle energies it would be possible to observe that each substance is saturated by human emanations, arising out of the psychic activity of man. The aura of the planet collects all the energies which constitute the essential manifestations of mankind. Therefore the purification of space is a task of prime importance on the path to the Fiery World.

381. How can one attain fiery initiation without actual struggle? How can one pass through life without a real battle? Only a low understanding can have a conception of higher attainment without tension. To pass through life and attain means to pass along the edge of the abyss, means to pass through sorrow and tension. Just as the Cosmic Laboratory transmutes these energies of the heart, so do human souls pass through purgatory on Earth. Without this fiery attachment to Cosmic Fire the heart cannot know initiation into the Higher World. On the path to the Fiery World one must remember about the purgatory of life.

382. The World is submerged in effects created by human deeds. Can one be surprised at what is taking place on the planet? Gases formed by the spiritual smotherings in human structures have dammed up space and enwrapped the planet in darkness. Human aspirations correspond to what is going on. The earthly and the supermundane strata are saturated with manifestations created by the evil-doings of mankind. The strata are in truth mutually infected. This is an obvious karmic action. On the path to the Fiery World measures must be taken for the affirmation of new karmic effects.

383. Cosmic energies have gathered flamingly around the planet and are piercing the thickness of the earthly atmosphere in concentrated currents. The state of humanity depends upon these currents, which

are physically and spiritually manifesting their effects. Physical and spiritual epidemics come from the thick stratifications, and one may trace their influence in the flow of events. Each epoch has its omens, which appear out of the accumulations of results of the actions of humanity. These stratifications can be sensed from out of space, becoming again sources of actions. In this manner does the law of eternal transmutation enter into life. On the path to the Fiery World let us manifest understanding of the law of eternal fiery transmutation.

384. A transport of the spirit is a fierily creative energy. Transport of the spirit saturates each manifestation with the best aspirations. In cultivation of the heart one should especially discern these creative energies, which saturate the spirit with the most subtle emanations. During ascent it is so important to refine all the senses. Building is always intensified by transport and striving of spirit and heart. The attraction of fiery energies from space has in its basis every exalted feeling. How important it is to awaken all fiery aspirations! On the path to the Fiery World let us strive for realization of joy in Service to the Great Hierarchy of Light.

385. The will which is impelled to creativeness with the Cosmic Magnet can erect many lofty constructions, for the consciously directed will creates intensely. Therefore, the choice of paths and the knowledge of the direction can saturate the spirit in fiery striving. Humanity does not accept this law of the consciously directed will; hence so many errors. It can be affirmed that each human action is begun without a true understanding of its application. Thus, in human life goal-fitness is conspicuously lacking. On the path to the Fiery World one must remember the great law of conscious direction of the will.

386. The conditions of existence place the spirit in dependence upon unification with cosmic currents. It is indeed necessary to develop the consciousness in this direction. When mankind will become intensely occupied in conscious labor, then will all energies be accessible to it. The vicious circle is indeed created by humanity itself, and the cul-de-sac is also a creation of man. Enlightenment can come only through a conscious relationship with cosmic energies. Isolation from the Higher Forces has led to certain events which have so strengthened their course. On the path to the Fiery World let us manifest a conscious relationship with the cosmic energies.

387. The most frightful bane of humanity is self-destruction for the sake of obvious selfhood. A man who affirms that in serving his own ideal he must destroy all others not coinciding with his path, is a destroyer of the fundamentals of evolution. The Cosmos requires expression of all that exists, and on the spiritual plane equalization cannot take place. All the higher Teachings have in their foundation the same Source, and will not destroy that which serves as spiritual food. Verily, he who demands the equalizing of all fundamentals, of all Teachings, reduces each great fundamental to dust. The scales do not waver much between atheism and hypocrisy. Thus, on the path to the Fiery World let us remember who tears down the foundations of construction.

388. During the decline of an epoch first of all is observed a split amidst inner structures. When spiritual downfall overcomes the national consciousness, these signs are especially clear. Looking over a chart of the World, one can easily be convinced that dissolution precedes the renascence which can be brought about only through regeneration of the spirit. Quests of the true renascence lead to renewal of the spirit and of principles, and thus a new constructiveness can be affirmed. New construction cannot be approved without a veritable renewal of the spirit. The Service to Light must inspire the spirit with courage to manifest fiery constructiveness.

389. The best definition for the harmonized aura is a subtle combination of energies. In this constituency can be found all creative energies, because when the aura is harmonized all the subtle ingredients can be held in conjunction. The harmonized aura unites the unified consciousness and the unified heart. In each tension of harmonization a particular current can pass without any injury when the forces of the poles are identical. The same law is applicable to sendings, for the sender and receiver must conform to one and the same vibration. Therefore the factor of the heart is so important. And if it is possible to act mentally at a distance, then the power of the heart is incomparable, for the heart can awaken all the dormant energies of remembrances and accumulations of the past. Thus is it needful to understand the power of the heart as a manifestation of the Fiery World.

390. Karma always manifests its signs. This coming year will manifest also its own requitals. The Karma of the World and the peoples' march will indicate the effects of world events. The Forces of Light imbue all world movements. On the Cosmic Scales will fluctuate self-renunciation and obvious ill will. Thus, in all reconstruction it will be possible to observe cosmic agitations which will reveal the Power of Light in the final Battle. Thus do We saturate space. A new step of saturation of construction is at hand. Thus by the tension of all forces will We conquer.

391. Receptivity to subtle energies is always accompanied by refinement of the organism. Besides, it must be remembered that the consciousness assists first of all, for the subtle energies can be perceived only through refinement of the organism. This principle must be thoroughly understood, because usually there results a mixture of concepts. And this misunderstanding and jumbling leads to very dangerous errors. During purification of the consciousness it is very necessary to discern these processes, for people are always disposed toward affirmation of psychism instead of the higher fiery concepts. The spirit who falls into this extremity may find himself so surrounded by psychic fluids that he cannot succeed, even though he may so desire, to be enwrapped by other, higher energies. And in this also let us point to the consciousness as to the salutary agent. Thus, on the path to the Fiery World it can be affirmed that the fiery consciousness will bestow the key to discrimination.

392. A conscious consideration of the force of one's own radiations can produce considerable saturation. A spirit striving for conscious application of its radiations must intensify the manifested power of the heart, for this sunlike source can reveal all paths. Conscious affirmation of radiations is indeed applicable when all higher fiery energies of the heart are kindled. On the path to the Fiery World let us affirm a conscious attitude toward the radiations of the heart.

393. Radiations of the heart have fiery qualities which manifest a powerful saturation throughout all space. If people could but learn to affirm construction through these fiery energies, much could be established in conformity with the Cosmic Magnet. Radiations of the heart have a constructive power, and nothing can be compared with fiery heart radiations, for to their mighty action even spatial energies are subordinated. On the path to the Fiery World one must manifest understanding of this Torch of Torches.

394. To feel the tension of the World is a proclivity of the fiery consciousness. The hidden ulcers of the World can be sensed by the fiery heart. Those vibrations which saturate space remain unnoticed by the consciousnesses which have fallen into the rut of world movements. Only the heart which consciously takes upon itself these ulcers can truly be called a co-worker of the Cosmic Magnet. The consciousness which is isolated from the Cosmic Battle does not draw near to the Fiery World, for this fundamental discernment is indispensable, when the World quivers in the conflict of the Forces of Light with darkness.

395. A particular property of the subtle spirit is recognition of the qualities and merits in man. The broader and subtler the consciousness, the more graciousness it contains, for only the limited consciousness deprives all of merit. A heart cannot be truly great without this fiery quality. Truly, the fiery heart knows how to affirm the tribute of the giving and generous heart. Saturation of the heart by these fiery qualities manifests its own strife. Great is the injury to the spirit when a physical affirmation takes precedence over the fiery essence. The fiery heart knows how to manifest recognition of fiery constructiveness, for on this foundation can be erected staunch pillars. Leaders and kings have been affirmed by this fiery quality alone. In the world structure there have been many destructions when this fiery quality was absent. On the path to the Fiery World this fiery property must be remembered.

396. I affirm how needful it is to manifest the fiery

quality of recognition of merits, for without it the new structure cannot be affirmed. This must be very steadfastly remembered; throughout the entire line of Hierarchy it must be followed. An action of Karma heavily atones for each expression of ingratitude, and even the Forces of Light abandon a spirit to its own resources when these fundamentals are scorned. And up to the highest steps the law is one and the same, for this quality must be attained by inner fire, and the spirit itself must develop this property. We do not intrude into the consciousness when We see the absence of this fiery fundamental.

397. Innumerable are the causes of diseases, and science must analyze these causes. In this it is necessary to have in view the structure of all planetary life. Analyzing diseases one should study the spiritual and physical currents. Likewise the environment has its influence, for group aura proves to have a strong effect on a sensitive organism. We have often heard that during epidemics the better people are the first to depart into the Subtle World, and such diseases often carry off many sensitive spirits. This needs to be investigated, for not always is insufficiency of psychic energy the cause of falling ill. "Microbes" of spiritual infection which saturate space actually overburden the sensitive organism which provides a large store of psychic energy. It can be traced how often in critical moments an illness solves the accumulating drama of life, and often a third spirit takes upon himself a burden created near him, bearing it voluntarily and with tense care. Physicians must very attentively investigate the circumstances surrounding and preceding illnesses, for they may discover a hidden key to many sicknesses.

398. So, too, the fire which menaced the Mother

of Agni Yoga on the heights was a synthetic discharge of spatial fire. Besides fiery transmutation, this fire, as it were, transmuted all the surrounding atmosphere. This occult and physical fire, verily, expiated all the manifestations which had been accumulated in that space. The subtle organism has many functions. The functions of the fiery spirit are so diverse. The Agni Yogi unburdens space and absorbs all emanations. He is a mighty warrior, battling with darkness, and he is that power which the dark pack is endeavoring to destroy.

399. The rise and fall of psychic energy is conditioned by various causes. The most important factor must be understood to be the actual quality of spirit of the bearer of psychic energy. As for the fiery spirit, even during the largest decline of psychic energy, its store is never completely exhausted. But the earthly spirit is affirmed only by the lowest energies, which very easily swallow up small stores of psychic energy; since this higher Fire is brought forth by the tension of the higher centers, by higher aspirations and higher feelings. The manifestation of psychic energy is, as it were, crystallized during a decline, but the fiery spirit is able to inflame these crystals by heart tension. A transport of the spirit can even manifest the potential of the store of psychic energy. Therefore the fiery spirit cannot exhaust its store of psychic energy. This store can burst ablaze during an inflammation of the centers. It can practically disappear during expenditure in battles and during sendings at far distances, but this sacred crystal cannot entirely disappear. Its action only alters its rhythm and its properties, as well as its tension.

400. The store of psychic energy is inexhaustible, and during spiritual strivings its strength is multiplied. At the time of spiritual aspiration this energy becomes a constructive impulse for new supplies. The properties of this fiery energy are thus multiform, and its potential surpasses every other energy, because the life contained in it can transmute all other energies. Psychic energy in its activity can overcome each opposition if it be consciously directed. The manifest source becomes exhausted only when it is not supported by conscious striving. Through attainment of the spirit, through fiery saturation, this sacred fiery source of life intensifies all vital functions.

401. The crystal of psychic energy can, as it were, grow dim during great tensions. But this temporary condition does not mean extinguishment, for, while there is compression from without, there is fieriness of spirit, because the potential of the crystal is, as it were, manifested in the fire which flares up from the very seed of the spirit. Psychic energy also gives form to the subtle body. When psychic energy compresses an energy, then that energy correspondingly compresses the subtle body. Clairaudience through fieriness depends upon the state of psychic energy. True, it is necessary to pay attention to each expenditure of psychic energy, for it must be remembered that one and the same source of psychic energy creates at distances and on all the other planes. Thus should be affirmed this fiery source, for in it is contained the dynamics of Fire.

402. The means for compressing psychic energy are highly multiform. Exalted thought or joy of aspiration, transports of the spirit and each inner saturation with power, can multiply the manifestations of psychic energy. Precisely, it is from within that this sacred source can be replenished. During great agitations or grave illnesses the crystal of psychic energy may be filled with new power through those energies which are nourished by the higher centers and by exalted feelings. Therefore faith, directed toward the Source of Light, verily works miracles.

403. During the kindling of the centers it is possible to observe different saturations by psychic energy. Fiery transmutation engulfs, as it were, and condenses the crystals of psychic energy. Labor of the centers engulfs all energies, and after a working over the crystals are condensed by new ingredients which contribute their saturations. These saturations are manifested in various functions of the centers. Psychic energy is distinguished also by its quality, and its refinement can permeate the higher manifestations of vital functions which are intensified on various steps by different qualities. And similarly, as creative Fire spreads out over the Universe, so does psychic energy pass through its many stages in being refined. Thus, the source of creative power depends upon affirmation of the force of psychic energy in all its potentiality. The development of the forces of the spirit is actually the potential of psychic energy.

404. Psychic energy also manifests in other forms, and it can be transmitted by means of a magnetic current. However, such transmission can take place only when currents and auras are harmonized, but when counteractions result psychic energy is swallowed up from without. These engulfments may take place as a result of anything from vampirism up to conscious destruction. Likewise, thoughts which saturate the atmosphere can either compress psychic energy or destroy it. Spatial Fire contains these crystals. Often the aura of places, where occur irritations or creative actions, is saturated with corresponding crystals. The quality of energy conformably saturates space.

405. Psychic energy intensifies centers during their transmutation. A state of tension in one center naturally diminishes the influx of psychic energy to the other centers, hence a feeling of imbalance. But after each transmutation the influx of psychic energy is stronger. The manifestation of psychic energy takes on a special quality after transmutation. The contact with Cosmic Fires has a powerful reaction, and psychic energy is then subjected to a greater tension. This permits the spirit to make use of psychic energy consciously during sendings. Thus, tension of the centers is revealed as a great transmutation of psychic energy.

406. Saturation of the centers by higher Fire intensifies psychic energy. When the Fire of the centers is raging, psychic energy is also found to be in a state of highest tension. Balancing these fiery forces after transmutation results in a new kindling of the centers. The process of compressing psychic energy proceeds in conformity with the transmutation. The centers collect within themselves crystals of psychic energy which affirm the power of the transmutation. The Agni Yogi manifests a powerful straining of energy, which creates in conformity with manifested spatial Fire. The treasure of psychic energy can create a powerful panacea. The consciousness which assists the striving of the spirit toward transmutation of the centers performs a fiery action.

407. It is not always possible to know immediately whither a current of psychic energy has been directed. It is impossible to decide immediately, when the currents are going in different directions and exercise the same influence, for the expenditure of psychic energy in creative actions emanates from one source. The current of psychic energy is reflected on the heart and on the whole organism, therefore it is difficult at any one moment to determine the direction in which psychic energy is creating its saturations. Heart anguish can be the result of many causes, but one should not attribute it only to the weight of the burdensome manifestations of life, for the cause may be the opposite. When a current of psychic energy is directed into space, a sensation of heartache is inevitable. One must carefully discriminate in these wonder-working manifestations and not confuse them with forebodings.

408. Directed psychic energy is particularly intensified by the Fire of the spirit. Tension of the will multiplies the supply and forces of psychic energy. One may become convinced in life how a manifestation of tensed psychic energy resists and counteracts different barriers. Currents of psychic energy are capable of magnetizing the surrounding atmosphere to such an extent that, indeed, there is established round about a sort of fiery current which shatters all encroaching evil energies. Conscious tension of the psychic energy of fearlessness is a great armor. Conscious application of these saturations erects a fiery wall which protects the affirmed position. The creative power of psychic energy is infinite.

409. The consciousness can intensify those levers which are requisite for the strengthening of psychic energy. But for this there is needed a very subtle discernment, because the subtle consciousness makes use of forces in creative tension, but the gross consciousness and the destroying spirit force the levers toward evil doings. Psychic energy in human hands is a most fearful weapon.

410. During cosmic eclipses manifestations of dark forces are made tense for the reinforcement of their actions, because equilibrium is upset and it is precisely in this state of disturbance that the dark entities manifest their force. Cosmic eclipses particularly accentuate events, for they help provocative forces to manifest. The action of the battle is enhanced and the events become accelerated; the darkness thickens, but the Light conquers and the new Star glows more brightly.

411. The condition of humanity, deprived of a store of psychic energy, is clearly expressed in events which heighten the clash of the Forces of Light and darkness. All currents are so obviously being forced in different directions, which indicates how little the source of psychic energy saturates the peoples. Surely spiritual death, the exhaustion of psychic energy, the destruction of higher aspirations, all denote that condition in which humanity finds itself. Striving for higher attainments gives wings to the spirit and compresses a store of psychic energy. Of course, the flame-like psychic energy is in need of actual application, therefore fiery aspiration appears as such a powerful accumulator of psychic energy.

412. It is indeed impossible to build with faint-heartedness, for it brings dissolution everywhere. An intensified constructiveness requires an act of highest striving—there is either brimful victory or worthless faint-heartedness. If it could be made clear to the human mind how harmful are half-way measures and compromises, the process of construction would proceed differently. But humanity is ailing with these horrible ulcers and We are obliged to exhude bloody sweat in corrective measures. This is the state of tension in which the Hierarchy of Light works. Verily, bloody sweat covers Our brow.

413. Transports of the spirit or sudden misfortune are equally effective in forcing the flow of psychic energy. This manifestation is easily understandable

during transports of spirit, but during misfortune many subtle reasons can be perceived. In time of confusion, of course, psychic energy cannot be condensed so as to begin to act. But through daring of the spirit psychic energy can burst forth as a powerful flame, forming, as it were, a shield against encroaching evil. One can take exercises in these concentrations of psychic energy and find that the tensed will is able to compress a store of it. Cowardice can, indeed, only extinguish the supply of psychic energy. Therefore, develop a store of psychic energy and sharpen daring, for in this source is contained so much power!

414. The heart especially intensifies psychic energy, and each heart experience is reflected on the store of psychic energy. One may speak about the chemical death of a man when the supply of psychic energy is exhausted. One may speak about resurrection when psychic energy begins to be accumulated. By a subtle study of methods it would be possible to discover means of intensifying psychic energy, but for this one should know the condition of the spirit. But a fiery composition of psychic energy can be compressed only through a fiery stimulus. In combating illnesses it is possible to focus psychic energy as a powerful factor. Through purification of the consciousness it is possible to intensify forces of the spirit which are revealed as motive powers of space. In the heart can be found levers for the fiery resurrection of psychic energy.

415. The spirit which realizes in life the power of tension of psychic energy can count upon the strength of psychic energy also during the crossing into the Subtle World. Our subtle body is fed by these saturations, and the fluids of psychic energy form the subtle body. Indeed, through transmutation of the centers psychic energy acts increasingly strongly, and the centers gather these powerful fluids for strengthening of the subtle body. When psychic energy is accumulated by exalted feelings, the transmutation of the subtle body is correspondingly saturated with fiery energies. Thus, it is important to intensify one's forces in a fixed understanding of the power of psychic energy. The action of fiery energy intensifies all the succeeding manifestations of life.

416. Psychic energy penetrates all tissues, establishing equilibrium throughout the organism. During sickness psychic energy flows away from a certain center, weakening the function of the glands. Psychic energy is then impelled to those centers which are able to support and maintain equilibrium. The glands depend so much upon psychic energy. Swelling of the glands may be explained as an ebbing of psychic energy. The weaker the flow of psychic energy, the greater the swelling of the glands, because the physical development is being affirmed without control. Therefore all growths, up to cancer, can be attributed to the ebbing of psychic energy. Spiritual equilibrium can help to eradicate many illnesses. The more prolonged the ebbing of psychic energy, the more malignant will be the diseases.

417. The establishment of equilibrium in the growth of psychic energy can be attained by different means, but the chief one will be spiritual conditioning. During the assault by hostile forces, one can observe how a spiritual transport begins to focus psychic energy, and the process of concentration of fiery manifestations is multiplied. But there may also occur an attack wherein, as it were, the entire store of psychic energy is depleted. This is usually connected with inability to raise the fiery sword of purification. Amidst manifestations of cosmic growth of psychic energy one should distinguish growth from within, and particularly when it is accentuated by self-activity of the centers. The condition of the fiery centers corresponds to that Cosmic power which condenses prana. Thus Macrocosm and microcosm are expressed in the fiery action. Through fiery transmutation the properties of the centers come to resemble the subtlest manifestations in the Cosmos. Through the compression of psychic energy the heart becomes sunlike.

418. The currents of space are subject to the influence of psychic energy. It is possible to compress or discharge currents according to the inclination of the will. The currents of space are subtle conductors of our psychic energy. It is possible to carry out various experiments with powerful sendings of psychic energy. Just as tensed psychic energy makes invulnerable currents in space, so also can weakened psychic energy strew broken threads in space. Spirit and heart are powerful sources for the condensation of psychic energy.

419. When psychic energy is propelled into space there is an intercompression of currents, creating a powerful impulse. When the spirit is strained in sendings of psychic energy, directing its entire forces to one goal, then the currents of space respond to the tension of the psychic energy, and harmony results in the way of mutual compression. Consonances of currents are those channels which can isolate the sendings of psychic energy; and that is why We say that the spirit can play upon the currents of space. Each fiery saturation of the centers is such a powerful resonator of space. Currents are subject to these powerful intercompressions. The manifestation of a harmonized unified aura can verily work miracles. Verily, the spirit plays upon the currents of space.

420. The spirit plays upon the currents of space

under varying conditions. The saturation of space by psychic energy during sendings at a distance intensifies the currents of space. During rarefaction of space the currents are also tensed with psychic energy. A conscious attitude toward the processes of psychic energy will reveal many marvelous manifestations, for it will be possible to establish a mutual pressure of psychic energy and the currents of space. Thought-creativeness is saturated with these mutual tensions in conformity with cosmic conditions and with the spiritual state. The power of psychic energy is unlimited in its manifestations.

421. The heart governs psychic energy. The crystal can multiply its force, which is saturated with fiery energy. In striving to compress psychic energy one should discern subtly which impulses actually create. Because upon the quality of the impulse will depend the tension of psychic energy. Thus, fearlessness and fiery striving for achievement will produce crystals of psychic energy. These crystals are soluble with difficulty, for they consist of the most fiery substances. Therefore, manifestations of the fiery centers can be revealed only to the spirit which knows fearlessness and the power of fiery aspiration toward achievement.

422. Harmonious currents form channels in space which enable sendings to reach their destinations. Through these channels psychic energy can be sent, and the currents will be correspondingly intensified. Spatial Fires can be unified with manifested sendings of the spirit. Harmonized currents create powerfully. Psychic energy saturates each structure. Verily it can be affirmed that to intensify psychic energy in a fiery transport means to affirm each construction. In the heart are laid powerful levers of creative power,

and upon this sun of suns depend the processes of creativeness.

423. Not seldom is a fiery miracle concealed in the heart, but it can be revealed only through continuous striving for its manifestation. Pure Fire glows brightly when the joy about a miracle is born. It should not be supposed that it is possible to attain only through a temporary recollection. But pure Fire, without ashes, can shine when all is filled with aspiration.

424. It is asked—what most of all hinders every good beginning? Reply—precisely absence of magnanimity. No creative attainment, no cooperation, in fact no community is possible without magnanimity. One can observe how through magnanimity labor is made tenfold easier and, it would seem, nothing could be simpler during an inspired work than to wish only for the good and for success of one's neighbor! Joy is the result of manifested labor. Joy is a great helper.

425. Here is a hastening disciple, bearing a chalice filled with possibilities; if he stumbles, violating the laws of trust and magnanimity, what becomes of the possibilities?

426. Only in unity is strength. This has been known since time immemorial, yet people have always transgressed this law. Precisely unity is needed in order to carry out a difficult task. If humanity were willing, it could work miracles through unified striving. But the small, sporadic efforts at saving the planet are very weak. Again We are obliged to repeat about the necessity of unity.

427. Victory in the spirit predetermines the outcome. Therefore it is so important to find the basic approach which is right. So much strength and time can be saved, and so much so-called grief avoided.

428. The Great Toilers in the Spiritual Domain are

the beauty and joy of the planet. Humanity must render gratitude to these Helpers.

429. Humanity must study more carefully its thinking. It is necessary to establish in schools the science of thinking, not as an abstract psychology but as the practical fundamentals of memory, attention, and concentration.

Actually, besides the four named branches of the science of thinking, many qualities require development—clarity, speed, the power of synthesis, originality, and others. It is likewise possible to cure irritability. If even a portion of the efforts spent on sports in schools were allotted to thinking, the results would soon be amazing.

Indeed, the lives and sayings of heroes and the Great Toilers in the Spiritual Domain must be made known in all schools.

As darkness is the absence of Light, so is ignorance absence of knowledge.

430. The necessity of concentration has been often spoken about. In the face of constant problems concentration is for co-workers an indispensable quality. It is needful to display concentration in all small works as well.

In antiquity concentration was considered a manifestation of first degree importance. All Teachings repeat about concentration, regarding it as an indispensable quality.

431. The grandeur of the Cosmos is so little realized. At best, people speak about the warmth of the sun. But the solar system is in the Cosmos as an atom in the sun!

432. The process of cosmic impact is constantly growing, yet the adaptability of the Earth grows worse. One may observe that scholars are beginning to recognize the effects of cosmic currents. It is not to be wondered at, since the currents are becoming so much stronger! The manifestations of the heaven's radiations, and even the rainbow, have a big significance for the surroundings. But I speak precisely about manifestations not subject to measurement by present day apparatus.

Subterranean fire is in an uproar, but how little attention do scholars pay to this significant circumstance! True study in fact must be more than a mechanical recording of force reflections.

433. The appearance of new and unexpected menacing world events is at hand. The manifestation of unexpectedness must be especially noted in the impending epoch.

If one compares the world of the twenties with the present, and applies the same rate of progress to the future, then it is obvious how difficult it is for people to form an idea of the future of the World.

434. The New World has new conditions and requires new actions. It is impossible to enter the New World with the old methods, therefore do I thus summon to regeneration of the consciousness.

Some the New World fills with terror. Some the New World appalls with work. In some the heart palpitates at mention of the New World—seek the latter.

435. It is especially difficult for people to understand the fiery nature of things. Each stone is filled with fire. Each tree is saturated with fire. Each cliff is as a pillar of flame. Who, then, believes this? But so long as people do not realize the fiery basis of nature, they cannot draw near to certain energies. Great is the significance of realization or even of admission or affirmation of the manifestation of Fire. One can speak about Fire as the source of light and warmth, but such a concept will be only belittling the greatness of Fire. With the radiance of each object are the Worlds connected. But few have convinced themselves of this radiance. Sojourn in darkness prevents understanding of the Light.

436. There is a great misunderstanding about the idea of the fieriness of actions. People assume that fieriness is contained in impetuous outcries and movements, but, as a matter of fact, Fire is expressed completely otherwise. Remember how the expression and the fulfillment of certain wishes did not at all conform to the crude human understanding. The most noisy and tearful desire was not fulfilled, but the calm thought received fulfillment. The Fiery World is far removed from earthly demands. The element of Fire is so subtle that it is in accord with the energy of thought. A word can already prevent the access of Fire. Therefore ancient invocations were based on rhythm, and only later, in the course of time, were perverted by cries and groans. What was indicated was heart prayer. One may become more speedily united with highest Fire in silence than in a verbal request. Thus upon all manifestations of life one may learn how to come close to highest Fire.

437. Intuition and so-called sensitivity will pertain to the Fiery World. People are not occupied with the question why only certain persons are gifted with sensitiveness. In an apparatus indicating fieriness it is possible to observe also the endowment of intuition. Likewise, the manifestation of the oscillations of a pendulum denotes straight-knowledge, in other words, fieriness. Not seldom do We speak about the same thing under different names. It is not easy to fix in the consciousness the fact that such a distant fieriness is close to all life.

438. Clairvoyants cannot see at a command. The disciple understands that conditions of higher receptivity cannot be demanded in coarse language. A step of higher development is reached when the disciple begins to value each supermundane chord. But even while flying away into the Supermundane the disciple does not abandon the Earth. Such a concurrence is called a proper bonfire. Its flame arises without any curvature. But few can uplift such a weight. How can one fly without breaking away from the Earth? Does this not mean that one must lift with himself the whole Earth? But how to understand such an impossibility? When the fiery basis of all that exists is realized, then there is no such thing as gravity or weight. By augmenting one's thought about the Fiery World it becomes possible to lift great weights. But one must remember the law of co-measurement.

439. Who is he, who is prepared to fly? Only the man who has not debased his own fiery merit. Not many are the Upholders of the Earth. People have managed to forget the Giants who uphold the Earth. With what words and forms is it possible to recall to mind the nature of things? We shall not weary of repeating.

440. The Fiery World has its expression under the name of psychic energy. Thus will people understand more readily. Everyone will agree that there exists within him something for which there is no name in any language. Force or energy will be more readily accepted than a fiery spark. Humanity is highly opposed to Fire. Fire consumes but does not create—so people think. Therefore, at first, name it psychic energy, and only to a developed consciousness speak about Fire. It is more acceptable to say that musk, phosphorus, or amber are close to psychic energy than to say they are close to Fire. The first consideration, in everything, is not to create impediments.

441. The Fiery World easily enters the consciousness of a man who has to do with minerals, since he has often been surrounded by sparks given off by solid bodies. His consciousness apprehends more easily and more graphically the Fire of space.

442. All the secretions of man are too little studied. They can call to mind so much about psychic energy! Already the remarkable contents of saliva have been spoken about. It can yield the same evidences as photographs of radiations. One has but to separate the saliva of man into its various constituents to see its different phases. Furthermore, at times something indeterminable in its composition will be noted. Something reminding one of psychic energy. In some particular cases a significant deduction may be drawn. How useful is the cooperation of the observant physician!

443. One should again and again repeat about the power of observation. Not often is it put into practice, but only acuteness of observation is of assistance in distinguishing the sparks of the Fiery World. Do not hesitate to use a variety of expressions in reminding friends about the power of observation.

444. Ponder that Karma does not by-pass traitors. Not vengeance but justice is irrevocable. One should understand how Karma turns and strikes unexpectedly. One should be a steadfast warrior. In My lives I was rarely killed, avoiding it by means of vigilance. Thus preserve Me in the heart as a talisman. The manifestation of confusion is not fitting for the Fiery World.

445. All is first built in the Fiery World, then lowered into the subtle body. Hence, whatever is created upon Earth is only a shadow of the Fiery World. One should firmly keep in mind this order of creation.

People must know that a great deal of that which is created in the Fiery World has not been as yet lowered into earthly delineations. Therefore the ignorant judge according to earthly evidence, but the wise smile, knowing the reality. This order in creativeness is simple but is not very intelligible to the ignorant. But even they know that statues are obtained by pouring a mass melted by fire into a fragile form.

446. Much of that which has not reached earthly solidity has already been completed in the Fiery World. Therefore seers know that which must be, even though it is still invisible to the eye of limited vision. For the same reason much dark dross is being formed around significant manifestations. People sometimes understand that a particular good is, as it were, plagued by a particular evil. The process of casting metals can remind about the transfusion of fiery decisions into earthly forms.

447. The Fiery World is, as it were, drawn in spirally by the events taking place on the Earth. But not many will apprehend why there are certain unavoidable intervals between fiery decisions and their earthly embodiment. Indeed, the chief factor lies in the fieriness of the primary structure.

448. If a psychiatrist were to collect cases of unusual ailments he undoubtedly would perceive points of contact with the Fiery World. If a specialist in neurology would assemble the facts about inexplicable occurrences, he could assist in the study of psychic energy. Even the apparatus of our physiologist in Calcutta can furnish hints toward the same energy. Different names are employed but the meaning is the same. People do not like to hold to already existing terms, and thus they merely complicate the study.

449. To reflect upon true causes will already mean

a contact with the Fiery World. Thus it is needful to strengthen one's penetration into the causes of cosmic manifestations. Will not the human spirit participate in them? It is especially necessary to observe the conduct of those people to whom assistance has been rendered. Whoever rejected St. Germain has had a dismal destiny. Rejected assistance is turned into an enormous burden—this is the law.

450. People inquire about the causes of infection, about the properties of blood and sperm, but they completely forget that at the base of these lies psychic energy. It preserves against infection; it is found in the properties of secretions. It is useless to take into consideration a mechanical summary of collected information if attention is not given to the participation of psychic energy. People call a certain immunity an influx of faith, but not without reason is a state of ecstasy called the radiance of the Fiery World. And such a radiance protects man against infection. It purifies the secretions, it is as a shield. Therefore a state of joy and exaltation is the best prophylaxis. Whoever knows rapture of spirit has already been cleansed against many dangers. Even ordinary physicians know how changeable is the condition of the blood and secretions. But few connect this with the spiritual condition.

451. One should not be enslaved by statistics; one can fall into error. It was not so long ago that the mental level was calculated according to the dimensions of the skull. Thus psychic energy has been largely forgotten.

452. One cannot study about the Fiery World without investigating how man conducts himself in moments of so-called misfortune. The spirit which has undergone preparation says—we shall conquer, and dons its fiery armor. But the weak and pitiful in spirit is crestfallen and thus admits a great infection. Do not think that this simple truth should not be repeated, the majority of people are in need of it.

453. People often do not understand the necessity of imagination. But how otherwise to represent to oneself the imminence of Fiery Images? All is born in Fire and cools down in flesh. One must be able to imagine the path to fiery germination out of the dense World. Only such a fearless representation makes Fire non-consuming.

454. Fiery conception leads to simplification of the very essence of earthly life. So it was when Fire began to condense manifested forms. Likewise, learn to understand references to revertible state: the fiery in the dense, the dense in the fiery.

455. Certain forms are invisible and cannot be detected by the eye. Thus must one understand many gradations of images.

456. The Hierarchic bond is one of the manifestations of the Fiery World. Actually only fiery hearts are able to understand the significance of such a bond; only they can perceive the web of the bond, which maintains the regular order of the World. Chaos does not weary of making attempts against these bonds. In addition to dissolute chaos, the forces of evil also attempt to break in and tear the threads apart. Such battles should be accepted as inevitable. Only understanding of the conflict can bestow true courage. Victory is then when one knows what precisely must be saved. Yet the Hierarchic bond is already the greatest Victory. It is necessary not only to submit to this bond but also to grow to love it as the only Shield.

457. Betrayal is first of all a violation of Hierarchy. It is inadmissible, as it means opening the gates to darkness. When betrayal is mentioned in each book, it means that this monstrous thing must be apprehended from all sides. It can reveal itself during the Call and Illumination, and on the New Path, and amid Fire and Infinity; it can strike at Hierarchy, and injure the Heart, and even contend with the Fiery World. The viper of betrayal can creep into all paths, and everywhere can be put to rout.

458. Any benevolent unity is desirable. But it is not unity when upheld by a rotten thread. If a cricket can disturb a structure it means that the striving has not been great. Amid the fiery battle an inviolable unity is imperative; only thus is an unassailable monolith set up. Such monoliths are needed.

459. In ancient Teachings the Fiery World was far more often mentioned than at present. The peoples have a concept of Fire not as a higher element but as a most ordinary circumstance. Science and the newest discoveries proclaim much about the fiery power. It is a matter of complete indifference by what paths will the cognizance of the Fiery World again return. But in evolution it must be revealed as the basis of further advancement.

460. One should not talk about anything in a way that completely disengages it from what has gone before. Spiral rings must almost touch each other, otherwise the spiral is not a strong one. Therefore introduce the new almost imperceptibly; it is no calamity if someone says—all this is old! The new will be accepted thus more readily. Often you may refer to the fiery basis of all discoveries. Let them be called by different names, but the essence will be the same. So many mishaps result from obstinacy in the matter of names! Therefore, never insist upon a particular name.

461. One may imagine a man who by the path of science has stumbled upon the presence of a fiery substance, but has not the imagination to bring it into life. Indeed, how unfortunate is such a blind man! He has heard supermundane voices, yet space for him remains empty. Precisely, he fails to realize that he is like a blind man in the middle of a completely filled amphitheater, who takes the whispering of the crowd for the murmurs of the sea. No one can convince him that he is mistaken. People consider that mechanical means of cognition are entirely sufficient, but these will not lead people to a transformation of life.

462. They are right who try to depict reality by means of luminous points. They awaken a consciousness of the fullness of space.

463. The mind does not love fire, for it is always contending with the heart. The mind does not love wisdom for it fears Infinity. The mind attempts to limit itself with laws, because it does not rely upon flights. Thus it is possible to discover the earthly principle, and also flights into the Fiery World.

464. Each solemnity is already a union with Fire. Who then can overcome you? Against Us no one is strong. Yet We love battle; otherwise it is converted into torment. Let there be found patience greater than Ours! But darkness is impatient. In this it is finite. Labor is in everything, and battle is already an affirmation of labor. Affirmation is courage, therefore We are so concerned about it.

465. He can have visions who will admit them and whose heart can endure them. Fiery visions can be withstood only very rarely. Even the subtle bodies inspire terror. People should not complain at the absence of subtle visions. Even the beginning of their approach already fills one with terror. But none of the good beings will frighten one. On the contrary, they

will guard against evil entities. Thus, the dense world is not accustomed to fiery perception.

466. Already various societies are in session for the purpose of becoming acquainted with the Subtle World. But usually those present are afraid, and thus they reduce the manifestations. Fear is a fire extinguisher. Thus it is time to accustom oneself to the Supermundane World. Fear spreads throughout the aura and acts widely. Indeed, one who is afraid already weakens all those present. Courage must be natural. Mere suggested courage is of little effect. Let us keep this in mind, for daring emanates from broad realization. Once such a step has been attained, it never forsakes a man.

467. One may observe examples of cruel obsession. It is needful that physicians fully understand such a beastly condition in order to know how to cut off the infection. It is right to isolate the obsessed similarly as lepers. Certain degrees of obsession may be incurable. Brain and heart may degenerate from dual pressure, but the steadfast, upright, cognizing spirit knows not obsession.

468. An awesome manifestation will again shake the Earth. Let people ponder—why? An ancient tale relates—"A king became unjustly angry and his best city fell in ruins. But the king did not reflect about the cause of it and again became filled with unjust anger. And lightning devoured his best harvest. But even then the king did not come to his senses, and he became so incensed that a plague carried off his people. Then began to shine a miraculous sign on which was written 'Murderer'. And the unjust king fell lifeless and condemned." Thus knew the ancients about the effects of injustice.

469. Without reason do people consider the

boundary lines of the supermundane spheres to be far distant. No one is aware of the exact boundary with the Subtle World; the consciousness cannot grasp it. And likewise that between the Subtle and the Fiery World. But these boundaries are immeasurably close!

470. The ignorant are contemptuous of fire-worship, yet they themselves surround their shrines with fires. Of course they do this in order to surround that which is most sacred with that which is most pure. Light and Higher Power attract the human consciousness. Not fire-worship, but cognition of the quality of the pure creative element. The sculptor cherishes marble and clay but he does not worship them.

471. There was a time when the earth opened and swallowed up traitors. Who then can picture the tenfold worse fate of contemporary traitors? They themselves least of all understand it. An evil destiny! The manifestation grows, and subterranean wrath is growling.

472. Can a worthy man meet on the path viper or scorpion or tarantula? Indeed he can. The longer the path, the more encounters. The difference is merely in this, that the faint-hearted can be stung, but the courageous will not be hurt. Thus, let us not consider that the best messengers will not be marked by the dark creatures. Let us call to mind all the examples.

473. Manifestations can be either subtle or connected with the dense world. Not rarely do dark entities strengthen themselves by the presence of creatures of earth which they attract. Thus, there may appear some stray dogs or cats or mice or annoying insects. Dark entities strengthen their substance from animals. Repeatedly has the Teaching pointed out the participation of the animal world in subtle and low manifestations. Sometimes they cannot manifest without the participation of animals. But for the courageous spirit all such manifestations are as nought. Let the tarantulas crawl, but it is very important for science to know these connections of animals with the Subtle World. I do not advise having animals in bedrooms. Certain people themselves sense the practicality of such vital precautions, but others, on the contrary, aspire, as it were, to attract invisible guests.

474. Let us say to all traitors—you have convicted yourselves. The fate of traitors is indeed self-imposed. Unendurable is the yoke of a traitor. Whither then so many unfortunate ones? They are disguised as beggars, thieves, murderers. Usually in their pouch are to be found old debts. The traitors do not understand what debts they are paying. But manifestly they bear the weight of payment.

475. The Fiery World is atremble from betrayal. This onslaught of chaos is against everything manifested.

476. Often the right concepts are uttered, but without true realization. The flaming glance very rightly calls to mind fiery energy, which is sent in the glance. The strong, warm handclasp is told about; again rightly, because it recalls the very same energy which fills all emanations. But people do not attribute the power of the glance to Fire; they think about the flash of the eyes or the muscles of the hand. Thus are forgotten the definitions which were taught at one time. Forgotten are many true concepts and many have been distorted. People simply reiterate, not attaching significance to very necessary denominations.

477. The World is atremble. Again the depths of the seas are restless. But these depths are not being taken into consideration. The dates for many submarine shifts draw near, but it is not customary to think

about such processes. If people knew how to think about the elements and the supermundane Spheres, their thinking would be turned more easily toward the fundamentals. Why can only a few think about the most essential?

478. One who has been chilled by frost brings cold with him. Mothers caution their children—don't go near the cold man. One who has been warmed by the sun carries warmth with him. People wish to warm themselves in proximity to him. Is it not the same with the flaming heart which is in communion with the Fiery World? People hasten to the glowing heart to warm themselves, and avoid the deadly cold—thus it is in all Existence. Simple and close is the presence of the Higher World, but earthly consciousnesses drive away the ethereal flame with stone blocks.

479. Accustom children to detect the currents of life-giving warmth. Help the children to smile joyfully at a true manifestation of Existence. Keep them from the worship of phantoms. Not necessary are fictions when the World reveals its marvelous structure. Thus, all space is filled with the rays of the wondrous Worlds.

480. Some people strive for knowledge while others are afraid of the Light. Is it not better to search for the cause along the boundary line of Fire?

481. Nothing ever turns back, but all is impelled infinitely. Happiness is indeed in infinity. Each limitation is already a wrong against higher creativeness. Limitation is a prison, but flight into Infinity already creates the swan wings. Thus, not without reason has been used the name—Swan.

482. The moon is only good for one order of manifestations, as actually in others it is not beneficial. Over and above its reflected rays one can better study the radiations of the Fiery World. Repeat to lovers of the moon about the low order of its rays.

483. Everyone knows how difficult it is to discover the cause of failure in a very complicated apparatus; somewhere something has been bent, and its performance yields no results. No one observed precisely when took place some small negligence. But it has taken place, and it is not only necessary to stop all operation but also to take the whole apparatus apart. So it is in the Fiery World: resist it with the least carnal desire and all relationship will be violated. But worry not the little ones, otherwise they will begin to fear such an element. Fire loves courage and impetuousness. But the courageous hero will not belittle himself with carnal thoughts. Impetuousness will help one to fly over the dark abysses. There is much darkness, many chasms, many dark traitors. Let Light shine above the darkness!

484. Steadfastness is an attribute of the shield; the strength is not in it, but in the directing hand. Fire is manifested to the eye but realized by the heart.

485. Let us rejoice at the manifestation of victory. People will still not see it for some time, but it is already here. Wait, impatient ones, not the eye but the heart determines victory. When a fiery structure is already realized in the Subtle World, then may the hearts of the builders rejoice. Those who sleep do not feel it if they are carried out of the house, but space is already singing.

486. Why do I insist that notes be taken down each day? So that the rhythm be not violated. Whoever has absorbed the value of constancy is already close to the Fiery Gates. One must prepare oneself for constancy in everything. Thence comes indefatigability, thence comes invincibility.

487. People love to talk about a miracle, but are afraid of each approach to the Subtle World. We divide people into three categories—the dense ones, those who admit the Subtle World, and those who cognize the Fiery World. Divide those whom you meet along these lines.

488. A remarkable year draws near. But many do not grasp the significance of current events. Even those who have heard are wishing that events would be carried out according to their own imagination. Usually each one wishes according to his nature, but observe current events without prejudice. Fix your attention honestly, knowing that a great date is ensuing. Doves will bring you not only an olive branch but also a leaf of oak and laurel. Likewise Our sacrificial offerings are not a chance occurrence but are as steps of the future. Indeed, unalterable are the dates of great knowledge. Learn to love creative conflict. Know how to put your ear to the Earth and to illumine your hearts in great expectancy. Let the ignorant desire evil, yet the dates weave the fabric of the World. Learn to discern. Learn to fly toward the ordained. Many are the garments and the veils, but the meaning is one. The pre-ordained year draws near.

489. People are wondering of what use are such small conquests of the elements as levitation, passing through fire, sitting on the water, or being buried underground? Only a symbol of mastery is indicated in these exercises of discipline. But the Fiery World is not attained by a test of the heels or by breathing exercises. The World of Beauty is attainable only through the heart. Let us not censure all those who devote themselves to severe practices of discipline, but let us hasten by the path of heart exaltation and rapture.

490. Austerely and tensely, yet also joyfully, should

this year be passed on the Earth for those who are wise. I affirm a powerful rotation of energies, yet there too it is possible to awaken sleeping ones. Not obviously does the King of Glory arrive, but by the wise His step is heard. Leave the dead to bury the dead, and rejoice in the formation of life. Say to friends—take notice, observe sharply.

491. Certain perspicacious people speak about the approaching end of the World. In describing it they talk as they were taught to think in elementary schools. They are little to be blamed in this, since their heads have been filled from childhood with the most monstrous ideas. And yet, they do sense some sort of end of something. Though dimly seen, still their spirit has a presentiment of some kind of change. They are called false prophets, but such a judgment is not fair, for in their own way they sense the end of an obsolete World. Only, they are unable to distinguish the external signs. Indeed, near is the hour when superfluous scales begin to fall, and the World of Light begins to come into being in joy. The most important processes can be carried out visibly-invisibly.

492. When forewarnings are given, it is easier to distinguish events. Already something is being born, but the crowds are occupied with amusements. Already an explosion is prepared, yet the crowds rush into the hippodromes. And ancient seers knew of many changes which are now clear to historians. But their contemporaries only knew how to stone all those who were far-seeing. Is it not thus also today?

493. It is difficult to think about the Fiery World without mobility of mind. He cannot take in all the sparks who does not know how to turn about in resourcefulness. Thus one must reflect upon the fiery link with each manifestation of life. People little study the manifestation and reaction of electricity on the nervous system. Each man can investigate upon himself how a current of electricity reacts on the quality of his pulse. Spatial electricity and condensed magnetization will react differently. The pulse will show a quality of significant tension. In general one should not reject any observations made upon oneself. People may be lacking in power of observation, but knowledge of oneself is instructive.

494. Consider this problem: if longevity is increased, and diseases will cease to be, the birthrate may be doubled. Calculate the situation then on Earth within a hundred years, and a thousand. In this way you will apprehend why some things are not being overcome. In addition, you will apprehend why life of the spirit is placed at the head of the future. The appearance of a new measuring rod of existence can save the Earth. But present understanding is especially far from the Truth. The past year has disclosed unprecedented gaps in the consciousness of people.

495. Prayer is expression of best thought. All beliefs prescribe praying to the Highest, in the best expressions. It is correct to advise people to approach the Highest with the most exalted thoughts. We always point out the high utility of exalted thinking. To whom then can one send thoughts if not to the very Highest? I advise to let no time be lost when it is possible to converse about striving toward Light. Not a petition, nor a dispute with irritation, but an aspiring heart-exchange multiples lofty Grace. People must learn to think, meaning that it is proper to affirm thought about the Highest—some clearly, some hazily, yet all by the same Fiery path.

496. The guiding teacher will not censure a neighbor and thus make difficult the path of those whom he leads. Each teacher will rejoice when his disciples hasten forward and find delight on the path in thought about the Highest. It is not necessary to employ compulsion where there is a flame. The best action is that of the heart. Very carefully guard the heart quality. This quality comes by way of many sufferings, but the Fire of the heart is sacred Fire.

497. The ignorant are exasperated by sufferings, but those who are familiar with the great examples understand bitterness as sweetness. Thus knowledge is the fiery path. Is it not inspiring to know how near is the path to the Fiery World?

498. Is it possible to want to have false thoughts? When the day of photographing the aura comes, many will attempt to replace their habitual thoughts with something more beautiful just invented. Indeed, people know how to shed simulated tears. Petty cunning individuals will try to conceal their essential natures, but the film will prove to be quite revealing. A remarkable experiment will take place. Hypocritical thought will only make the picture worse, spattering it, as it were, with dark spots. Thus, new cunning will not be successful. Sincere, inherent thought produces clear rays. The needed sacred aspirations will have clear colors. Soon advancement will be made in the photographing of the aura. But it is difficult to reconcile the polarity of the photographer with the photographed person. Many trials will be required. Likewise is needed a particular, as it were, ozonising apparatus, for purifying the surrounding atmosphere.

499. Spirituality is both an earned and natural quality. On the middle steps it can be cultivated, but it is necessary to begin such transformation from birth. One must provide a pure atmosphere, not darken the imagination with base views, learn to rejoice at the truly highest and beautiful, eschew luxury and any form of filth. The spiritual man will not be a hypocrite, nor will he be liar nor coward. He will cognize labor as an indispensable means of perfectionment, but his heart prayer will be flamingly beautiful.

500. The worst of all is to understand humility as mediocrity. Humility is the worthy carrying out of Service. Is standing guard before the trusted gates insignificant? Not insignificant is a resolution to perform better labor. Standing before the Fiery World cannot be of no account. But true Service lies in the toil of patient endurance and perfectionment. Such quality pertains to the Fiery Path.

501. You already know that objects can be made to change place by thought or psychic energy. The ignorant ask—why is not the fiery energy of thought subject to everyone and at all times? Ignorance can even reach the extent of such nonsense. A child asks help of an adult where his own strength is inadequate, but ignoramuses are not ashamed to ask such silly questions. In the Subtle World everything is moved by thought, but the dense World only rarely admits subtle qualities. The laws of such admissions are complex and not always are such invasions into the Subtle World admitted. Apparatus which can confirm the physical reaction to thought can be only very primitive, because the nature of employment of fiery energy lies not in the domain of the will but in that of the heart. The heart does not admit evil, but the will can occasion calamities. When the World will come to realize the value of the heart life, then will the flesh be transformed and draw near to the laws of the Subtle World.

502. It is important to understand to what extent people's consciousness has become petrified. Therefore, do not give it food which it cannot assimilate.

Side by side with the difficult give also the easy; otherwise people will not listen. The letters of the Teacher are inevitably diverse, because directed to different consciousnesses. This is not contradiction but simply the best way. Thus, accustom yourselves to deal carefully with consciousnesses, as with fire.

503. It can be observed that children not only use the words they have heard but introduce words of their own. These will provide clues as to the nature of the inheritance from previous incarnations. One can easily observe the true inherited character and gather evidence of some valuable peculiarities. Even from among the very first expressions of an infant it is possible to form an idea of its inner consciousness. It has not by accident turned its attention to this or that object. Also very significant are the unexpected words uttered in its very infancy. We have already spoken about practically the same thing, but now We are mentioning it from the standpoint of fiery energy. It can be observed that in childhood there is much electricity in the body, relatively the same quantity as in adults, which means that the elements of the fiery body have been fully implanted. The seed of the spirit has been already embedded.

Mothers, remember that children observe and are conscious of more things than you surmise. And many manifestations escape notice: for example, a frequent glowing of the child's body, as well as gestures and occurrences of anger or repose. Erroneously people think that the child's aura is inexpressive. One may see in it not a little of the burden it has brought back.

504. Taking certain remedies is tantamount to poisoning. It is necessary to reexamine the field of medical compounds. Side by side with these poisons there are such medicines as precious balsam, and others of which you know, which have been forgotten. One must not reject life-giving substances, no matter how the adversaries rise against them.

505. The silver thread is a radiant symbol of the link and of trust. It is possible to bring the concept of the bond into such a state of clarity that the thread will be almost perceptible. The appearance of the Image of the Guide will no more forsake one than will the thread of the bond. But the will is free; it can snap the strings of any harp whatsoever. I already have told you how lamentably sound the strings which are forever broken. Verily, even in the raging of the most frightful obsession are heard the wailings of the broken strings. Amid chaos, most shocking indeed are the moanings from such ruined threads. Diseases are born of such criminal actions. Traitors break the most sacred threads. That is why betrayal is the worst offense against the Fiery World. What, then, can be more shameful?

506. People lose sight of the fact that rays fill space. Can one sever a ray? Can one cleave the lightning? The eye of man can sometimes pierce a stone wall, so strong is even the ray which is subject to man. But is it possible to apprehend the power of spatial rays? Therefore it is needful for people to understand responsibility for their actions.

507. A certain king sent his army into battle and awaited on a hill the outcome. There he saw horsemen hastening away and exclaimed, "Victory, the enemy is fleeing!" But those near him said, "Alas, that is our own beaten army." The king smiled, "My warriors carry spears, but these horsemen have neither spears nor banners." But his advisers whispered. "They have already thrown away their weapons." Thus the defeated king for a long time imagined himself victor. Likewise it may happen that the victor erroneously thinks himself beaten for a considerable length of time. The dates of sowing and of harvest are not the same. But the fiery heart may have a premonition for which there is no supporting evidence. The Fiery World is reality.

508. Why call fiery energy psychic? Only for better assimilation by the majority of people. They can still reconcile themselves to the manifestation of psychic energy, but the concept of Fire is completely inadmissible to them. Do not frighten those who are already afraid. Let them enter through their own doors. A layer of names does not disturb the essential nature of realization. People fear that which from childhood they have been told is dangerous. But it is not possible for the great energy to have only one appellation.

509. Whoever cannot pass around an observed object on all sides is no investigator.

510. Only an invincible attraction enables one to cognize the inexhaustible Teaching.

511. To the dark ones all appears finite—therein lies their darkness.

512. Do you not think that audible discharges, as drops of dew, are also from fiery energy? When you become accustomed to perceive everywhere the presence of fiery energy, then everything in life will be transformed.

513. There is consolation in Infinity and in realization of the constant presence of the Higher Force.

514. It is possible to augment fieriness by direct or indirect means. Indirect means include the rhythm of movements, of singing of lamentations, but simpler and more natural is the bonfire of the heart. All indirect means can be reflected on the organism. Even massage can help one limb and disturb the equilibrium of others. The same imbalance is observed in the tightening of the skin to destroy wrinkles. This is but temporary, as they will thus the more quickly become apparent. Obviously, equilibrium must be upheld by natural paths. Not a squeezing out by the muscles, but fieriness, nurtured by the heart, is useful. Equilibrium between heart and muscles is the problem of the future race.

515. Little does man think about his inheritance, about reconstruction. His mind is swayed between two extremes, and the path of prudence is abandoned. The process of employing fiery energy is being presented by the fakirs, and evokes only an empty curiosity.

516. One may add a most useful exercise—to preserve silence and direct one's thoughts to the Most High. A wonderful warmth suffuses one. Indeed, not the fire of combustion is needed but the higher, creative Warmth. The wise gardener does not set fire to a beloved blossom.

517. Does not a fiery gaze compel people to turn around and even to tremble? Any tremor is already near to Fire. But there can be Fire of a hot body and of a cold one. During high temperature the extremities can become numb; this condition accompanies the great Warmth of the heart.

518. A state of silence is sometimes filled with discharges and lights, but there can be a deep silence when nothing stirs—which is the greater?

519. Among the interpretations of the pyramids pay attention to that one which delineates the three Worlds. The top represents the Fiery World, where all is one; the middle part represents the Subtle World, where the essences are already separated; and the base is the dense World. This division is the most profound, and the gradations between the Worlds are symbolically portrayed by the pyramid. Such a symbol is truly significative. The dense World so widely separates the natures that it is even difficult to perceive how they can be fused into one on the Fiery summit. Yet the pyramid was built for the summit. Its foundation was laid only to bring all sides harmoniously together and to completion. Let each one ponder on how many times the point of the summit will be contained in the foundation. The fiery point must rule the unbridled, rudimentary stones upon the earth's surface. A great deal of just care must be applied in order to safeguard the Fiery completion. One must think about the summit. One should not be concerned that already in the Subtle World the essences are clearly separated. The edge of the pyramid may be divided into four parts, also into five, seven, eight, or any other number, but the three Worlds will remain the foundation of the basic division. One may imagine over the visible pyramid the identical invisible one, in an infinitely expanded concept. But this is beyond earthly language.

520. Often people complain about the monotony of their external life. But any external life whatever depends upon the riches of the inner life. The external life is but a hundredth part of the inner. Therefore the inner life is the true one.

521. When I say—guard the health, by that I am not sending you to a physician, and I urge you not to be alarmed. By no means would We develop a sickly hypochondria. We wish to preserve your health. No one can say that it is unnecessary to guard the health. The carriage must roll along the ordained path toward the beautiful goal. Take away everything pertaining to Karma and the goal will be really beautiful. But with which do people mold the larger Karma—the inner or the outer life?

522. The inner life influences Karma a hundred times more. Examine any crime whatever, and it appears small in view of the inner preparation. How protracted is such preparation! So many near-by consciousnesses have been poisoned by such creeping preparations, and so many better possibilities rejected—yet people do not think about this wrong. Again remote from the consciousness is the fiery energy, which alone can put an end to this crawling corruption. So easy is it to arrest decomposition by timely cauterization.

523. The dispute about allopathy and homeopathy must also lead to synthesis. The wise physician knows where it is advantageous to apply one or the other principle. Even sweetened water may be applied with benefit. Let us not forget that spatial rays are highly allopathic and it is impossible to avoid the doses administered by Nature. The laboratory of the human organism is likewise highly allopathic. However, in such disputes let us be conciliatory.

524. Try asking someone how he senses within him the action of fiery energy. Perhaps first of all he will mention a burning sensation in the esophagus. Thus, little attention is paid to the significant manifestation of the organism, as first of all people turn their attention to the consequences of their own excesses. How to explain to them where lies the line of good sense? People are afraid of good sense because it may prove them guilty.

525. The Teacher has been asked what is concealed behind the Fiery Veil. When He pronounced the word Aum—no one perceived its full significance of Highest Power. People have asked whether this Superfiery Force can be manifested also among earthly creations. It has been stated that it can. People were again confused, for if this Power lies outside of the elements it would seem impossible for one to embrace it. The Teacher has said that there are no earthly words for

expressing the Highest Radiances, but sometimes their signs can be observed. Let us learn attentiveness.

526. The Teacher will show how the disciples can avoid dangers when the link is strong. The link must be understood in all its vitality, not only on holidays but amid all labors. Indeed, such constancy is inaccessible to many. The Sacred Fire must always be alight.

527. Everyone has met people who emphatically denied the existence of the Subtle World. Their argument was that they had never seen it. But, likewise, many people have not seen the inhabitants of some remote parts of the planet yet none the less a remarkable life has been flowing there. Therefore it is foolish to ridicule the investigators. Though they may not have made mathematical calculations, still their heart knows the right direction. At the call of the heart do the Fires of enlightenment flare up.

528. In the Subtle World only at times do the Lights of the Fiery World glow. The inhabitants of the Subtle World revere such manifestations as salutary sacred shortenings of the path. Thus, even the Subtle World understands the higher step as a very rare manifestation. But on the Earth contacts with the Subtle World are not so rare; and even the radiances of the Fiery World occur there. Why, then, are the incarnate dwellers so filled with negation?

529. Clouds rush along, but the ship reaches the harbor. Yet the sailor must not think about the watery depths under the hull of his ship. Likewise, there are abysses around, and one should not be frightened by them.

530. It is right to assign to co-workers the collecting of parts from the Books of the Teaching pertaining to separate subjects. Thus two results will be achieved—they will read the books more attentively and they will ponder as to what is pertinent to each different subject. In time one could collate these excerpts for inexpensive separate publications. The Teaching of "Living Ethics" is needed in diverse strata of people. One could combine the simpler themes and pass them on to those requiring preliminary knowledge. With each passing day people are more in need of a greater aspiration toward the understanding of the spiritual life. The confusion of the World demands new paths.

531. For what reason then are people being tormented here? Why are sufferings not diminished? Why is hatred so strongly in possession of hearts? The shield of the spirit has been forgotten. There is nothing supernatural in a reminder about the Fiery World, where the coarse knags are being burned away. People consider bodily cleanliness necessary, but after ablution by water there is need of one by Fire. One may understand that water pertains to subtle ingress, but further along Fire is needed.

532. Though earthly fire may go out, the Fire of space is never extinguished. Is not the elemental conductor eternal? Not without reason are torches used even in the daylight processions.

533. More attention should be paid to longevity, to change of character, lack of electricity, new kinds of diseases, and other things noticed by a vigilant mind. The Teaching alludes to many changes, but also in life there can be seen the unusual. Though people may not admit the chemism of the Luminaries, it nevertheless exists and creates the various periods of life.

534. Note this remarkable fact: when a man begins to notice around himself a manifestation of spiritual life, he never fails to call himself an occultist. Whereas it is simpler to consider oneself able to see. Occultists are rather those who remain in darkness, in secrecy.

Hence, there should be given an essential cleansing to some concepts. Otherwise many may fall into the abyss of conceit and insanity. Affirm everywhere that the spiritual signs are a part of natural existence. But those ignorant of them deny them, for they are blind. Much have those who see had to endure; the blind cannot stand talk about the Light. Therefore do not enrage those who do not see. So much is taking place just now that only those completely blind are paying no attention to the fiery signs.

535. The ability of the child about whom you spoke is a direct proof of what was said earlier. When a child makes use of pure psychic energy, it knows that which is inaudible to others. But when the will of the reason acts, then the current of basic energy is broken off. It has been prescribed—be simple in spirit, which means to allow pure energy to act. Do not impede its current; grasp the fact that violence by the reason only impoverishes one. Thus, a scientist knows which book he should take from the shelf not through reason but with straight-knowledge. People are right when they act by this unassailable straight-knowledge.

536. Soda is taken for the abatement of diabetes. A vegetarian diet is beneficial, especially oranges. Musk is not for diabetes, but it is useful for equilibrium. It is possible to cure diabetes in the beginning by suggestion, if the action is strong enough. Indeed, milk with soda is always good. Coffee and tea, as well as everything which generates internal alcohol, are not useful. This disease is often hereditary through a generation; therefore it is impossible to foresee the illness.

Likewise, it is inadvisable to trust in all the kinds of musk from various animals. Only the musk deer has the proper diet.

537. The dark ones should not vouch for their vic-

tory. They should not boast of their seizure. Already the axe has been revealed and the tree will not withstand the hand of justice.

538. Some people think that it is possible to change Teachers without danger, but they forget the three year period, and the seven-year, through which the bond is woven. You have read already about the ignominious end of apostates. Thus does the Fiery World safeguard the right of justice.

539. Reflect upon the confusion which encompasses the spirit of traitors. That most frightful, gloomy sinking into darkness, that most perilous breaking of the fiery bond. It is as if for traitors the sun and the moon were the same, and in their madness they would overthrow the sun. Indeed, the madness of traitors should be studied by psychiatrists. One may observe the paroxysms which are followed by terror. From the one side they appear to be ordinary people, but from the other they no longer belong to the planet, and the spirit knows what such a path is like!

540. Betrayal presupposes trust on the opposite side. And the greater the betrayal the stronger was the trust. As hammer and anvil produce a strong spark, so does creative trust obtain from betrayal a fiery force. Very ancient is the history of the reciprocity of opposite principles. Along with events of beneficent significance there are also taking place monstrous betrayals.

541. A true mechanic is he who does not turn the wheels of the machine of some one else. Because of his love for the work, a natural mechanic tries to improve each apparatus with which he works. Devotion to the Fiery World must include the refined observation of all its manifestations. But it is possible to pass by the most significant manifestations without paying attention to them. Space is linked with each human organism, but do many pay any attention to such reactions? If a sensitive organism re-echoes distant earthquakes and eruptions, and trembles at atmospheric manifestations, the same thing occurs before great events. Already long ago was it said that the better people will become specially sensitive, while the rubbish of Kali Yuga will grow deaf and dumb before the great events.

542. Why are people amazed at many cases of children who remember their past? Precisely nowadays are being born many such evident intermediaries between this and the Subtle World. They also remember about their sojourn between the earthly lives, but people do not know how to question them about this. The important thing is not that they remember about buried gold, but that they can tell about precious sensations. Thus takes place a rapprochement of the two Worlds, and this circumstance precedes great events. But for a long time not many will apprehend to what an extent everything is changed around them. Remember the old tale, how the king was being taken to execution but he was so far removed from reality that on the way he was much concerned about a stone that fell out of his crown.

543. A foundation of great events lies in the alteration of spatial rays, in the drawing together of the Worlds, in the renewal of consciousness, which will produce a new attitude toward life. Already much is being revealed.

544. Is it not indicative that music over the radio does not charm snakes? There is a great number of such proofs in small examples. At the root of it all is the very same psychic energy. Everywhere these manifestations can be observed.

545. It is true that mostly sick and so-called abnormal people are the ones who manifest a link with the

Supermundane, and therein lies a great reproach to humanity. Indeed, the healthy people ought to sense the nearness of the Subtle World. But the distinction between the sick and the healthy has become confused. People have covered their reason with a crust which has given rise to prejudices. Behind this fence the Subtle World is not visible. So-called abnormal people are usually free from prejudices, and because of this they do not lose contact with the Subtle World. Indeed, so often during illnesses do people see through both past and future; some have viewed their past lives and recovered forgotten aptitudes. A new boundary must be laid between the state of torpor and true health. New discoveries are of no help. People must receive such shocks that they are rendered able, without any fever, to preserve the memory about the past and that which is ordained.

546. During extraordinary dangers clairvoyance flashes out, which means that it is possible for something to shake up the sediments of the consciousness. The same thing occurs during epilepsy, when in the words of the afflicted the heavens are opened to him. It also means that clairvoyance is possible amid earthly conditions. Indeed it is instantaneous, too quick to be marked off by earthly time. And also in this lightning timelessness there is apparent a quality of the Subtle World. Of course, dreams are also timeless, and yet they may contain a great number of events. By various examples we can recall that which formerly was quite known to everyone.

547. It is asked why so much evil is permitted. How conceited are such utterances! Who can judge how much darkness has been burned up and how much help extended? You, too, send many good thoughts, and help through them. It is possible to kindle many

Fires, not knowing where nor how. It is precisely as when letters addressed to a blind man eventually reach and help some one who can see. One should send arrows of fiery justice. The Fiery World is maintained by justice.

548. I hear the question—why so many words about betrayal? Precisely for the reason that there are so many betrayals. When a cobra creeps into the house there is much said about it. Before an earthquake serpents crawl forth. Just now there are many such snakes.

549. Experienced telegraphers can, without employing the voice, talk to each other by scarcely noticeable touches. So too in the Subtle World, the voice is not needed and is replaced by swift thought, but sound does not leave the World. What could be more beautiful than the music of the spheres? And people forbid conversation during music. They are right—the sound is so subtle that the noises of speech can produce the most irritating dissonances. The Subtle World in its higher spheres sounds indeed beautifully. When it is so burdensome on the Earth, thought can lift itself up to the Supermundane Spheres.

550. One can observe that there are appearing whole groups of people formerly connected with each other. One can likewise perceive that during a certain incarnation a common interest toward the past creations of a person begins. One can notice, as it were, a spiral of manifestation and concealment of creativeness. One should observe such paths, for such attention brings closer the understanding of the Subtle World. So, too, do appearances of groups merit study; as indeed not only friends but also enemies may come together. Here you notice a friend who retains his disposition of long ago. Likewise you see ill-wishers, who, while they do not harm you personally, hinder those

243

near to you. The entire complex interweaving clearly indicates the strong bonds which take many lives to live through.

551. Some will not understand about the necessity of indicating the Subtle World and then later forewarning against it. Yet there is no contradiction. The higher spheres of the Subtle World deserve attention and respect, but the lower ones can be harmful. The pure in heart are not subject to the infection of obsession, but tainted hearts can attract frightful entities. Also, there should be no discordance in understanding of the Subtle World when the Fiery is mentioned. The very summits of the Subtle World are almost touching the Fiery World. Similarly, under certain circumstances the dense World is close to the Subtle. Thus, let us once and for all apprehend the bond of the Worlds as steps of Infinity.

552. Observe that at present people are talking about the beyond more than ever before. A deeper understanding is showing itself. Do not judge severely the peculiarity of many manifestations. People are ashamed to appear to be thinking of something besides the bazaar. But spatial currents are acting invisibly. Actually there is taking place a continuous, directed, lucid preoccupation with that which was not thought about formerly. Side by side with madness, touching searches go on. You may guess what country I have in mind. Wonderful sprouts may be expected.

553. Many times have the words been spoken about the necessity for expelling any fear—it is paralyzing. But especially should one free oneself from fear before the Subtle and the Fiery Worlds. For fear before the Supermundane Spheres is the most harmful. One must transform it into joy. Only a few will apprehend this joy. Even though they agree verbally,

nevertheless an inner tremor will chill the warmth of rapture. Precisely warmth and light are needed for an easy entrance into the fine garden. Above this fine garden will shine the Fiery Heavens in all their glory. Equally fearlessly should one meet new neighbors. In fact, luminous courage saves one from disagreeable entities. On the earthly plane people try to hide their fear, but out there it cannot be concealed.

554. Despair is called darkness. Such a definition is precise; indeed, it extinguishes radiation and the Fire of the heart grows dim. Such a state is not only harmful, it is unworthy of man; he becomes lower than an animal. It is possible to brave the condition of despair. The most frightful entities employ it. Behind it stalks terror itself. Where then will be the garden of beauty?

555. One should study psychic forces in different situations. Sometimes a complete repose is useful, but often tension is needed in order to attain a manifestation. Not without reason were different genuflections indicated in monasteries. Likewise, from deep antiquity has the value of silence been known. It must be broadly understood how the dense World serves the Subtle.

556. If, reading writings about the Fiery World, one remembers even the two words—Fiery World—that in itself is good. There could also be a dangerous trend of thought in which one would say—if the Fiery World exists... In this "if" is already contained a great mistrust. No good words could cover such deadly doubt. It means that such a traveller must pass through a great deal before he views the Fiery Heavens. There are many such remarks about the Fiery World; even from people who consider themselves initiated or enlightened. It is of no value to shake the fingers or to whirl in the round-dance, when the heart is silent in coldness.

Such a small number wish to prepare themselves for the distant journey.

557. You know that one should speak simply, but people expect the very simplest. One may receive questions such as one is even ashamed to answer. But every mother knows of these questions from her children. The mother conquers her irritation and finds a kind word for the child.

558. Knowing how to bring one's consciousness down to another's level is already compassion. Washing a wound is also not always pleasant. But it is still more insufferable to see treachery, yet even such an abomination can be contended with. Victory is so needed for the path. Victory in the spirit is already advancement.

559. Does one become cognizant of the Teaching only in order to tremble at every shadow? It is sometimes helpful to ask oneself how much of the Teaching has been so far applied in life. It is useful to suggest this thought to friends. Let them reflect and write down. Worn out thinking is cleansed by such writings, it is like taking an oath before oneself.

560. The Teacher who has not overcome intolerance cannot mold the future. The Teaching is given for the future. The spirit cannot advance without forging perfectionment. Thus, it is possible to command the attention of listeners, but it is far more necessary to arouse a movement forward. The Teacher does not forbid reading different books. Everyone who fears puts limitations on himself, but the leader summons to a broad cognition. He will not restrain one from good in all of its aspects. This liberality of spirit is indispensable. He who does not even wish to listen is already afraid of something. Thus, the fiery condition requires broad gates and the speediest of wings.

561. A sensitive dog follows from afar the traces of his master. So too in man exists this fiery sensitiveness, but he tries to suppress it with reasoning. Whereas not a few people will acknowledge that they sometimes sense inexplicable odors. Perhaps it is that the Subtle World sends aromas but they are rarely noticed. People are more quickly conscious of an animal scent than of supermundane aromas.

562. Accounts of wereleopards are correct. The Teaching has already given attention to the indisputable fact of the bond between man and animals. One may see that the fate of such animals is reflected on certain people. Instead of listening to tales about witches one should investigate reports of such wereanimals, of which there are not a few. Verily, the World is full of marvels! Today a man is burned and lives, tomorrow he is buried and lives; then comes a little girl who relates about her former incarnation—thus is life broadened.

563. Reverence is affirmed by indignation of the spirit—this most ancient means is common to all peoples.

564. Is it possible for a most worthy inhabitant of the Subtle World to rise thence into the Fiery World? It is, and his transformation will be beautiful. Through the process of purification, the subtle body begins to shine. Fire begins to spread, and finally the shell falls away like a light layer of ash. Since the fiery essence cannot remain in its former stratum it ascends into the Fiery World. That which was in the Subtle World an insufferable effulgence becomes in the Fiery World the dimmest—such is the ladder. One must become accustomed to imagining many strata of the Subtle World. From deep red flame to the most beautiful radiance of the rainbow, like an agitated sea, these facets are effused and weave all possible combinations. But for the darkness, for the lower abysses, this radiance will look like a distant heat-lightning. Let him who longs for Light not fear to be fiery. A burning on Earth is a symbol of superb transformation.

565. The reality of the force of thought is beyond dispute. Thought creates. But in each book it is needful to review the fact that not every thought is effective. A vivid thought is equal in force to lightning. But each duplicity is destructive and will not produce the desired result. On the contrary, each duplicity produces deformities and most besetting monsters, which remains as horrible nightmares. By various thoughts there are created inhabitants of space which are like troublesome insects! Often people whisk away from the forehead an invisible fly. Often they sense a cobweb. Should one not then be reminded about the consequences of thought?

566. Often disputes take place about the length of stay in the Subtle World. Long periods have been mentioned, but also there can be noted some very brief ones. How to reconcile this difference? Yet in the great multiform Universe all is possible. The inhabitants of the Subtle World can be divided into several kinds: some try to prolong their sojourn from a desire to develop the utmost usefulness—they are the hardest workers. Others try to remain longer in order not to take on the earthly trial. A third group stay on because of their love for the Subtle World. A fourth exert every effort to return more quickly to the earthly experience. It is true, children often incarnate quickly, but they can be observed to be striving toward many different tasks. It is touching to see children who wish to do better and who are afraid of former conditions; they should be particularly helped. Of course such strivings do not resemble those of a pauper who, because of the loss of his earthly treasures in a former life, wishes to become a rich man. But the chief happiness in the Subtle World is to preserve the purity and clarity of one's thinking. One must know precisely what one desires.

567. It is of no help for people not to think about the future. Each day it is possible to meditate beautifully about a better life beyond the limits of Earth. The more beautiful the imagination, the better are the possibilities engendered there where thought rules.

568. You have seen a toy in which there were many spheres, one fitting into another. The Chinese thus wished to call to mind the sacred Worlds. It is difficult for man to understand the supermundane, inexpressible dimensions. But whoever has seen the color of the Subtle World and heard its resounding, understands that for such a World the best definition is—The Subtlest.

569. Santana, the current of life, transforms and predetermines a great deal, yet there remains a place for free-will. The Rays of the Luminaries determine much, but the bond with the Higher World is strong, and in this respect it will have the greater significance. It may be understood that the Teaching about Guides has a great importance in all faiths. People must realize that to them is given the possibility of passing through the melee and through all straits with the help of the Higher Guides, but that they must not reject the helping Hand. One must come to love the Guide with all one's heart. Not by earthly means does the Guide bring help—therefore one must be sensitively conscious of this fiery thread. Throughout one's entire life can be seen the wonderful protection, if one's eyes are opened. Thus Santana itself is no stronger than the manifestation of the Higher Worlds.

570. What is more dangerous than the boomerang? When it touches the Teacher himself, the weapon then returns with frightful effect. Therefore the concept of the Guru is so strongly guarded. When the manifestation of the Guru is threatened, the evil weapon returns with deadly force. This is not punishment but merely one's being one's own judge. Therefore let us be very careful with the higher concepts, in them we touch Fire.

571. The black lodge has the sole aim of harming Our works and disrupting the planet. People are usually enticed into the black lodge by promises of long life, for great is the fear of death, and also by promises of riches and of great power. Especially nowadays is being developed a desire for long life. People do not think about the life of the Supermundane Spheres as they are greatly attached to the Earth. Among the dark suggestions passion and greed will be apparent; out of them is born the very lowest treachery.

572. Not from poison did the scientist die, but from conjuration. Thoughts attached to a definite object live for a long time. One can learn how in antiquity thoughts were stratified on an object by particular conjurations continued over a long period of time. The object did not leave the hands of the conjurer, who himself placed it in a secret place. Very remarkable is the experiment of conjuration for lengthy periods.

573. The Teaching of Good must be the friend of Good in all its manifestations. This truth appears simple, yet evil intention continually tries to distort it. The Teacher of Good must be grieved, seeing how the workers of Good become twisted and how they exclude each other. Such a mutilation of Good takes place when someone bears a burden of Good which is too much for him and someone else attempts to carry a double load. And if someone will dare to think about a triple load, he will not find many helpers. Millions of years have not been enough for humanity to learn to rejoice at Good, to grow to love it as something of the utmost utility. The Teaching must stimulate in all the bearers of Good a feeling of broad sympathy. Otherwise it will not be the Teaching of Good but a teaching of egoism.

574. The Fiery Battle—such an expression may be found in many beliefs. Such expression is correct— love, courage, self-renunciation, devotion, all the best qualities are linked with Fire. On the other hand igno- rance, anger, irritation, malice, malevolence, and envy also evoke Fire; albeit scarlet and dark, yet neverthe- less Fire. Thus the battle of Good and evil will be a conflict of Fires. During such a clash one can see how very different are the Fires engendered by higher feel- ings and lower passions. Let this division into feelings and passions be accepted. Many can in no wise imag- ine the distinction, but the color of the Fire will easily indicate the engenderment.

575. It is needful to speak about the dark lodges because there are so very many of them. Often peo- ple who are themselves good do not even admit the thought that such an abomination can exist. But one can see the most monstrous transgressions. One can see how the dark ones invade different strata of peo- ple in the guise of the most respectable servitors of the general welfare.

576. Pure hearts will perceive the Highest. Only it must be remembered that the purity of accepted concepts depends upon free will. People begin a pure life, as in the home, and also in the heart, according to their own decision. Thus the Guide cannot compel purifying the heart, if there is no desire for it. The best cleansing is through Fire.

577. People often do not know for a long time what goes on in the house of a neighbor. Still longer remains unknown what is happening in another country. Therefore it is not astonishing that that which takes place on another plane is unknown. Thus secret are causes and effects. The material World perceives only a transitory Maya. The more is it sensible to pin hopes upon the future. Our Decree is concerned with real results.

578. A certain warrior came under the protection of a revered hermit. After a victory he came to the hermit and expressed his gratitude for two marvelous rescues. But the hermit said: "Ungrateful warrior, you were saved not two but twelve times. You did not recognize the most important rescues." Usually people notice the lesser rather than the greater.

579. The Living Ethics is a bridge to all Worlds. Only in its living application is created an invulnerable crossing. Nothing can pierce the fiery armor. One does not have to be disturbed by the weeds of metaphysics when the spirit knows the path of living thought. Only the measure of good manifests the Fire of Light. With such a lamp it is possible to enter firmly upon the great bridge. Only for the distant journey is the Living Ethics given. One must love it as an aid in the journey.

580. You know that the concussion from a shell or other explosion may be worse than a visible wound, because from concussion a man may lose his balance forever. The same thing results from shock by invisible forces. Each physician can observe identical symptoms resulting from concussion and from invisible shocks. They even speak about the noise of thought or about gusts of warm or cold wind. It is correct that thought can make noise or create a wind. And such an action

will be a fiery one, but rarely do people notice such manifestations.

581. Often people talk about contradictions, putting in this category many cases not understood by them. On a hot day people may see a traveler dressed in warm clothing and laugh at the inconsistency. But they do not think about the cold night. Contradictions are usually due to meager thinking. A great number of misfortunes have resulted from unwillingness to think. Not contradictions, but the empty utterance of thoughtless words clutters life.

582. Vairaga is the very sacred flame of renunciation of corporeal things. Forbearance is more difficult in thought than in action. In action even the muscles can assist abstinence, but the thought centers are so subtle that the man who has not attained the art of thinking will not know how to follow the reflexes of these centers. It is said that the Subtle World is far from the material, yet each thought process is already a process of the Subtle World. According to the subtlety of thinking is it possible to imagine the film of the Subtle World. The subtle body is also ponderable, but in the most minute measurements. But the fiery body is already beyond measurement. Scientists can assist in revealing the Subtle World. In all domains is it possible to observe that thought multiplies the other energies; thus new cooperations take place.

583. Who, then, will presume to say that emptiness does exist? Yet so often is this word repeated in ignorance that people become accustomed to it from childhood. It is difficult to extricate meaningless words from the language, yet such a cleansing is imperative; otherwise consciousness will become obstructed with rubbish.

584. Knowing how to purge the consciousness of

unneeded concepts means already to get set for the distant journey. Only in such a liberated state is it possible to think about a new consciousness. Joy is born when Vairaga is shining.

585. It has been said—"Ignorance is Hell." Few understand this. Whereas, precisely devouring Fire is the result of ignorance. But one may exchange evil for good and thus alter the properties of the Fire. A wonderful gift is possessed by man in that he can alter the properties of the element. Yet how can humanity enter upon such action if it fails to think altogether about the elements? The Teaching of Living Ethics must set the direction in which the mind of man is to be propelled. Let us not violate free will, let each one make haste in his own rhythm, let each one sense the great vibrations in his own way, but let him sense it and make haste.

586. Never does an evil heart draw near the Fiery World. Like a black stove-lid stands a charred heart. Only malice burns up the life devoted to the ruin of others. Therefore, so much more needed is the sword of Light which, without malice, sheathed in justice, stands on guard.

587. It is always good to talk about the heart. It is timely to speak of that which is urgently needed. Precisely there where is heart is also Fire. The wayfarer does not sally forth without his flint, for he does not forget that he stands in need of it at night. Thus, without heart the night of the spirit approaches. Not so frightening are the impediments, but a stony heartlessness is terrible. No man is without heart, nor animal, nor plant, nor even stone. This means that heartlessness is no longer in the manifested World but in chaos.

588. Worry is a chasm of misery. He who gives himself up to worry is like a man in a burning house. Waves of flame almost consume him. He is full of

a desire only to escape from the house. Scraps of thought are tossing about and fill him with irritation. In this chaos fear is born, and the will becomes paralyzed. Hence, one must avoid worry. Yet calmness is not absence of feeling nor inaction.

589. Very dangerous are all adaptations for artificial super-sensation. Humanity resembles a superficial braggart. Only natural achievements are of value. Besides, any artificial adaptations in filthy hands can only lead to monstrous actions. Accompanying filthy thinking, all images will be filthy. The principle element in everything is quality.

590. A nonsensical act often sprouts deep roots. From a small visibility is born a great invisibility. People do not think about beauty and consequently surround themselves with ugliness. First of all—thinking.

591. You already know how necessary it is to reiterate, but repetition itself is in need of art. It is almost, but not quite, the same as the rug on the stairs. To be wearied by the mere fact of repetition itself is impossible, as witness a pavement of identical stones. And those to whom endless repetition is offered may proceed as calmly as they walk along the pavement where each stone has been laid with care.

592. Too often are words used in an incorrect meaning. People speak about the supernatural instead of saying the unusual. The supernatural does not exist in any of the Worlds. Perhaps a certain thing is unusual for the ignorant, but even this definition is conditional, as that something is unusual only under certain conditions. Thus it would be possible to revise dictionaries considerably. We have often spoken about this, and in translations into other languages you see how needful are various shades of meaning. People do not like to search for better definitions, yet diverse old dialects demonstrate that it is not easy to rejuvenate a dictionary with befitting expressions. It is especially difficult in the case of concepts of earthly and heavenly Fire. There are so many visible and invisible Fires that far more subtle definitions are needed.

593. Around the place of manufacture of high explosives people do not smoke, they wear special soft footwear, they avoid any metallic objects, they do not even speak loudly, and they do not breathe in the ordinary manner. There, where danger threatens their flesh, people are ready to renounce habits, but it never enters their heads that thought can result in a far more dangerous explosion, invisible yet irreparable. Terror helps people to guard themselves against bodily dangers. But the entire spatial life does not exist for them. They can blaspheme at the Great Forces and rejoice at the misfortunes of others, if their own ruin is not immediately visible to them. The loss of spatial co-measurement in Infinity consumes all the better possibilities. Whereas, the present time is precisely the last chance to join the dense with the subtle and even with the fiery. One should begin to think persistently and clearly in the direction of the merging of Worlds.

594. Even the rays have been discovered which make objects invisible. Is it possible that such a discovery does not call to mind the invisible Subtle World? The smallest discovery could be protracted into Infinity. One can see how such a discovery can alter all earthly life. All state foundations could be unsettled by such discovery. The kingdom of machines can be broken up by one ray. Thus, the most ingenious mechanisms can be stopped by an invisible ray. Some may be fearful of such possibilities but others cover them with powerful straight-knowledge. Fire of the heart is stronger than such rays.

595. Soda is useful, and its usefulness is linked with Fire. Soda fields themselves have been called the ashes of a great Conflagration. Thus already in antiquity people knew the significance of soda. The surface of the Earth is covered with soda, for broad usage. Likewise oil of Artemisia (wormwood), is a powerful strengthener of the nervous system. It does not destroy, but fierily cleanses of injurious deposits.

596. Not in temples only was valerian added to the wine, but many Greek wines knew this admixture. Thus, musk and valerian and soda can be combined.

597. It can be observed everywhere how people dismember one concept in their own many ways. Psychic energy is subtle, fiery, divine, Aum. Thus variously is the same principle called, and with each variation it is assumed that a better definition is introduced. Doubling our attention, we see that such dismemberments are not useful. It is again time to begin to synthesize. One should strongly affirm the meaning of earthly existence. It is needful to simplify it. Above all cares one should remember that the path is long, and that it will be necessary to be supplied with patience and with the thought about everything useful on the path. But this necessity should be found full of joy for oneself. Without this quality the heart will still be confused and thus weakness brought in. Likewise, one should realize that courage is inseparable from joy. Even the most difficult achievement cannot be low-spirited. A slave can toil in depression, but the fiery spirit transforms everything by very luminous joy. And warmth flows out from joy. But call to mind that joy, warmth, and fire live in the heart. Be not averse to reminding about such dwellers of the heart. After all, people do remember about the heart, and each one loves warmth, calling it cordiality. Therefore, know how to speak to everyone about the most joyous, in the simplest words and in the expressions most fitting for all. Thus knock at the fiery door of the human soul.

598. It is instructive to observe how the dark ones, in springing upon everything, merely trying to cause harm, only expose in their fury their own weaknesses. Evil makes a poor adviser.

599. You remember the remarkable case of the small boy who, while blind-folded, performed amazing things. But the solution is simple—he was blind from birth. People did not appreciate his aptitude when his blindness was revealed to them. As if, in view of his condition, he really had no capacities. It can often be seen how people pay attention to the most non-essential circumstances, ignoring the principal one. Certain aptitudes of the blind are wonderful and worthy of observation. Such a state is sometimes called the fiery sight.

600. A hermit wished to progress further in his training in the matter of silence, and, not trusting himself, he patiently and firmly bound his mouth. One day he saw a child on the edge of a cliff, but he didn't succeed in removing his complicated bandage quickly enough to warn of the danger. By the time he unbound his mouth the child had been already carried away by the current. Not in invented bonds lies achievement! Only then do we attain when we cannot but do. He who does not because he cannot, attains nothing. Thus it is in bodily and in spiritual existence. In addition to not doing shameful things, one must also account to oneself why such doings are inadmissible. Thought must be at work. In such creativeness the force of thought is needed. Evolution without thought is impossible. If in the near-by Subtle and in the Fiery World all is moved by thought, then it is not difficult to recognize the continuity of thought. In Infinity, spiral rings, whole cycles of thought, are engaged in manifestation. The most insignificant earthly object represents a transformation of thought. Cannot the very same thing take place in space on a large scale? Thought is Fire. Thought is the engendering of the creative vortex and explosion. Thought is Light and radiance. Thus must Fiery Thought be respected.

601. Artificial calculations, not illumined by the fire of the heart, bring misfortunes and confusion to the world. People lose the meaning of life. Not only for themselves but for all generations to come they leave a heritage of smoke and poisonous fumes. Thus is it needful to turn to thought as the creative path. Each one possesses sufficiency in thoughts, if only he were reminded from childhood about the treasure, manifested and ordained.

602. Each day passed in unity is already an offering of treasure. It is not difficult to cooperate, it is not difficult not to disturb space. Thus, it is each day possible to fill the sacred storehouse.

603. Thought is sometimes compared with the ocean—the comparison is plausible. Each man has three basic currents of thought. A superficial one—from the flesh, connected with muscular reflections, obvious in the external life. The second already concerns the heart, and contributes to improvement and progress in the subtle feelings. And finally, in the depths of the consciousness is being conceived the achievement of self-renunciation—here the Fiery World will be near. Each man can touch all Worlds; even in the routine of his everyday life he can choose the type of thinking he desires. In order to harken to the voice of the heart it is not necessary to be poor or rich, lofty or lowly; it is not even necessary to be very learned. Verily, thought is an ocean with all its currents.

604. People are inquisitive as to why fiery manifestations are so rare. Let us reply that it is because the heart of the dense world cannot endure such fiery vortexes. Ask those very rare individuals who have had such manifestations. They will tell you that they were almost dead after the fiery Visitations. Through the training of right thinking one can accustom oneself to the possibility of such Communion. But it is a long way from the flesh to fiery vision. Only most uncommon hearts can undergo them.

605. Rock crystals are formed from one fire, yet all are different. One should ponder over such fiery formations. To have them about will be a good reminder of that world of Light whither each one is permitted to aspire.

606. Earthly fire more quickly swallows up a tree which is cracked than a whole sturdy trunk, and the same holds true in all approaches of the Fiery World. When I forewarn about the harm of any fissures, I already foresee how important it is to restrain humanity from any folly. The crevices themselves, as it were, attract and draw in the lower flame. One must avoid all infections, and heartache will diminish. All-embracing thought will be the curative principle. Ask a physician how much longer will run the course of sickness of a man who wishes to be ill. Thus does personal desire indicate the power of thought.

607. The Fiery World is both difficult and easy to imagine. There is no break between the Worlds. The Subtle World bears the same relation to the Fiery as does the dense to the Subtle. Besides visible manifestations there can be invisible approaches. Likewise in the earthly World, sometimes only the pulsing of the heart denotes the presence of a subtle being. The eye very rarely notices, as it were, certain flashes, usually attributing them to chance. Likewise in the case of the rarest spiritual people, it is possible to see a sort of diadem of light above their heads. Such a manifestation is very rare and denotes the crystal of spirituality. The aura itself seems to roll up into a ring. Hence the ancient idea of the crown, as a sign of distinction, had a deep significance. One should not be astonished that lofty manifestations can become apparent in the most difficult hours. The Laws of the Fiery World are inexpressible.

608. The centers produce ring-shaped radiations. They can begin to shine all at once when the spirit is helping at far distances. Great are such tensions. Not the muscles, not the nerves become tense—the strings of the heart resound. Such a sounding can even be heard. But such tension is frightful for a man who is not accustomed to think about the Higher Worlds. Experienced thinking will apprehend calmly even such manifestation of the crown, and will observe it as something very unusual but valuable. Not often will such tension occur.

609. Astrology is a great science, but it can be ruled by the forces of thought. Thought can indeed have a significance in astrology. Thought creates; thought is a chemist; thought even has an influence on Karma. With such powerful laws does thought contend.

610. Especial attention is paid to dwarfs. As a special race they appear everywhere. One may observe in them not only bodily peculiarities but also a special psychology. No one discerns the cause of appearance of such small creatures; the more so since side by side with them, in the same conditions and families, appear people of lofty stature. But it has already been observed that there do occur unexpected materializations of very tiny beings. Even a clumsily embellished story from the life of Paracelsus recalls how he tried to preserve such small creatures. Of course the experiment was unsuccessful. But even now imprints of very tiny extremities are known. They must be looked upon purely scientifically. The solution will lie in a property of the ectoplasm—hence come both giants and dwarfs. But giants have already been forgotten. Few of them are of interest to anyone and few exceed two meters; and the materialization of giants is rare. But the tiny creatures reveal definitely their similarity and singularity. The dwarfs of southern India and Africa, and the Eskimo pigmies will be very reminiscent of their European brethren. When ectoplasm shall be diligently studied, then its specific properties will be discovered. And in relationship to the Fiery World such study will be a great attainment.

611. A manifestation of eyes can be a distinctive sign of the Fiery World. Thus, not without reason may it be asked why of all the human organism stands out the image of the eyes? It is very simple, for the centers of the eyes are a conduit of fiery energy. The very structure of the eyes appears to be the subtlest among the structures of the dense World. Thus it preserves also the singularities of the Higher World. When a single eye is seen, it will not be merely a symbol but a concrete manifestation which has been seen by others.

612. And in the constitution of races, ectoplasm has its significance. It is linked with the rays of far-off Worlds. Indeed, it can be of lofty or low quality. Likewise it depends upon the burning of the heart. One can observe in the case of lymphatic people a low quality of ectoplasm, and this makes possible the strange dwarf-like formations. Mediums are frequently lymphatic.

613. The same lymphatic quality can be of assistance to black magic. One must guard against it in every possible way. Do not think that there is only a little of black magic. It makes its nests with the people and also in governing circles. Let science look very deeply into such corrupting endeavors.

614. The curative force of suggestion is very great, yet it can be still more reinforced. To the inner fire can be added the vibrations of Spatial Fire. Under such Fire is understood magnetic force and electricity. Various kinds of paralysis can be cured under such threefold influence. Naturally the magnet above the head of the patient must be of considerable strength. Electrization must be twofold, that is, both bodily and aerial. One may be convinced that through the suggestion of such power even a chronic case of paralysis can be improved. It is urgently needed to study hypnosis. It must be understood that brief suggestions bring small benefit, as prolonged suggestion is required; for the time being the hypnotist should even live near the patient, in order to harmonize the auras. Among other things, this condition of harmonization is altogether not being observed. A strange man may be brought in, surrounded perhaps by harmful tendencies, and the wonder-working force is given a half-hour to show its effect. Any sensible man should understand that from such a casual treatment nothing but harm can come. The fiery force requires a thoughtful consideration toward itself.

615. Even dullness from nervous causes can be cured by the same triple action. Only in such case the suggestion must be very soothing, whereas in the case of paralysis it must be imperative. Many cases of mild insanity can be cured and a healthy condition restored. So many unfortunate ones languish in confinement!

616. Mild insanity is, as it were, a local paralysis. One must establish a friendly contact with brain and heart. Rarely does such heart contact take place. People either fear or scorn the patient. Yet the illness might have resulted not from any fault of the patient himself; a hostile arrow might have stunned him. There are many such cases, where the man himself is not at fault but a malignant arrow has pierced him. It is possible to cure many cases of this kind of madness, arising, as it were, from concussion.

617. It is better when there is plenty of spatial electricity in the air; otherwise the subterranean fire becomes too unbalanced. There is much malice in space, therefore I so urge to guard the health.

618. A therapeutic-psychic treatment must be applied not only after much consideration but resolutely to the very end. Half-way measures, as in everything, are dangerous. It is possible to open up the centers, but to impose upon them any influence so that, instead of a cure, irritation and new infection set in, is impermissible. The employment of increased suggestion requires also the consent of the patient himself. Every counteraction is dangerous for it could in the end overstrain his forces. It can also be seen that the unconscious condition is also undesirable, as the patient's strong desire and cooperation through will is required. Not only during medical treatments, but in all the manifestations of life, the same conditions are needed. Without them how can one think about the Fiery World? The Subtle World can be reached even in semi-conscious state, but the Fiery World can be approached only in clear and full consciousness.

No one can say that thought about the Fiery World is destructive, negative or anarchistic. No harm can result from aspiring to the Higher Worlds. There will be only co-measurement and a desire for perfectionment. Thus, after reading "The Signs of the Fiery World," nothing will be rejected and profaned. On the contrary, the thinker will learn and attain a joy over and above earthly existence.

We shall return again to the Fiery World, when We shall speak about the higher energies. But until that time let friends learn to love the Fiery World, the World of Light, the World of Beauty!

AGNI YOGA SERIES

Leaves of Morya's Garden I (The Call)   1924
Leaves of Morya's Garden II (Illumination)   1925
New Era Community   1926

Signs of Agni Yoga

Agni Yoga   1929
Infinity I   1930
Infinity II   1930
Hierarchy   1931
Heart   1932
Fiery World I   1933
Fiery World II   1934
Fiery World III   1935
Aum   1936
Brotherhood   1937
Supermundane (in 3 volumes) 1938

Agni Yoga Society
www.agniyoga.org

9 781946 742216